Taiko Boom

ASIA: LOCAL STUDIES/GLOBAL THEMES

Jeffrey N. Wasserstrom, Kären Wigen, and Hue-Tam Ho Tai, Editors

Taiko Boom

JAPANESE DRUMMING IN PLACE AND MOTION

Shawn Bender

UNIVERSITY OF CALIFORNIA PRESS

BERKELEY LOS ANGELES LONDON

University of California Press, one of the most distinguished university presses in the United States, enriches lives around the world by advancing scholarship in the humanities, social sciences, and natural sciences. Its activities are supported by the UC Press Foundation and by philanthropic contributions from individuals and institutions. For more information, visit www.ucpress.edu.

University of California Press
Berkeley and Los Angeles, California

University of California Press, Ltd.
London, England

Library of Congress Cataloging-in-Publication Data

Bender, Shawn Morgan.
    Taiko boom : Japanese drumming in place and motion / Shawn Bender. — 1st ed.
        p.   cm. — (Asia : local studies/global themes ; 23)
    Includes bibliographical references and index.
    ISBN 978-0-520-27241-5 (cloth : alk. paper) —
    ISBN 978-0-520-27242-2 (pbk. : alk. paper)
    1. Taiko—Japan—History.   2. Taiko (Drum ensemble)—Japan—History.   3. Music—Japan.   4. Musical instruments—Japan.
5. Japan—Social life and customs.   I. Title.
    ML1038.T35B46   2012
    786.90952—dc23   2012010917

21   20   19   18   17   16   15   14   13   12
10   9   8   7   6   5   4   3   2   1

To my family, for their love and support

CONTENTS

List of Illustrations ix

Acknowledgments xi

Note on Translation, Japanese Names, and Romanization xv

Introduction 1

PART ONE

THE EMERGENCE AND POPULARIZATION OF TAIKO

1 · Taiko Drums and Taiko Drum Makers 25

2 · Genealogies of Taiko I:
Osuwa Daiko, Sukeroku Daiko, Ondekoza 48

3 · Genealogies of Taiko II:
Ondekoza to Kodo 73

4 · Placing Ensemble Taiko in Japan:
Festival Creation and the Taiko Boom 105

PART TWO

DISCOURSES OF CONTEMPORARY TAIKO

5 · (Dis)Locating Drumming: Taiko Training,
Embodiment, and the Aesthetics of Race and Place 119

6 · Woman Unbound? Body and Gender in Japanese Taiko 142

7 · The Sound of Militarism? New Texts, Old Nationalism, and the Disembodiment of Taiko Technique   170

Epilogue: Taiko at Home and Abroad   190

Notes   203
References   227
Index   241

ILLUSTRATIONS

Map of Tokyo's *shitamachi* area *55*

FIGURES

1. Varieties of ensemble taiko 1 *3*
2. Varieties of ensemble taiko 2 *4*
3. Festival drums *29*
4. *Ōdaiko* *30*
5. *Okedō-daiko* (or *daibyōshi*) *31*
6. *Chū-daiko* (or *miya-daiko*) *33*
7. Cartoon of *buraku* drummers *43*
8. *Kumi-daiko* versus drum set *51*
9. Sukeroku Daiko *59*
10. Kodo's "Yatai-bayashi" *76*
11. Muhōmatsu plays *Kokura gion daiko* *89*
12. Ondekoza debuts "Ōdaiko" *89*
13. Kodo's "Ōdaiko" in 1997 *94*
14. Festival poster in a Tokyo neighborhood *109*
15. Kodo apprentices practice "Yatai-bayashi" *138*
16. "Women Play Taiko" poster *143*
17. Members of Honō Daiko in their costumes, highlighting their muscular physiques *160*

18. A female drummer for Amanojaku posing before an *ōdaiko* *161*

19. Members of cocon in their stage costumes *168*

20. Cover of Nippon Taiko Foundation brochure *183*

For additional images related to this book, visit
www.ucpress.edu/go/taikoboom

ACKNOWLEDGMENTS

My first encounter with taiko drumming occurred quite by chance during my first visit to Japan in 1992. Out of an awareness of my interest in drums and perhaps some annoyance at the incessant finger tapping on the table in our shared office, a work colleague suggested that I check out a Japanese drum workshop he saw advertised at a community center in Kyoto. Little did I know at the time that this one-day taiko workshop would turn into a book project that would take over ten years to complete. Along the way, my passion for the subject has been stoked and supported by a great number of people to whom I remain deeply indebted.

David K. Jordan has been enthusiastic about my research on taiko since I first proposed it as a doctoral dissertation topic. He has been a constant voice of reason and a tireless editor, and this book is much improved as a result of his constructive criticism. Many of the intellectual perspectives that guide the book were developed first in graduate seminars at the University of California, San Diego, with Michael Meeker, who challenged me to think in new ways about theory, anthropology, and scholarship. I am also grateful to Japanese studies faculty at UCSD, especially Stefan Tanaka and Christena Turner, for sharing with me their insights into Japanese society. As part of my doctoral committee, Suzanne Brenner and George Lipsitz offered helpful suggestions that encouraged me to think in new ways about my research. The Interfaculty Initiative in Information Studies at the University of Tokyo hosted me during the sabbatical year in which I completed this book. Over the year, Jason Karlin lent a sympathetic ear and offered precious feedback on many of the chapters that follow.

Freddy Bailey, Jeffrey Bass, Marc Moskowitz, James Ellison, Alex Bates, and Christopher Bondy kindly gave me comments on early drafts of chapters, and the book is much better for their suggestions. Mizuho Zako of Oedo Sukeroku Daiko and Melanie Taylor of Kodo proofread portions of the text and saved me from many embarrassing errors. David Leheny, David T. Johnson, and Greg Noble gave me sage advice as the book neared completion. The development of the ideas presented here has also benefited from conversations over the years with Sharla Blank, Bambi Chapin, Steven Carlisle, Zachary Orend, Laura Gonzalez, Ethan Scheiner, Sherry Martin, Richard Miller, Deborah Wong, Riikka Länsisalmi, Yoshitaka Terada, Toshio Ochi, Eri Yoshikawa, Takahiro Sakayama, Gill Steel, Helene Lee, Erik Love, and Suman Ambwani. E. Taylor Atkins, Jennifer Milioto Matsue, and one anonymous reviewer read through the complete manuscript, and their thoughtful comments helped improve it considerably. All errors that remain are, of course, my own.

Research for this book was funded by grants from the Japan Foundation, the Social Science Research Council/Japanese Society for the Promotion of Science, the Japanese Ministry of Education (Monbusho), the UCSD Department of Anthropology and Japanese Studies Program, and the Dickinson College Research and Development Committee. I have been fortunate to receive support in this project from many members of the North American taiko community, especially Roy and P. J. Hirabayashi, Alan and Merle Okada, and Wynn and Brian Yamami. I am thankful to the members of Kodo for granting me access to their organization and for lending me time for interviews over the course of my extended research with them. Satō Ryūji, Negishi Toshiaki, and Nishita Tarō each took an exceptionally strong interest in my research and gave generously of their time. And though their stories don't appear on these pages, my hosts on Sado Island, the Kusaka family, who put a roof over my head and taught me much about life in rural Japan, deserve thanks for their warm hospitality.

Kiyomi Kushida of the Inter-University Center for Japanese Studies helped arrange institutional support for me at the University of Tokyo, provided me with a wealth of scholarly data on the Japanese folk performing arts, and pushed me to improve my understanding of classical and folk performance in Japan. Yoshitaka Terada shared with me his knowledge of *buraku* taiko and introduced me to the drummers of Taiko Ikari, for which I am deeply grateful. I also appreciate the cooperation of Nitagai Kamon and Robert "Robin" Early, who were both integral to the smooth start of my fieldwork in Tokyo, and to the members of Sukeroku Daiko, Nihon Taiko Dōjō, and the group I call Miyamoto Daiko for accepting me into their ranks as a beginning drummer. Osuwa Daiko, Oedo Sukeroku Taiko, Kodo, Miyamoto Unosuke Company, Asano Taiko Corporation, Hayashi Eitestu, and Kenny Endo graciously gave me permission to use their beautiful images in this book and on the book's website. Back home, the analysis of my research data would have taken much longer without the transcription of Japanese interviews by my research assistants Nakamachi Midori, Osone Riiko, Shinohara Emi, and Takazawa Chie.

A version of chapter 5 was published previously as "Of Roots and Race: Discourses of Body and Place in Japanese Taiko Drumming" (*Social Science Japan Journal* 8:197–212), and sections of chapter 3 provided the basis for the article "Drumming from Screen to Stage: Ondekoza *Ōdaiko* and the Reimaging of Japanese Taiko" (*Journal of Asian Studies* 69:843–867).

I would like to thank my family, to whom this book is dedicated, and the many friends who have encouraged me over the years as I pursued this project. Their gentle prodding helped make this book a reality. Finally, I want to express my gratitude to my many editors at the University of California Press, especially Kären Wigen and Reed Malcolm. Their enthusiasm, patience, and professionalism were much appreciated as this book made its way through the process of publication.

NOTE ON TRANSLATION, JAPANESE NAMES, AND ROMANIZATION

Unless otherwise noted, all translations from Japanese are my own.

I have worked throughout the book to preserve the anonymity of those who shared their thoughts on taiko with me. Individuals who have been interviewed for other publications or who gave me formal permission to use their names in print appear here with first and last names. In keeping with Japanese convention, these names are written last name first, except in cases where the individual is well known in the West. All other names are pseudonyms. In addition, the names of professional Japanese taiko groups, such as Osuwa Daiko, Oedo Sukeroku Taiko, and Kodo, are written in the groups' preferred style of romanization.

Introduction

Ducking inside the rehearsal hall brings relief from yet another sweltering summer day on Sado, the island in northern Japan I have called home for the past several months. I step over the jumble of shoes lining the entrance and make my way up a steep staircase to a high perch on a balcony inside the hall. A seat there offers a view of the scene below: drums and instruments ring the hardwood floor of the hall, roughly the size of a middle school gymnasium; apprentices dressed in casual workout clothes nervously shuffle in, trying their best to remain inconspicuous; managers and staff sit on foldout chairs at the edge of the room, with clipboards firmly in hand and faces focused on the center of the floor. There, seven male drummers are arranged in a row, each sitting cross-legged behind a small shime-daiko *drum. Their bodies are still and drawn tight, their expressions blank as if they are fixed in meditation.*

The loose bustle of preparation recedes to tense anticipation. Silence slowly envelops the hall, punctuated only by the buzz of cicadas outside and the dull whirr of electric fans. Still, the air is thick with heat and humidity. I tug at my shirt and carefully unfurl a folding fan.

In unison, the drummers place their sticks on the drums in front of them. Almost imperceptibly, a light tapping begins, rapid fire—Te-Ke-Te-Ke-Te-Ke-Te-Ke. The motion of hands alternating right-left, right-left soon becomes visible. The sound grows heavier and fuller. Lightly tapping hands quickly become pounding arms. The drummers push their sticks down toward the center of the drums. Hitting the rim and drum simultaneously, they drive the sound to an ear-splitting crescendo—TA-KA-TA-KA-TA-KA-TA-KA. Their flailing arms become a blur of vertical lines framed by their rigid bodies. Sound swirls around the interior of the hall, slicing like a knife at the planks supporting me. Overwhelmed, I cover my ears. Still, the sound reverberates through me. Just

as quickly, sound and movement recede to nearly imperceptible once more—
Te-Ke-Te-Ke-Te-Ke-Te-Ke. *Piercing the silence, the drummers alternate quick staccato rolls. Right to left, left to right, a cascade of furious drumming builds, washing back and forth like waves crashing on waves, until the lead drummer slices through the din*—DON-DON-DON-DON.

Silence.

Drummers freeze. Echoes fade. Hair stands on end. Crack! Crack Crack! *Drumming begins again, erratically this time. Smacking. Chopping. Slapping. Chaotic strikes replace ordered rhythm until one by one the drummers fall into the steady, synchronized cadence that marks the denouement of "Monochrome"*—TA-KA-TA-KA-TA-KA-TA-KA.

FINDING TAIKO IN JAPAN

I have seen Kodo perform "Monochrome" countless times, but it never fails to move me as viscerally as it did that summer day. A troupe of drummers and dancers, Kodo established a performance base on Sado Island in the late 1960s. (At the time they performed under the name Ondekoza.)[1] Led by their charismatic founder, the troupe sought to breathe new life into Japan's folk performing arts by converting folk motifs into dynamic stage performances. They quickly came to be distinguished as much for the intensity of their training regimen as for the impact of their drumming: their American debut performance in 1975 took place soon after they crossed the finish line at the Boston Marathon. Observing this strenuous training regimen and building on a history of domestic and international performance that spans three decades, Kodo has earned a place at the apex of a genre of Japanese performance called *kumi-daiko*, "ensemble taiko drumming."[2]

Taiko ensembles arrange barrel-shaped wooden drums *(taiko)* of various sizes and shapes for stage performance, much like an orchestral percussion section. However, the relatively large size of these drums and their strategic placement on stage encourages much more vigorous use of the body in performance than orchestral drumming would. In creating stage performances that explore both the musicality of the taiko drum and the muscularity of taiko drummers, postwar taiko ensembles broke with centuries of Japanese custom whereby these drums were relegated to primarily supporting roles in religious rituals and festival performances. At the same time, these groups resist easy classification as musical alone, since the intricately choreographed

FIGURE I. Varieties of ensemble taiko I: drums in this group are arranged like a drum set and then organized into an ensemble. Photo by Nishita Tarō.

movement of performers on stage, typically associated with dance, is a distinctive feature of the new genre (figures I and 2).

In the closing decades of the twentieth century, the physically intense and visually spectacular music-cum-dance performances of taiko ensembles drew enthusiastic audiences across Japan, ushering in a veritable "taiko boom."[3] From just a few dozen in the 1950s and 1960s, the number of taiko groups rose into the thousands by the close of the millennium.[4] The largest national organization of taiko groups in Japan, the Nippon Taiko Foundation, now counts more than eight hundred groups on its membership rolls. As exhilarating expressions of contemporary culture, taiko groups have performed at major national and international sporting events: exhibitions of drumming at the Nagano Winter Olympics in 1998 and at the FIFA World Cup cohosted by Korea and Japan in 2002 followed influential debut performances at the 1964 Tokyo Olympics and 1970 Osaka World Expo. Popularity at home has been met with enthusiasm abroad. Professional ensembles routinely tour Europe and the United States, and hundreds of locally based taiko groups have formed in North and South America, Europe, Southeast Asia, and Australia (Terada 2001). Taiko has become a crowd-pleasing staple at Japanese cultural festivals and events around the world. Building on this popular appeal, it has even been

FIGURE 2. Varieties of ensemble taiko 2: drums in this ensemble are separated out by pitch and timbre in a manner similar to that of an orchestral percussion section. Photo by author.

converted into a video game. In "Taiko no Tatsujin" (Taiko Master), an arcade game created by the Japanese company Namco, players use wooden mallets to tap along with a mixture of festival and pop music on an electronic drum shaped like a taiko. The company has released software and hardware home-console versions of "Taiko Master," along the lines of the "Guitar Hero" and "Rock Band" series of video games.[5] Clearly popular domestically, taiko drumming has arguably become Japan's most globally successful performing art.

Yet, despite this apparent popularity at home and abroad, it can sometimes be difficult to find taiko in Japan. Weekly event magazines like *Pia* only recently began to advertise the performances of more than a few professional taiko groups. Even in the 1990s, Kodo recordings were shelved in the "world music" section of Japanese record stores.[6] While it is still common for Japanese record chains to divide music into Japanese and Western genres, the placement of Kodo CDs in bins for non-Japanese (and non-Western) music not only defied intuition but also effectively marginalized taiko from both the East and West. More recently, taiko's classification appears to have brought it closer to the Japanese mainstream, albeit in inconsistent ways. In 2008, one foreign chain, Tower Records, kept Kodo CDs alongside the CDs of Japan's "J-Pop" (Japanese pop music) stars.[7] A few blocks away, a Japanese chain, JEUGIA, filed the same CDs along with performers of *koto, shamisen,* and *shakuhachi* in the "traditional Japanese music" section. Another Japanese retail outlet, Miyako Music Market, simply placed them in the section marked "miscellaneous," sandwiched between a string quartet from Shanghai and the New Age pianist George Winston.

Figuring out exactly how taiko fits within the categories of Japanese music retail and advertising clearly remains a problem. (Admittedly, corporate outlets are probably not the most reliable place to look for consistent categorizations of music.) More troubling is that it is equally difficult to locate taiko within scholarship on Japanese music. Recent comprehensive treatments of Japanese music in English provide little to no information on this rapidly expanding genre of Japanese performance culture.[8] Perhaps the postwar emergence of taiko groups has contributed to a classification of taiko drumming as Japanese *popular* music, which these texts have tended to cover less thoroughly. But while there has been a burgeoning academic literature on Japanese popular music in recent years (Aoyagi 2005; Atkins 2001; Condry 2006; Matsue 2009; Sterling 2010; Stevens 2007; Yano 2002), the many anthologies on Japanese popular culture or its increasingly global presence have failed to devote sustained attention to taiko ensembles.[9] The lack of Western instrumentation or recognizably foreign influence has likely led scholars not to identify taiko groups with contemporary Japanese music. As a result, there is currently more English-language scholarship on taiko drumming *outside* Japan than in Japan, a significant gap that I seek to redress with this book.[10]

Indeed, part of the difficulty in assigning taiko a place within Japanese musicality is that it confounds popular and scholarly divisions among musical genres. Professional taiko ensembles perform on stages in clubs or concert halls, participating in the same circuits of commodity capitalism as pop or rock groups. At the same time, taiko groups often make exclusive use of instruments and motifs associated with "traditional" genres of Japanese performance, eschewing the kinds of visible East-West hybridity associated with *enka* singing (Yano 2002) and the genre of Western-influenced classical Japanese music called *gendai hōgaku* (Herd 2008). Yet, like popular music groups and in contrast to the inherited forms from which they often take inspiration, taiko ensembles tend to emphasize creativity, adaptation, and innovation, rather than preservation or conservation. In fact, few contemporary taiko ensembles claim to be passing on any particular "tradition."[11] Moreover, in contrast to the majority of inherited folk performances in Japan, which have suffered from a lack of young recruits as Japan's population has continued to decline (Brumann 2009; Thornbury 1997), the taiko "boom" indicates that these groups have popular appeal.

Failing to fall neatly within categorical conventions has thus led to the marginalization of taiko drumming in Japanese commerce and in academic scholarship, even as its popularity and global reach place it squarely in the musical mainstream.[12] However, it is precisely this marginality that makes taiko a rich site for examining how contemporary Japanese negotiate distinctions between native and foreign, popular and traditional, and local and national through expressive culture. How does taiko fit into contemporary Japanese and international performance as an intensely physical expressive art form? Through what processes did it emerge, and how has it increased in popularity? What has it come to mean for practitioners and enthusiasts alike?

In order to investigate such questions and begin carving an intellectual place for taiko, I conducted intensive ethnographic fieldwork in Japan from 1999 to 2001. This research built on preliminary work conducted over the academic year from 1997 to 1998 in Japan and the United States and involved observation of dozens of taiko concerts and festival performances, interviews with players and influential individuals within the taiko community, visits to sites of folk performance, as well as collection and analysis of articles, books, magazines, and documentaries on taiko. This initial extended research trip was supplemented by additional research in Japan in the summer of 1998, during a short trip there in 2004, and over extended stays in 2008, 2009, and 2010 to 2011.

In the course of this research, I found that my desire to locate an intellectual place for taiko mirrored a concern with performing local place among the taiko groups I studied. The most influential styles of taiko drumming emerged within either evolving religio-communal celebrations or efforts to establish new forms of community. In addition, the spread of taiko across Japan occurred in tandem with government investment in local festivity, a connection that is not merely incidental but evident in the structures and practices of the genre. Instruments and regalia were borrowed from folk festivals and given new life in taiko ensembles, while traditions of oral transmission were applied to entirely new kinds of physically demanding drumming. Taiko groups thus conserved the link between specific bodily movements and specific localities that defined older performance forms. At the same time, as hereditary barriers to participation in festival performance gave way, territorial boundaries intensified. While gender-exclusive obstacles to participation were relaxed, masculine performance norms took root. Having broken down traditional norms of performance and participation, Japan's emergent taiko drummers also became subject to new, localized techniques of bodily discipline, as well as normalizing ideologies of aesthetics and gender.

Importantly, this process of localization did not take place in isolation but in the midst of a great deal of movement. Performative celebrations of local identity in fact depended on national and international circulations of media, knowledge, and people. Drummers seeking inspiration for new performances traveled to local areas to witness "authentic" displays of inherited folk techniques. Regional practitioners of folk performance in turn visited metropolitan areas to teach their authoritative versions. Amateur drum groups not only performed at local celebrations but also traveled to neighboring festivals and national events. Audiovisual recordings of older festival drumming and newer ensembles flowed where people did not. (A key historical event in the popularization of taiko in Japan, for example, was the televised performance of Oguchi Daihachi's taiko group Osuwa Daiko at the 1964 Tokyo Olympics.) What's more, this national circulation of local culture in Japan coincided symbiotically with an emerging global fetish for local culture, as illustrated by new markets for cultural tourism and world music in the 1980s and 1990s. Global demand led professional taiko groups to tour both internationally and domestically. In such new spaces of consumption, "the world becomes an array of localities" (Tilly 1997, 74), performed for audiences and tourists alike. Taiko groups became not only exemplars of local community expression at home but also representatives of "local" Japan in sites of global performance abroad (Fujie 2001).

Kodo epitomizes the process of performing locality within national and global cultural flows. To create its repertoire, Kodo's antecedent group, Onde-koza, built on a foundation of folk motifs acquired through visits to regional locations or through study with visiting local teachers. Rigorous, physically demanding apprentice programs were designed to retrain the bodies of young Japanese such that they would be able to recapture the vigor of Japan's rapidly desiccating folk art forms while reinterpreting those art forms on stage. Performances of these newly localized bodies were marketed to audiences abroad in order to build an "artisan academy" (which would later become Kodo Village) on Sado, transforming the cultural capital of their exotica on the world stage into economic and social capital back home. The result has been not only the founding of Kodo Village on Sado Island but also the emergence of Kodo as a symbol of Japanese musical distinction in the global music scene. The group has been featured as a local instantiation of the global impulse to drum in publications like Mickey Hart's *Planet Drum* (1991) and in the film *Pulse: A Stomp Odyssey* (Cresswell and McNicholas 2002). Capitalizing on a global network cultivated over years of touring worldwide, Kodo has helped transform "local" Sado into a cosmopolitan site of intercultural interaction by hosting its own world music festival (called "Earth Celebration") on the island every summer since 1988. Even the piece "Monochrome," to which I noted my reactions at the beginning of this chapter, is the product of global-local articulation: it was written by Maki Ishii, a Japanese avant-garde composer based in Germany, after he was introduced to the group by Seiji Ozawa, the expatriate Japanese conductor of the Boston Symphony Orchestra. In contrast to the orally transmitted forms of the many folk performing arts from which Kodo takes inspiration, the piece is entirely scripted, with every seemingly random strike of the drum notated. In the delicate interplay between traveling global routes and establishing local roots, Kodo thus presents in stark relief processes at work more generally in taiko ensembles throughout Japan.

GLOBAL FLOWS, LOCAL PROJECTS

The articulation between global flow and local emplacement that taiko groups like Kodo exemplify resonates with shifting anthropological conceptions of the production of culture and place in our current era of globalization. Anthropologists have argued that the local in this era of the global can no longer be examined in isolation, but, rather, must be understood in the context of accelerated national and international flows of people, capital, and culture (Gupta and Ferguson 1997).[13] This scholarship has begun to trace the increasingly rootless nature of living in the contemporary world. Whether at rest or propelled into motion, people seem to be bound up ever more in maintaining connections over distances and durations that are rapidly being compressed by advancing technology (Harvey 1989), even as physical mobility continues to be significantly conditioned by class and wealth (Ong 1999, 11). For anthropologists, this implies that the process of making meaning out of social life, a defining feature of culture, takes place in a variety of forms, often mediated, across larger spaces and shorter intervals.[14] Boundaries that once seemed fixed have loosened, ushering in an era in which cultural mixture appears more the norm than cultural purity. Given the increased permeability of societies to cultural flows, the scope, substance, and sense of local community can no longer be taken as natural and universal but rather must be considered an ongoing product of discourse and practice (Appadurai 1996, 178–199; Gupta and Ferguson 1997; R. Robertson 1995). Building a sense of attachment to one's local community, however defined, applies as much to those who remain within officially recognized boundaries (Allison 2006, 184) as it does to voluntary diasporic and involuntary refugee communities (Malkki 1992). What's more, the "local" can be culturally constructed through materials from nearby or from a diffuse global "elsewhere" (Luvaas 2009, 266).

In performing the local—that is, by bringing it into social action—artistic performance is a particularly fruitful site in which to examine localization in a world of flux and flow. According to Marc Schade-Poulsen (1997, 59), "Music . . . is seemingly one of the 'things' in the world that most easily 'flows,' becomes 'creolized,' 'syncretized,' [or] 'heterogenized'" within particular places. Indeed, scholars of Japanese music have already begun to examine how foreign (specifically American) popular music has been incorporated within Japan (Atkins 2001; Condry 2006; Matsue 2009), though their analyses of this process differ.[15] By exploring how global-local interaction in Japanese popular culture puts meaning and music into play beyond mere imitation, these studies convincingly demonstrate that the constitution of Japaneseness in the twenty-first century differs from that of previous eras. Nevertheless, this research has not pushed the boundaries of the "local" far beyond the immediate context of observation. The primary settings for this research (and for that of most other forms of Japanese popular culture) are urban sites of transience, play, and leisure (for example, jazz clubs, nightclubs, and underground bars). Surely, much negotiation of global and local culture takes place within these sites of leisure, but little scholarly discussion focuses on how this process extends to the less transient neighborhoods and communities that remain after shows end. In other words, it is clear that these forms of performance *take place* in local sites; it is less clear how they contribute to establishing local sites as *lived places.*

TAIKO AS A NEW FOLK PERFORMING ART

The close connection between taiko drumming and projects of localization lend it utility as a site in which to address such questions. Japan anthropologists have noted that, from the late 1970s to the early 1990s, the dominant idiom of localization in Japan was the *furusato,* or "old village."[16] This term took on greater salience in Japan in the wake of the massive postwar economic growth of the 1950s and 1960s. During this time, in a continuation of prewar trends, millions of Japanese flocked to Japan's expanding urban areas while leaving the rural periphery depleted of people and resources. The rapid transformation of city and country led large numbers of metropolitan Japanese to take nostalgic interest in the "vanishing" (Ivy 1995) people, culture, and *furusato* of Japan's past (interpreted spatially as its rural periphery), generating a "*furusato* boom" in the 1970s and 1980s (Ben-Ari 1992, 204). *Furusato* rhetoric and imagery were utilized extensively by elites in urban and suburban areas in community revitalization projects, and in rural areas to help stimulate tourism and economic development.[17] Although there are exceptions (Ben-Ari 1992; Brumann 2009), scholars have tended to be critical of these projects. The *furusato* projects have been blamed for generating new forms of social exclusion (J. Robertson 1991), distorting inherited folk customs, and fostering fabricated "traditions" (see Brumann 2009 for a critique of this literature).

While place making in Japan does have problematic aspects, it is precisely these kinds of local projects, particularly the new festival celebrations created within them, that have generated demand and supplied performance venues for new taiko drumming groups. Moreover, the simultaneous circulation of taiko groups both nationally and globally highlights an aspect of Japanese place making implied by recent anthropological scholarship—namely, that projects of localization coincide with processes of nationalization and globalization. Touristic projects to make local places "native places" encourage not just domestic tourism but also foreign tourism; cultural objects produced by such efforts similarly circulate not just domestically but also internationally. A concern with local culture in *furusato* making thus invites comparisons between the local, the national, and the international.[18] From this perspective, Kodo's double move—making a place in Japan's rural periphery while traveling across the world's stages—looks less capricious and more like a logical extension of Japanese desires to internationalize while localizing. As forms of performance shaped by attempts to generate new kinds of communal affiliations in a context of ever-greater circulations of people and culture, taiko ensembles are more than merely degenerate simulations of folkloric performance. Instead, they are better understood as performative expressions of Japan's new, globalizing communities—Japan's "new folk."

Since the end of World War II, scholars have called the expressive culture of local communities in Japan "folk performing arts" *(minzoku geinō)*. The term denotes performed content and performative context as well as practices of technical instruction, transmission, and generation. Most commonly, however, these art forms are defined negatively: they are neither traditional performing arts of the stage *(koten geinō)*, such as Noh or kabuki (what I prefer to call "classical stage performances"), nor are they "popular" art forms produced for mass consumption and distribution. Instead, the word *folk* signifies a group of nonelites living in a particular community; folk performing arts are the kinds of expressive culture that emerge organically among these community members over time. Most often, "folk communities" have been identified spatially with villages on the rural periphery and temporally with cultural vestiges of communities (even in contemporary urban areas) that existed before the influx of Western modernity in the late nineteenth century.

While the Japanese notion of a mythohistorical "folk" from which all contemporary Japanese are believed to descend has been rightly criticized as a problematic modern formulation (Harootunian 1991), if used narrowly, the term "folk performing art" retains analytic utility. It centers attention on performance culture that is presumed to be a communal possession, expressive of that community, transmitted orally within it, managed by it, and owned by no one community member more than another. This is not to say that there are no hierarchies or gender or class divisions among the managers of folk performing arts, or that there are no interruptions in transmission. Rather, the assumption of a tie between community and expressive form analytically distinguishes a "folk performing art" from popular music or classical stage performance.[19] Furthermore, although the idea that folk performing arts continue only old traditions is still widespread (Thornbury 1997, 14), there is no reason why this must be the case. On the contrary, as the context of a communal performance shifts, so should its content; the performative expression of a community, large or small, logically should reflect the nature, even one that is in flux, of that community.

In fact, recent shifts in official attitudes toward the folk performing arts suggest that a concern with historicity is waning. Since the folk performing arts became eligible for public protection in Japan (in the form of preservation and financial support) as "intangible cultural properties" in 1975, it has been incumbent on local inheritors to provide documentation of how a particular folk performance was adapted by them and how it changed in the community prior to World War II (Thornbury 1997, 58). However, with the passage of the so-called Festival Law in 1992, pressure on localities to provide evidence of longstanding (prewar) historicity has eased.[20] This law, which was part of a national effort to encourage domestic tourism by developing local festivals into tourist events, extends eligibility for official public support to what it calls "regional traditional performing arts." The 1993 "Directive on Developing Basic Plans in Accordance with the Festival Law" states that if regional performing arts "have taken root in a specific region, and are passed along among the people of that region, they need not necessarily possess a long history" to receive public support (quoted in Hashimoto 1998, 40). The directive thus shifts governmental attention away from the historicity of a performance (retaining the term "traditional" to signify a form of transmission rather than prewar emergence) to the location in which it is performed. Even though some confusion about how to define folk performance remains within official circles, Japanese authorities appear to be grappling with the changing nature of local community and local performance culture in an era of domestic and international cultural tourism.

Categorizing taiko ensembles as "new folk performing arts" avoids terminological confusion and highlights the close connection of these groups to projects of localization.[21] Born as they were within the context of local festivity and in the search for new forms of communality, taiko ensembles function within a social space previously occupied by older, orally transmitted folk performing arts. At the same time, the innovation, creativity, and openness to change exhibited by taiko ensembles distinguish them from older forms of inherited folk performance from which they take inspiration. Taiko ensembles also circulate in broader national and global channels of commercial and cultural exchange, incorporating influences from around the world while participating in the expansion of Japan's new musical culture abroad. Furthermore, by bringing a previously marginal instrument, the taiko (these groups were the first to explore its *musical* potential), used within a marginalized form of performance (the folk performing arts), into the mainstream of Japanese performance, taiko ensembles have also brought into the spotlight previously marginalized groups, such as nonhereditary performers and women. This process has generated discussion about the status of taiko within the wider field of Japan's performing arts and debates about new performance hierarchies and standards.

In framing this field of performance anew, the category of "new folk performing art" moves analysis away from a modernist concern with temporal progress—Japan emerging out of tradition into modernity; Japanese preserving tradition in the face of change—toward a postmodern perspective, in which the signs, symbols, and objects of the past and present are combined in creative ways. Such a perspective draws attention to the process of localization in a context in which a past of inherited traditions is as accessible as a present of global culture. To use contemporary parlance, it aims to explore how taiko has "remixed" the global and local in Japan.

STUDYING TAIKO IN THE FIELD

The connections among taiko, localization, and globalization that feature prominently in this book became apparent to me soon after I started organizing my field research on taiko in Japan. Initially, I believed that the best way to learn about Japanese taiko drumming would be to spend time with Kodo as a participant-observer. Kodo has a two-year apprentice program to train incoming players and staff, and I thought that joining the group as a pseudo-apprentice for a period of one year would be the easiest way to facilitate my entry into the group as a researcher while giving me a fruitful vantage point from which to conduct my study. In addition, Kodo's home base on Sado Island provided a fixed geographical location within which to study groups elsewhere that meet only intermittently to prepare for festivals or concerts. As with most fieldwork in cultural anthropology, however, chance and circumstance played a larger role than rational planning in determining the eventual scope and methods of my research. In the end, my single-sited project grew into a multisited one (Marcus 1995), better suited to the highly mobile character of contemporary taiko.

In fact, my first encounter with Kodo was facilitated by the very transnational circuits of culture discussed earlier. In the summer of 1997, a small contingent of Kodo members traveled to Los Angeles to attend the first North American taiko conference. The inaugural conference attested to the popularity of taiko abroad, and Kodo's participation indicated its desire to maintain transnational connections. At the conference, a member of San Jose Taiko, a Japanese American taiko group based in California, kindly introduced me to Tatsu, a Kodo staff member and apprentice program codirector. Tatsu listened politely to my research proposal and expressed a desire to help me achieve my objectives. But he stressed that his group had received similar requests from other researchers in the past, and never for such a long period of time. Before granting my request, Tatsu told me, he would have to bring the matter in front of the entire group for their approval. A former graduate student in economics at the University of California, Santa Barbara, he also asked me to send him a copy of the English text of my research proposal for reference.

By the time that Kodo reached its decision in October of that year, I was already in Japan undertaking advanced language study. Tatsu told me that the group had approved my proposal on a preliminary basis, but that I should plan on visiting Sado Island to work out the details and acquaint myself with Kodo's headquarters, Kodo Village. I arranged to visit the group during a break in my language study at the end of December. The timing was hardly fortuitous. Sado, which is located in the northern Japan Sea, has brutally cold winters, and December is one of its chilliest months. Strong winds and large waves often interrupt ferry service to the island during this time of year, especially to the small port nearest Kodo Village. Fortunately, weather permitted, and I made the two-and-a-half-hour ferry ride to meet with Tatsu.

The visit marked the beginning of a fundamental shift in my conception of the Kodo organization. As Tatsu and I descended the serpentine road leading to the group's main office and rehearsal hall, it became apparent that Kodo Village was a "village" only in a very generous sense of the word. Along with the two buildings in immediate view, Kodo Village included a small dormitory, a guesthouse where the managing director maintained an office, and a transplanted local house that functioned as a part-time apprentice training facility and banquet hall. Other than the dormitory, there did not appear to be any homes in the area. It was quiet and still. All that interrupted the white blanket of snow covering the tree-ringed ground around us were the black lines of windshield wipers left jutting up on the cars of touring members to ease snow removal. As we approached the entrance of the office building, a couple of dogs huddling together for warmth halfheartedly barked a welcome. A small wooden sign left unobtrusively beside the entrance announced "Kodo" in both English and Japanese.

Tatsu slid the door open, and we walked inside the three-story office building, which was constructed almost entirely out of wood (without, he told me, the use of a single nail). We passed the administrative center, which was a collection of desks and Power Macs, and went down through the back to the dormitory where I would stay for the evening. Tatsu showed me to my room, which was barren except for a futon spread out in the center of the hardwood floor and a low-slung table left by some former occupant. I dropped off my small bag and paused a moment to watch the wispy trail of my breath evaporate as I exhaled. "I'll have them bring in a *sutōbu* [gas heater]," Tatsu said. Relieved, I followed him back into the office building to the dining hall, where a couple of female probationary members were finishing up their dinner. Tatsu left me with them to eat and chat.

I was feeling excited, because this was my first opportunity to actually talk with the drummers about whom I had read and thought so much. From Kodo's promotional literature and its active participation in the global music scene, I anticipated that the group's members would be interested in the promotion of cultural exchange and the support of Japanese traditional performing arts. I had many questions, but I did not want to be too inquisitive or intrusive, for fear that it might jeopardize my chance to work with the group in the long term. I began by telling the women that I was a graduate student in anthropology. They asked what it means to be an anthropologist, and I told them that it meant I was interested in studying cultural difference. "For example," I said, "the differences in culture between the United States and Japan." Without a moment's hesitation, one of them shot back matter-of-factly, "Huh? I don't think there's any difference in culture between America and Japan." "Oh, really?" I replied. "Yeah, what's different?" she asked again, emboldened. "Well," I started, trying to simultaneously form Japanese words with my mouth and distill the language of cultural anthropology down to the level of dinnertime chat, "there are institutional differences, such as the religious basis of society, the educational system, the political system . . ." Mulling over my answer for a moment, she responded, "Hmmm . . . I still don't think they're that different. Southeast Asia, now *that's* a place with a different culture."

The answer seemed odd in a place ostensibly devoted to study of and engagement with Japanese folk culture. I attempted to steer the conversation in a direction that I thought would be less academic and more personal. I asked each of the women to tell me why they had decided to become Kodo apprentices. Their answers came as something of a surprise. "I want to travel around the world, and I thought this would be a great way to do it," one replied. (I learned later that this is a popular reason for apprentices to join the group.) "I see, but wouldn't it be easier to just save up money and travel around the world by yourself?" I suggested gently, thinking that this was a rather arduous way to travel the globe. "No, I like taiko, too." Just as I was weighing the implied order of importance, the other woman shared her answer with me: "I like performing on stage, having people listen and making them happy." "With taiko?" I asked for clarification. "Not necessarily, I like dancing, too." Dancing? We chatted for a few minutes longer, until they had to leave to return to practice. Tatsu fetched me shortly thereafter and I retired to my room. My brief conversation with these two young women had started me wondering about my preconceived notions about the group. They hardly seemed like the wide-eyed idealists dedicated to cultural revitalization that I had expected to encounter.

The following morning, Tatsu drove me out to Kodo's Apprentice Centre, which is located about forty-five minutes by car from Kodo Village in Kakino-ura, a small hamlet then under the administrative jurisdiction of Ryōtsu City.[22] The Apprentice Centre is housed in a converted junior high school that the group began renting from the city after it was closed for lack of students—a not uncommon phenomenon in the depopulated rural communities of Japan. Our stay there was brief. We left soon after looking in on several apprentices, who were gathered in the one room that had a heater, assiduously carving Noh masks and other objects for display. On the drive back, I realized that the visit was meant to be more intimidating than instructive. My heart sank as Tatsu began to indicate that my plan to join the group as an apprentice was impracticable. "We've had a number of foreigners try to go through our apprentice program and virtually all of them have failed. They find it culturally too unfamiliar, maybe 'too Japanese' to bear," he began.[23] I assured him that this "unfamiliarity" was precisely what I was interested in, yet to no avail. "But you don't intend to join our group, do you?" he asked. "No," I said, "I don't." To paraphrase his answer: "We are a professional group. This is how we make our living. Our apprentice program is very competitive. Let's say you came in as a first-year apprentice. What would justify our spending time on you? If you don't understand something, if you can't do something, if our teachers have to spend more time with you—a person who has no intention of joining our group—at the expense of other apprentices, the others will start to complain and you'll get in the way. Think about it for a moment: would you ask to join the Bolshoi Ballet as an apprentice for a year?"

Of course not, I thought. I did not know what to say. I felt that I had unintentionally misapprehended, offended, and threatened my potential hosts before even meeting them. I had not expected that they would accept my research proposal without modification, but I did not anticipate that it would be interpreted as insulting. Not entirely sure how to respond, I suggested that I mainly observe, rather than participate with, the apprentices as they proceeded through their training program, and that I interview and observe the stage performers to the extent that it did not interfere with their practice sessions.

With the prospect of my future fieldwork with Kodo still uncertain, I returned to Sado the following summer to live and work at Kodo Village on a trial basis. My job responsibilities included some translation but primarily evolved into working with a bilingual Japanese employee to create a website for the group. I had never done this kind of work, and it was a challenge to learn the intricacies of web design and HTML with Japanese texts. But after several failed attempts and much trial and error, the two of us were able to produce a prototype that the group ultimately accepted (in fact, they continue to use its basic layout as of this writing). I became a part of life at Kodo Village, buying food and cooking (unfortunately not very delicious) meals for everyone, cleaning the office and dormitory daily, and helping with garbage disposal, among other quotidian tasks. I also observed several taiko workshops that the group held locally that summer and sat in occasionally on practice sessions and informal performances with the probationary members of the group (not with the apprentices, though, since I lacked the car and license necessary to get to the Apprentice Centre). At the conclusion of this two-month period, Tatsu informed me that I had been able to integrate myself into the group well enough that returning to do a longer-term study would not cause problems.

Meeting the probationary members, negotiating with Tatsu, and working in the office provided revelatory glimpses into Kodo's place at the turn of the twenty-first century. What I had imagined as a group of artists interested in revitalizing local performance culture and performing it around the world included a number of young players interested as much, if not more, in the latter than the former. At all levels of the organization, Kodo members' interests clearly differed from those of local performers across Japan entrusted with maintaining the integrity of inherited folk performing traditions. For the former, cultivating artistic connections with local performers across Japan and affirming a place on Sado Island equaled in importance the cultivation of contacts with world music performers outside Japan. In this sense, my brief stint as a web programmer was highly symbolic. On the cusp of the information century, I had journeyed to Kodo just as the group had begun to expand global (virtual) access to its village through the "new" technology of the Internet.

FIELD SITES AND METHODS

After returning home at the conclusion of my summer stay with the group, I received a two-year grant to support research on Japanese taiko. The grant period was scheduled to begin the following year on the first of April, a date that coincided nicely with the start of Kodo's apprentice program. Shortly before I was to depart for Japan, however, I found out that receipt of the grant depended on first completing several months of compulsory Japanese language study at my host institution in Tokyo, thus throwing all my research plans into disarray. But what I saw initially as a burden turned out to be a blessing. On the first day of language study at the University of Tokyo, I met a fellow American student who was a member of an amateur taiko group, Miyamoto Daiko, in neighboring Saitama Prefecture. With his introduction, I was able to join and begin participating in a taiko group not more than two weeks after setting foot in Japan. Contacts in that group led to introductions to two semiprofessional taiko groups—Sukeroku Daiko and Nihon Taiko Dōjō—that ran training programs in the Tokyo area. I decided to stay in Tokyo for the year with my three main field sites thus established, and I split my time among them: twice per week at Sukeroku Daiko, twice per week at Nihon Taiko Dōjō, and once per week at Miyamoto Daiko.

The first group, Miyamoto Daiko, is based in a suburban community in Saitama Prefecture, one of the prefectures that borders Tokyo City and about a thirty-minute train ride from Ikebukoro Station in western Tokyo. Many of the members of the group set up residence here because of its proximity. In fact, most commuted daily to Tokyo for work. The group was composed of about thirteen performing members: nine men (myself included) and four women. Several other individuals, mostly older men who were former members, maintained peripheral advisory roles with the group and occasionally performed with us. Miyamoto Daiko's repertoire consisted of a mix of a few original compositions and a much greater number of pieces borrowed from other taiko groups, such as Tokyo's Sukeroku Daiko, and folk drum styles from a variety of regional locations in Japan.

Sukeroku Daiko is a professional group composed of about five or six performing members. It is an offshoot of another group with the same name that was founded in the late 1950s by Kobayashi Seidō and three other young men in Tokyo's Bunkyō Ward. This ward is located in the affective heart of Tokyo, an area called *shitamachi* that constituted the urban center of Tokyo before 1868, when it was still called Edo. Imaizumi Yutaka, who later joined Sukeroku Daiko and became a featured performer, had a falling out with Kobayashi and founded the Sukeroku Daiko Hozonkai (Sukeroku Daiko Preservation Society). Kobayashi later founded the group Oedo Sukeroku Daiko. When Kobayashi formed this group, Imaizumi changed the name of his actively performing troupe back to Sukeroku Daiko and set up the affiliated preservation society for apprentices. It was this preservation society in which I took up lessons. Imaizumi himself rarely if ever engaged in actual instruction. Instead, he delegated teaching responsibilities to two young female apprentices and a male veteran who became my main teacher. True to the group's name, its repertoire is made up of a fixed set of pieces inherited from the original Sukeroku Daiko only a couple of decades earlier.

The last of these groups, Nihon Taiko Dōjō, is a semiprofessional group run by the drummer Onozato Motoe and supported in part by the Miyamoto Unosuke Taiko Company, which is based in another part of Tokyo's *shitama-chi,* Asakusa. Onozato, an original member of Sukeroku Daiko, had planned not to return to ensemble taiko after leaving that group in the early 1980s. But after seeing multitudes of taiko performers playing with what he deemed "poor technique," Onozato decided that he would open a school where he would teach the "proper way" to play ensemble taiko. Onozato was reputed to be a good teacher, and I decided to join his class. In the early stages of my research, the lax approach to taiko instruction at Miyamoto Daiko and the more doctrinaire approach of the Sukeroku Daiko Hozonkai made me feel that I was not getting sufficient exposure to a range of taiko.[24] Although there was a performance group (of the same name) attached to Onozato's teaching program, my primary experience at Nihon Taiko Dōjō came in group lessons geared toward beginning and intermediate taiko learners.

Of course, given the necessary time and money, I would have liked to join more ensemble taiko groups in the Tokyo area. But even if such funds and time had been available, the particular circumstances of ensemble taiko groups in Japan would have made this difficult. Belonging to more than one profes-sional, or even amateur, group is often openly discouraged. In fact, on my first day at Nihon Taiko Dōjō, Onozato asked me to confirm that I had received Imaizumi's approval. I had, and my special status as a researcher was the cen-tral factor in allowing this to happen.[25] There is a practical reason for this: per-formance dates for taiko groups often conflict, and choosing among them can not only impair the ability of a group to perform but also be the source of dis-sension within the group. Nevertheless, there is also a more symbolic reason for this parochialism. Upon entering a particular ensemble taiko group, one adopts the particular training methods, performance repertoire, instrumen-tation, and stage techniques that make that group distinctive. Approaches to each of these aspects of performance can differ fundamentally among groups and are closely connected to a sense of group identity. Joining another group while already affiliated with one is, therefore, tantamount to repudiating one's teacher or fellow group members and considered highly offensive.

While in Tokyo, I supplemented my direct experience and interviews with members of these three groups by conducting interviews with members of several additional amateur and professional groups, and I took in a wide assortment of ensemble taiko performances at concert halls and local festivals in the area. I also made short research trips to two islands, Miyake Island and Hachijō Island, that are renowned for their styles of folk drumming, and to Chichibu City in Saitama Prefecture. In Chichibu, I observed the night festival in which the much-copied *yatai-bayashi* (festival-cart drumming) originated. At the conclusion of this year of activity, I moved to Sado Island to begin long-term fieldwork with Kodo. In the interval since I had originally spoken with Tatsu, an American employee who had been doing translation and interpretation for Kodo had left his job, and I took up his former responsibilities as a volunteer in Kodo's main office. My time was thus split roughly in half between the Apprentice Centre and the main office. Because the main office is located next to Kodo's rehearsal hall, volunteering there facilitated access to the performing members of the group for informal conversation, interviews, and the observation of practices and rehearsals. A six-month research trip to western Japan in 2008 and a summer visit there in 2009 afforded me additional opportunities to learn about groups outside the areas of Tokyo and Sado.

Conducting long-term fieldwork with a range of taiko groups in both urban and rural locations generated a wealth of data with which to analyze the roots and implications of the taiko "boom." The process of entering the field provided useful information about the intricacies of negotiating fieldwork in contemporary Japan as well as the character of the groups I intended to study. Later, as I proceeded through this fieldwork, close observation of Kodo along with my own experiences playing with and observing groups in the Tokyo area brought home to me how centrally physical training figures in taiko performance. For the drummers I encountered, playing rhythmic patterns was just part of what it meant to be a good performer. The finely honed movements of bodies in the process of drumming were of much greater importance. Drummers spent a great deal of time criticizing and correcting these movements, and I found that debates about local identity, proper style and form, and good and bad taiko tended to revolve around degrees of bodily comportment. Particular body shapes and particular ways of moving those bodies to play drums were believed to distinguish taiko groups within Japan and Japanese taiko drumming from other varieties of drumming around the world.

I also found that this intense concentration on the body and the expression of locality through the embodiment of local style did not proceed without challenge. The increased popularity of taiko drumming among women brought to the surface gender inequities inherent in a form of performance based on an implicitly male standard of physicality and strength. In addition, members of the taiko community who were interested in legitimizing taiko drumming as a national style of performance began textualizing the hitherto oral (and visual) tradition of taiko instruction. While distilling the diversity of taiko drumming styles into standard techniques suitable for mass instruction makes taiko learning available to more people, it also has the effect of "disembodying" taiko pedagogy and reducing to mere variation the nuances of inherited drumming styles. At the beginning of the twenty-first century, the "new folk performing art" of taiko drumming thus reflects broader debates in Japanese society as well as the growing pains of a genre maturing in the wake of rapid popularization.

STRUCTURE OF THE BOOK

Part 1 examines the factors that led to the "taiko boom." It shows how taiko emerged within shifting patterns of community organization in Japan, opening up opportunities for previously marginalized Japanese to participate in civic culture and providing them with a new means of expression. Building on that analysis, part 2 examines the social and musical contours of this new participation, illustrating the extent to which many contemporary discourses on taiko revolve around issues of locality and embodiment. These discourses are generated in large part by the intense physicality of the art form itself as well as the social context of its emergence. The chapters depict a genre in the midst of change, in which distinctions of regional and national, masculine and feminine, and native and foreign are negotiated in pedagogy and performance.

Chapter 1 introduces the variety of drums used in Japan and begins a discussion of the "taiko boom" by demonstrating how it has helped bring taiko drums and taiko drum makers closer to the mainstream of Japanese cultural life. Chapters 2 and 3 trace the emergence of the four groups that contributed most significantly to the instrumentation, stage presentation, performance techniques, and repertoire of contemporary Japanese taiko: Osuwa Daiko, Sukeroku Daiko, Ondekoza, and Kodo. Each of these groups appropriated and rearranged styles of drumming inherited from the folk performing arts within the shifting contexts of local community in Japan. At the same time, they also embraced elements of contemporary musical trends and popular culture. Chapter 4 examines the close relationship between governmental support for community festivity and the spread of ensemble taiko groups throughout Japan. It builds on the insights of an anthropological literature that has detailed changes in the patterns of local festival performance throughout Japan, but it challenges the notion that new festivals represent only the failed imitation of older, "authentic" festivals based in religious celebration. Rather, new patterns of festivity reflect new patterns of community organization within the context of global-local place making.

Part 2 builds on the arguments advanced in part 1, exploring how the emergence and popularization of Japanese taiko is reflected in the experiences and concerns of taiko players. Chapter 5 discusses how centrally discourses of the body and embodiment figure in the instruction and localization of contemporary taiko. These discourses of the body have deeply gendered implications as well, as taiko emerged primarily around the male body and expressions of masculinity in Japan. In the past two decades, however, the number of female taiko players has risen dramatically. Chapter 6 focuses on the experiences of women who play taiko in Japan. Although taiko has become a new vehicle of self-expression for women, the masculine standards of strength and power institutionalized in taiko aesthetics continue to constrain them.

While chapters 5 and 6 explore the relationship between locality and discourses of the body, chapter 7 examines instead attempts to "disembody" and "delocalize" taiko techniques by a segment of the taiko community. Dismayed by a perceived degradation of technique and continued marginalization from traditional Japanese performing arts, some influential members of the taiko community attempted to standardize taiko pedagogy and establish taiko as a national performing art deserving of a place alongside older genres of classical Japanese performance. Importantly, transforming the diversity of styles into a national genre entailed the textualization of taiko technique—that is, its standardization and delocalization—as well as scholarly justifications for the inclusion of (new) taiko drumming alongside (older) inherited forms of folk performance. The chapter looks at how these forms of textualization link institutional relations of power and knowledge with the emergence of a nationally representative genre of taiko drumming.

PART ONE

The Emergence and Popularization of Taiko

ONE

Taiko Drums and Taiko Drum Makers

pa·ri·ah (noun) 1. an outcast. 2. any person or animal that is generally despised or avoided. 3. (initial capital letter) a member of a low caste in southern India and Burma. *Origin:* 1605–15; < Tamil *paṟaiyar,* pl. of *paṟaiyan* lit., drummer (from a hereditary duty of the caste); deriv. of *paṟai,* a festival drum

RANDOM HOUSE DICTIONARY, 2010

FOR MOST JAPANESE, *taiko* simply means "drum." In this book, the term is used in a more technical sense to signify a subset of Japanese percussion. Japanese drums are typically differentiated based on their size, shape, and material composition.[1] Drum shells hollowed out from blocks of wood are classified differently from drum bodies made up of individual wooden slats, like a wine barrel. Drums also differ based on the kind of dried animal skin used for playing surfaces and the methods of attaching skins to the drum body, either by ropes, tacks, or bolts. Drums also are sounded in distinct ways (by hands, sticks, or mallets) and are employed differently in the three main genres of Japanese performance: music of the imperial court *(gagaku),* music accompanying the classical stage performing arts *(koten geinō),* and music used in religious ritual or the folk performing arts *(minzoku geinō).*[2]

Prior to the emergence of ensemble taiko drumming, taiko drums were used most extensively within the folk performing arts. This historical context contributed significantly to the development of taiko in the postwar period. In contrast to the classical performing arts of the stage or music of the imperial court, the lack of strict control over performance and instruction within the folk performing arts gave individuals the flexibility to use these instruments for performance ensembles. The fact that there was specifically a *taiko* boom is therefore not merely coincidental but reflects the particular structural location of these instruments within Japanese musicality.

Just as the popularity of ensemble taiko has brought taiko from rare and restricted use in the classical arts to the focal point of dynamic stage performance, it has also raised the cultural standing of taiko makers in Japan.

Previously relegated to outcast status for the occupation of drum making, which for generations had been deemed "polluting," taiko makers from the latter decades of the twentieth century onward enjoyed both high demand for their drums and growing recognition for their art. The higher profile of the instruments and those who make them is both evidence for and a consequence of the taiko boom. Instruments and instrument makers have thus moved from marginal positions to the center of Japanese cultural life.

TYPES OF DRUMS AND DRUM PERFORMANCE

The Drums of "Gagaku": The Music of the Imperial Court

Gagaku is the music and dance of the Japanese imperial court. It has its origins in older court music from China and Korea, which was brought to Japan in the fifth century, and from India, which arrived in the seventh and eighth centuries. In 701, imperial authorities established an imperial music bureau to oversee performances of court music. At the time of the bureau's establishment, most musicians in the imperial court remained Chinese or Korean, and the creation of a distinctly Japanese variety of court music did not occur until the middle of the ninth century, when a group of noblemen under the leadership of former emperor Soga arranged the divergent mass of styles that made up contemporary gagaku into the form they take today (Malm 1959, 89).

Since the Soga reforms, court music performances have been divided into two parts: one devoted to music of Indian and Chinese origin (tōgaku) and the other to music of Korean and Manchurian origin (koma-gaku) (Malm 1959, 89). Each of these is further subdivided into instrumental music (kangen) and dance music (bugaku). The type of drums used changes depending on whether instrumental music or dance music is being played. For example, the dadaiko, the largest of all the gagaku drums, is used only in performances of dance music. It has a carved-out wooden body and is covered on each end by cowhide drum skins that are held to the drum by long ropes tensioned with wooden pegs. A decorative wooden flame envelops the front head of the drum, which is imprinted with a mitsudomoe pattern (a yin-yang symbol with an extra teardrop). When struck with a felt-tipped mallet, the drum produces a low and resounding boom. Impressive as it is, the drum is used sparingly for percussive effect (for example, when a dancer stomps his foot on the stage). In performances of instrumental music, a gaku-daiko is used in place of the dadaiko, to similar effect. The gaku-daiko, which is about half the size of the *dadaiko,* is suspended from a wooden frame, and its cowhide drum skins are held on by a series of drum tacks.

Gagaku ensembles also make use of two smaller drums, the *san-no-tsu-zumi* and the *kakko.* Like the *dadaiko* and *gaku-daiko,* these drums are used alternately in performances of *tōgaku* and *koma-gaku.* The *san-no-tsuzumi,* a small hourglass-shaped drum of Korean origin, is played only during performances of *koma-gaku.* Positioned on its side, the drum's front is struck with a thin stick in one of a limited number of short patterns. The *kakko* drum is a barrel-shaped drum of Indo-Chinese origin that has two rope-fastened deerhide heads. In contrast to the *san-no-tsuzumi,* the drum is struck on both sides during performances of *tōgaku* in one of three simple patterns: a slow descending roll, a tap with the right stick, or a press roll with the right hand.

In sum, the four drums of *gagaku* are used for effect more than for sophisticated timekeeping. Musicians and performances of *gagaku* are strictly regulated by the Music Department of the Imperial Household Agency. The regulations have helped preserve *gagaku* since the ninth century (much of the original Indian, Korean, and Chinese court music has long since disappeared), but they also have prevented significant innovation. Although some musicians have left official court music to experiment with combinations of court music and orchestral music (Lancashire 2003), to my knowledge no ensemble taiko group has integrated the instruments or motifs of court music into its performance. The ensembles of classical Japanese theater have been a much greater source of inspiration.

The Classical Performing Arts: Noh

Noh is a kind of Japanese theater that developed from folk theatricals in rural villages and towns (Malm 1959, 106). The first of these, *sarugaku,* or "monkey music," was a form of comic theater derived from ritual performances at Shinto shrines. *Sarugaku* was augmented in later years by the addition of Chinese acrobatics *(sangaku)* and the rice-planting dances of peasants *(dengaku).* These two forms of *sarugaku* remained virtually indistinguishable until they were formalized and stylized in the late fourteenth and fifteenth centuries by a father-son duo, Kannami Kiyotsugu and Zeami Motokiyo. Both men were affiliated with a shrine in Nara and were sent by the shogun at the time, Yoshimitsu, to Kyoto, where they combined contemporary *sangaku* with Buddhist chanting to create a new hybrid theatrical performance called *sarugaku-no-noh.*

Sarugaku-no-noh, which came to be called Noh, was heavily influenced by the Zen Buddhist emphasis on "restraint and allusion" (Malm 1959, 108). In its current form, performances of Noh include long periods of chanted dialogue ("song") and slow, highly scripted movements ("dance"). Songs and dances are accompanied by an ensemble (*hayashi*) made up of a flute called the *noh-kan* and three drums: *ko-tsuzumi, ō-tsuzumi,* and taiko. The *ko-tsuzumi* is the smallest of the three drums. It has an hourglass-shaped body made of zelkova wood, much like the *san-no-tsuzumi* used in court music, and two rope-fastened horsehide heads. The inner shell of the drum is carved with a special pattern to improve resonance and timbre, and a small piece of deerhide is applied to the center of the bottom drumhead to control reverberation. A *ko-tsuzumi* player places the drum on his left shoulder and strikes it with the fingers of his right hand. Tightening or loosening the tension on the ropes running the length of the drum raises or lowers the pitch of the drum. Skillful manipulation of rope tension, together with various finger strikes, produces the five basic *ko-tsuzumi* sounds.

The *ō-tsuzumi* is shaped like the *ko-tsuzumi* but is slightly larger. Two sets of ropes extend along the body of the *ō-tsuzumi* from cowhide heads on each side. One set holds the drumheads to the body; the other wraps around them and is tightened or loosened, as in the *ko-tsuzumi,* to raise or lower the pitch of the drum. The drum skins are made out of cowhide, not horsehide like the *ko-tsuzumi.* In contrast to the *ko-tsuzumi,* which is held by the left hand on the right shoulder and then struck with the right hand, the *ō-tsuzumi* rests on the performer's left hip and is struck with a sideways motion of the right hand. Deerskin thimbles are sometimes used to enhance the sounds produced by the drum, which are divided into three basic types, ranging from strong to weak.

The barrel-shaped body of the *noh taiko* differentiates it from the two hourglass-shaped *tsuzumi* and defines it as a type of taiko. A block of zelkova wood is carved out to fashion the body of the taiko, which is approximately six inches deep and twelve inches across. Two drum skins, made either of cowhide or horsehide, are held to its body by tightly drawn ropes. The drum rests horizontally on a stand that keeps it several inches from the floor, and it is struck with two lightweight sticks whose ends taper slightly. *Noh taiko* are, therefore, distinguished from *tsuzumi* drums not only by their barrel shape but also by the use of sticks, instead of hands, to produce sound. Varieties of *shime-daiko* used in the folk performing arts have slightly thicker heads, which allow for higher pitch and greater durability. Since Noh theater grew

FIGURE 3. Drums used in festival ensembles: *shime-daiko* (left) and *chū-daiko* (right). Photo courtesy of the Miyamoto Unosuke Company.

out of folk performing arts like *sarugaku,* it is appropriate to think of the *noh taiko* as a lighter-weight version of its more robust folk cousin (figure 3).

The Classical Performing Arts: Kabuki

Originating in the risqué riverbed dance-theater of a Kyoto shrine maiden named Okuni, kabuki evolved into a form of popular theater more suited to the urbane tastes of merchants and city dwellers than Noh (Foreman 2005, 38). Still, a debt to the Noh theater is evident in the conservation of the Noh ensemble in kabuki theater. Together with the *shamisen* (three-stringed Japanese lute), the instruments of the Noh ensemble are the major source of musical accompaniment for kabuki performances. Drummers in kabuki ensembles use drum calls *(kakegoe)* to mark time and coordinate their performance, as in Noh. In addition to this ensemble music, musicians concealed in an offstage area called the *geza* provide sound effects. The *geza* houses a myriad of percussion, including the drums of the Noh ensemble as well as the larger *ōdaiko* and *okedō-daiko*.

Like the *shime-daiko,* the barrel-shaped *ōdaiko* is carved out of a single block of wood, but it is much larger—approximately four to six feet in diameter and slightly smaller in height (figure 4). Its two cowhide drumheads

FIGURE 4. *Ōdaiko.* Photo courtesy of the Miyamoto Unosuke Company.

are fastened to its body by a ring of metal tacks, like the *gaku-daiko. Ōdaiko* were originally used to advertise kabuki performances. In those early days, the state of kabuki theater was so tenuous that audiences would not know whether performances would take place until they heard the sound of the *ōdaiko.* In contemporary kabuki, the *ōdaiko* is played in the concealed *geza* with long, thin bamboo rods to create sound effects, such as falling snow or rain.

The *okedō-daiko* (or *daibyōshi*) is cylindrical in shape, and it is constructed out of individual staves, not a hollowed-out shell. The staves are held together by two hoops, and the drumheads are fastened with ropes to the drum body, which has similar dimensions to the *ōdaiko* (figure 5). Evoking its origins in the folk performing arts, it is used in the *geza* to create the atmosphere of a "folk" festival. In size and form, the *okedō-daiko* and the *daibyōshi* are indistinguishable—the name *daibyōshi* being merely the lingo of *geza* musicians. Along with several types of gongs and mallet percussion, *geza* musicians augment the sounds of these two taiko with *gaku-daiko,* for scenes depicting war, and the *uchiwa-daiko,* a fan drum, for other percussive effects.

Noh and kabuki, along with court music, are classified together in Japan as *hōgaku,* or "music of the homeland." In common usage, *hōgaku* is opposed

FIGURE 5. *Okedō-daiko* (or *daibyōshi*). Photo courtesy of the Miyamoto Unosuke Company.

to *yōgaku,* or "Western music." In addition to its connection to stage theater or court music, musicianship in the world of *hōgaku* is strictly regulated—one usually cannot begin stage performance without passing through an apprenticeship of ten years or longer. The strict regulation of training and performance distinguishes Noh, kabuki, and court music from the music of Japanese ritual and festivity.

Folk and Religious Music

The music of Japanese ritual and festivity derives primarily from a collection of religious practices and worship in Japan dedicated to ancestors and supernatural spirits *(kami)* called Shinto (Kawano 2005). At structures enshrining particular spirits, formal rituals evolved into the sacred music and dance called *kagura,* or "god music." *Kagura* is typically divided into two types: music for Shinto functions or formal parts of ceremonies at local shrines *(mi-kagura),* and music that accompanies Shinto festivals *(sato-kagura)* conducted at important seasonal moments in the agricultural cycle. The often-spectacular grand processions associated with contemporary Japanese festivals descend from *sato-kagura*.

The music that accompanies these rituals and processions (there is no completely instrumental folk music) is provided by ensembles typically made up of two kinds of taiko (small *shime-daiko* and larger *chū-daiko*), Japanese flute *(fue),* and small brass gongs *(atarigane). Chū-daiko* are smaller versions of the *ōdaiko* used in the kabuki *geza. Chū-daiko,* also called *miya-daiko,* are the most extensively used variety of taiko in the contemporary taiko ensembles that are the subject of this book (figure 6).[3] The appellation *miya,* which means "shrine," derives from the near ubiquity of these drums in Shinto shrines. (They are also found commonly in Buddhist temples.) The extensive use of *chū-daiko* in *kagura,* festival processions, Bon dance, and other forms of the folk performing arts relates directly to the consolidation of the majority of the Japanese population under the religious institutions of Shinto and Buddhism.

Festival ensembles are often named for the areas where they originated, a custom that reflects the Shinto emphasis on marking place through ritual (see Kawano 2005). Although their rhythms can be complex, they are usually rather slow and timed to coincide either with dances or with movements in a procession (Malm 1959, 50). That said, of the three types of music discussed here, festival music is where taiko drums play the most central role. Organized around rhythmic cadences rather than harmonic motifs, the drumming of festival ensembles is more extensive than that found in other kinds of indigenous Japanese music, such that "the importance of the drum as a center of many Japanese folk dances is little realized by the casual visitor to Japan" (248).

Taiko, especially *chū-daiko,* also retain an important position in Buddhist ritual. *Shōmyō* chants, based on sacred Buddhist texts and hymns, are vocalized to the steady rhythm of the *chū-daiko* drum. During the annual summer Buddhist festival of O-Bon, *chū-daiko* drums accompany festival dancing and singing. In fact, it is from the musical accompaniment to this ritual that one influential style of ensemble taiko derives (see chapter 2). During the rituals of the Nichiren sect of Japanese Buddhism, fan drums, mentioned earlier in connection with the music of the kabuki theater, are also used to accompany enthusiastic chanting.

The division between folk performing arts and religiously inspired festival music is ambiguous, because most of what is called "folk music" in Japan, with the exception of some folk songs or work songs, is derived from religious

FIGURE 6. *Chū-daiko* (or *miya-daiko*). Photo courtesy of Miyamoto Unosuke Company.

festivals or worship. Yet the folk performing arts are usually considered distinct from religious music and the performing arts of the stage, even though classical performing arts like Noh and kabuki have roots in just these folk entertainments. Whether or not they are considered separate from or part of religious music, folk performing arts are distinct from the classical performing arts in several other respects.

First, classical Japanese music includes specific artistic styles indigenous to Japan that are performed on a stage. Although many folk performing arts are currently performed on a stage, they were not originally created for that purpose; rather, they were created by a particular community for that community, usually as a part of a religious festival or ceremony. Second, and as a corollary of the first, compositions in the classical performing arts typically have a specific author or composer. By virtue of their being created within a community sometime in the past, however, folk performing arts are by definition authorless. Third, classical stage music is typically notated, and performance is legitimated by proper reproduction of that score. Although notation often leaves much room for interpretation, which makes long-term study with a teacher important, texts continue to play an important role in the classical performing arts. In contrast, folk performing arts typically have little to no basis in notation and are usually transmitted orally. Lack of notation and the custom of oral transmission leave space for more play and individuality in performance. Finally, whereas the classical performing arts have taken root and developed in urban centers, the folk performing arts have historically been identified with rural communities, especially those that originated before the end of World War II.[4] Reflecting this provincial basis, folk performing arts have also been referred to as "local" or "regional" arts.

In sum, as one moves away from the realm of court music and classical theater toward the domain of the folk performing arts, the prominence of drums and drumming increases, especially on *chū-daiko*. When thinking about newer taiko ensembles, it is important not to ignore their ties to religious rituals and communal celebrations, both of which are distinct from the rarefied performances of court music and classical theatrical ensembles. For much of Japanese history, the customs and celebrations of the common "folk" were looked upon as crude and vulgar in comparison to the refinement of the classical stage arts, with lack of notation and unregulated transmission providing yet further testimony. However, in the aftermath of World War II, the transformation of these rude and vulgar customs into examples of national-cultural heritage paralleled the elevation of their central implement, the taiko, into a symbol of a new Japanese performance culture. This same elevation applies to those who have worked for generations to fashion these instruments for the use of ritual specialists and common folk.

DRUM MAKERS AND THE TAIKO BOOM

Asano Taiko

As we settled into the comfortable leather chairs in his spacious office, Yoshi, the general manager of Asano Taiko, told me the story of his company. One of the most successful taiko makers in Japan, Asano Taiko is a family-owned enterprise over four hundred years old. In 1609, not long after the powerful Tokugawa family seized control of Japan and ushered in over 250 years of relatively stable peace, a wealthy landowner of the Kaga clan sent Yoshi's ancestors to present-day Mattō City in Ishikawa Prefecture to establish a base for the manufacture of Noh drums as well as leather saddles, armor, and helmets for military use.[5] The business expanded to include folk and festival drums in the Meiji period (1868–1912) and now encompasses an even wider variety of standard Japanese instruments along with entirely new, custom-designed drums. Perhaps unsurprisingly, company advertising highlights this impressive longevity, stating proudly that Asano Taiko "maintains into the present traditional techniques passed down since first receiving its charge in the seventeenth century." Even with such a long history, Yoshi, a seventeenth-generation taiko maker himself, expressed to me how much his company had benefited from the postwar surge in ensemble taiko drumming. Proof of this, he told me, was manifest in the very buildings surrounding us.

Prior to the postwar emergence of ensemble taiko drumming, a single building housed the entire business, from production to sales. Now, the company grounds are a sprawling complex of several large buildings the manufacturer calls Asano Taiko Village. The "village" includes two state-of-the-art warehouses. The larger of the two is a multilevel, climate-controlled space where hollowed-out drum shells are left to air dry before being fashioned into drums. The other, smaller warehouse is packed tight with drums and filled with smoke. The smoke hastens the drying process, which is useful if a client needs a drum in less than the four or five years it normally takes to make one. There is also a large factory space full of blocks of wood, cowhides, and artisans working on drums at different stages in the manufacturing process. In addition to these manufacturing sites, the company headquarters also has a drum museum, which houses over one hundred drums from across the globe as well as taiko-related audiovisual materials, a product showroom, a high-tech practice space with vaulted ceilings and a specially soundproofed interior, a regular practice room for use by an Asano-sponsored professional taiko group and by students who come for workshops or weekly classes, and a "taiko culture research institute." The institute publishes the manufacturer's taiko-related journal, *Taikology,* along with other books on taiko history, production, and performance. Asano Taiko Village is not merely a location for the manufacture and sale of taiko drums, the promotional literature says, but a place where all things related to taiko can be "seen, heard, and learned."

Midway through our interview, Yoshi gave me a tour of the grounds. Stepping into the sunlight, we threaded our way through piles of huge tree trunks waiting to be cut and processed. Having made so many large *ōdaiko* drums to meet burgeoning domestic demand, the company has begun importing giant tree trunks from Africa. (As mentioned earlier, an *ōdaiko* is fashioned out of a single block of wood, not slats, so the size of the woodblock—the size of the tree—determines the size of the drum.) Once inside the factory, Yoshi showed me how processed blocks of wood are hollowed out into drum shells, and then after years of drying in the warehouse are carved by hand on the inside with distinctive patterns that enhance the resonance of the finished drum (the exact patterns used differ by manufacturer and are trade secrets). Several cowhides were hanging to dry from the ceiling, illuminated from behind. As we passed them, Yoshi paused a moment to point out how uneven the skin was. Here where the skin is thinner, he said, we will use it to make a smaller drum; here where it is rougher and thicker, we will stretch it over a larger drum that needs to withstand much more vigorous pounding. Years of experience had cultivated the now middle-aged manager's keen eye for the subtle properties of different skins—whether from bulls or cows, domestic or foreign cattle—as well as different kinds of wood. Once dry, he continued, the skins become hard and tough. They are stretched over drum shells with ropes and wooden dowels, and then they are tightened by hand until the appropriate tone is reached. (Knowing how much tension to apply requires considerable skill, because the timbre will continue to change slightly even after the drum is finished.) Once the appropriate tension is reached, artisans attach the hide to the drum with small metal rivets that are pounded neatly in two rows around the drumhead.

We sat down again for a cup of tea, and Yoshi told me how hard he had worked to bring about the current success of his company. Given the rapid and recent expansion of his Asano Taiko, the drum maker had needed to go outside the immediate family and hire locals to help out in the factory. Yoshi told me plainly that he had worked hard to make Asano Taiko a place where someone "wouldn't be ashamed to work," especially the young women who helped out in the factory and store. His parents had been sloppy account managers, hastily rushing to gather up financial papers when authorities arrived to examine them. Without hesitation, Yoshi gestured at two framed certificates hanging on the wall beside us. Beaming with pride, he told me that the certificates were from the national tax office. The company had received them as awards for outstanding tax preparation in two separate years.

Why would someone be ashamed to work at a taiko manufacturer, especially one as successful as Asano Taiko? And why of all things would the general manager be so proud of paying corporate taxes that he would hang these certificates on the wall and point them out to me? The answers to these questions lie in the fact that the Asano family, like virtually all taiko makers in Japan, belong to an outcast group called *burakumin,* or *buraku* people. The term literally means "hamlet people," and, although their exact origins are uncertain, most scholars agree that the *burakumin* trace back to another outcast group, called *senmin,* that coalesced in the Tokugawa period (1603–1867) (DeVos and Wagatsuma 1966; Donoghue 1978; Henshall 1999, 49). The *senmin* comprised mostly *eta* (literally, "great filth"), who worked in so-called polluting occupations such as butchery, tanning, leatherwork, and grave digging, and *hinin* ("non-persons"), who were social undesirables such as itinerant musicians, fugitives, beggars, and vagabonds. The Tokugawa authorities socially and legally marginalized these groups, effectively transforming them into outcasts. Because the construction of taiko involves handling the carcasses and skins of animals, the work was considered polluting by the Buddhist-influenced government and hence left to members of this new class.

Although official occupational discrimination was abolished with the passage of the Emancipation Edict in 1871 at the end of the Tokugawa shogunate, unofficial social discrimination against the *burakumin* has persisted into the contemporary era. Employers, as well as marriage agencies, have been known to check the family registers of applicants for evidence of residence in a known *buraku* community. *Buraku* youth continue to have lower rates of academic success and lower levels of occupational attainment than their peers (Henshall 1999, 50; Hill 2003, 81–82; Kitaguchi 1999). This alienation leads some *buraku* youth to turn to crime or violence; although reliable statistics are hard to find (Bondy 2010), estimates indicate a disproportional involvement of *buraku* youth in Japan's notorious *yakuza* crime families (Ames 1981; Henshall 1999, 52; Kaplan and DuBro 2003, 132–133). While many majority Japanese are sympathetic to the plight of the *buraku* people, the presumed association with violence and crime has contributed to a general unease and wariness toward them. It was to this prejudice against and generalized suspicion of *buraku* people that Yoshi referred in his discussion with me. In fact, he told me that his own family had to deal with issues associated with a family register check when his daughter married a few years earlier. Thus, the awards from the national tax office stood as official recognition of the integrity of his, a *buraku* person's, business.

Given the status of taiko makers as part of a historically segregated population, the four-hundred-year history of Asano Taiko Corporation represents not just the maintenance of an unbroken tradition of craftsmanship but also the legacy of generations of discrimination. Yet just as the drums the company makes have moved into a position of prominence in the wake of the taiko boom, taiko makers have been greeted by unprecedented demand for their instruments. This demand has not only engendered economic benefits; it has also enabled taiko makers (and *buraku* groups more generally) to reimagine their taiko-making techniques as Japanese "tradition" and to advocate for the elimination of all remaining discrimination against them. Perhaps the clearest illustration of these two aims is found among the residents of the Naniwa district in metropolitan Osaka City.

According to the general manager of Asano Taiko, there is approximately one taiko manufacturer per prefecture in contemporary Japan. (Some regions have more than one.) One of the largest concentrations of taiko manufacturers in Japan is found in the Naniwa Ward of Osaka City, an area located at the southern reaches of the Osaka Loop Line that also happens to be home to one of largest populations of *burakumin* in Japan. Naniwa Ward is an officially designated "assimilation area." Assimilation areas are former *buraku* areas that received special funding from the Japanese government to improve living conditions following the passage of the Special Measures Law for Assimilation Projects in 1969 (Neary 1997, 64). Known chiefly for the production of leather goods and, of course, taiko, Naniwa Ward is an economically depressed region of one of the urban areas hit hardest by Japan's prolonged recession. On my first visit there, I took a wrong turn and stumbled onto a series of dilapidated cardboard shacks shrouded in bright blue tarp, the temporary abodes of homeless people living under a busy elevated freeway.

Present-day Naniwa Ward encompasses a *buraku* area formerly known as Watanabe Village. As in other urban communities in Japan, local elites have worked to reclaim the "old village" *(furusato)* within the newly amalgamated urban space as a basis for civic community (Bestor 1989; Ivy 1995; J. Robertson 1991). Had I gone the other way on my first visit to the area, I would have been led toward the Osaka Human Rights Museum along the Road of Human Rights and Taiko (Jinken Taiko Rōdo). Opened in late 2003, the Road of Human Rights and Taiko is the result of efforts by the Osaka City government, the Naniwa branch of the Buraku Liberation League (BLL)—a major advocacy group for *buraku* issues—and other local groups. The road's construction was intended not only to help bring tourists to the area and the museum but also to reclaim the three-hundred-year history of drum making in the community.[6]

The impetus to create the road emerged in response to the success of an ensemble taiko group made up of local youth. This group, Taiko Ikari (literally, "Taiko Rage"), formed over a decade earlier as this younger generation became conscious of the loss of a tradition of taiko drumming in the area. The "rage" in the group's name reflects its mission to advocate through performance the elimination of all kinds of discrimination in Japan and throughout the world. Given the group's local roots and commitment to *buraku* issues, it is surprising that its founding was in fact a response to the activities of a taiko ensemble quite far away.

Prior to the formation of Ikari, a group of ensemble taiko drummers from Okinawa called Zampa Ufujishi Daiko visited the legendary taiko-making area of Naniwa in search of high-quality drums to use in their performances. Originally stimulated by new ensemble taiko groups from the mainland, the Okinawan drummers were surprised to find that there were no competent taiko players in an area known widely for its abundance of taiko manufacturers. Zampa's inquiries prompted elites in the area to reflect on the irony of this situation. The local chapter of the BLL subsequently invited Zampa to perform a concert in support of rights for *burakumin* and Okinawans living in the Osaka area. Inspired by the example of the Okinawan drummers, several younger members of the community began playing taiko themselves, carefully mimicking the movements they saw on videotapes of Zampa's performances. Eager to support what appeared to be a nascent local taiko ensemble, the BLL helped provide material and financial assistance to the group. Although many of the young drummers had initially joined out of a desire to stand out, look cool, and gain status in the neighborhood, once they saw the strong emotional reactions of their older neighbors they began to take more seriously their newfound roles—*buraku* drummers playing instruments that their *buraku* ancestors had suffered to produce. The fact that there were no impressive taiko drummers in the community, they reasoned, was "nothing more than a manifestation of the long history of discrimination" (Terada 2008, 311) directed against members of the community. No longer content to remain in the background while their instruments were taken up enthusiastically by other Japanese, in locations as far away as Okinawa, they resolved to play, with the purpose of revealing and overcoming all forms of discrimination (310–311).

In an interview, the current leader of the group recalled an experience of one group member. A son of a taiko maker in the community hoped to marry someone from outside the community, but his fiancée's father opposed the marriage on the grounds of the young man's status as a *burakumin*. After seeing a performance by Taiko Ikari, however, the father changed his mind. Realizing his prejudice, he told the boy that he would feel silly if he continued to resist the marriage. He had found Ikari's performance to be full of spirit and passion and was impressed by how much it moved the audience. He now recognized the importance of taiko making and performance. When the man thanked the group and told them this story, they wept openly and recognized anew the power of their performance. An older member of the community confirmed the young leader's account in a recent documentary: "I know the story sounds like something out of a movie, but it actually happened!" (Terada 2011).

Despite its passion, the early Taiko Ikari had far more pride than skill. This became clear a few years after the group began performing, when they received a visit from Jishōya Ichiro, a former leader of Ondekoza who happened to live nearby. As a member of Ikari put it to me, after Jishōya made just a few strikes on the big ōdaiko drum, the group members realized his skill. After learning about his performance background, the drummers asked him to help them improve. Jishōya admired their enthusiasm but commented that their performance left the audience more "tired" than inspired. He taught them new pieces, many of which they still play, and new approaches to playing that dramatically improved the quality of their performances.[7]

With an increased local profile, stronger sense of mission, and enhanced set of taiko skills, Taiko Ikari came to serve as a model for other groups. Other BLL chapters soon started taiko groups, but the shared experience of oppression did not lead easily toward cooperation. As the ethnomusicologist Yoshitaka Terada states, "There is a strong tendency among Buraku people . . . to distrust outsiders, presumably in order to protect themselves from discrimination. This tendency is found even among Buraku people and . . . [has led to] sectional rivalry . . . [that] has prevented [Buraku-based] taiko groups from interacting with each other." Still, attempts have been made to overcome these differences through performance. One concert in 1999 featured eleven different *buraku* groups and over one hundred drummers (Terada 2008, 313).

I attended a similar concert in late July 2008 that featured four *buraku* groups from the Osaka area. In the rehearsal, the performance, and the after-party, unity was the prevailing theme. The groups took direction from one another in practice, shared drummers across pieces during the concert, and swapped stories in the jocular atmosphere of the party. Even so, during the after-party, a hint of physical competition broke with the general spirit of camaraderie. A series of arm-wrestling matches began between members of different groups (into which even this out-of-shape anthropologist was drafted). Nevertheless, the conversations I had with drummers, along with the satisfied smiles on the faces of young drummers and more senior organizers of the event, indicated to me that the performance was greeted enthusiastically by many involved. This bodes well for a future in which drumming continues to provide a shared basis for advocating equality and eliminating discrimination against the *burakumin* and other minority groups in Japan.

Along with providing a new form of advocacy, the (re)appropriation of taiko drumming by the descendants of taiko makers is yet another tangible manifestation of the taiko boom and its positive effect on the formerly marginalized individuals, like the employees of Asano Taiko Corporation, who make the instruments at the center of ensemble taiko performance. If the interest of an Okinawan group had not been stimulated by the popular new taiko drumming of the mainland, it is likely that Taiko Ikari would not have emerged when and how it did. If the development of compelling performance techniques by new taiko professionals like Jishōya Ichiro had not occurred, Taiko Ikari clearly would not look and sound like it does. If the success of the early ensemble taiko groups had not begun to generate popular national and international interest in Japanese taiko drumming, Taiko Ikari would have encountered greater difficulty gaining visibility and securing performance opportunities. This in turn would likely have delayed the utilization of ensemble taiko in other *buraku* areas. Of course, Taiko Ikari received early and significant financial support from local governmental and nongovernmental organizations. In this respect, the emergence of Taiko Ikari parallels patterns seen elsewhere in Japan. Nevertheless, the unique relationship of the descendants of *buraku* taiko makers to the new genre of ensemble taiko drumming adds a level of meaning and significance to their performance activities not found among other taiko groups in Japan. It also represents a point of pride for the community of Naniwa Ward, pride that is made publicly visible in the aforementioned Road of Human Rights and Taiko.

The Road of Human Rights and Taiko

Just as Taiko Ikari represents a movement to reappropriate a "lost" drumming tradition (in a novel form, of course), the Road of Human Rights and Taiko (hereafter, the Taiko Road) signifies a move to bring into public view, and thus to memorialize and celebrate, a long history of drum making in the community that had formerly been hidden out of shame. But the Taiko Road does not merely pause to reflect publicly on the past; it also looks toward the future, imaging a Naniwa community based on the protection of human rights and the elimination of all forms of discrimination. This combination of a concern for drum-making culture and for human rights may seem odd, but it makes sense in the context of recent shifts among *buraku* groups to couch narrower local concerns within the universalist discourse of global human rights (Neary 1997, 75).[8] In this sense, claims for *buraku* rights and for recognition of *buraku* heritage are tantamount to the claims of any oppressed minority for its human rights. The Taiko Road connects the heritage of the Naniwa community with a broad understanding of human rights that includes advocacy for other minority groups. In this manner, it extends the goals of Taiko Ikari into the form of a public "field museum," as it is called. A new folk culture of drumming is appropriated to reflect on the past and present Naniwa community and to provide the basis for shared advocacy on behalf of Osaka's other major minority groups (figure 7).

The Taiko Road is made up of nine zones that surround a central axis.[9] This central axis, the Taiko Maker Zone, leads visitors on a five-hundred-meter path from Ashiharabashi Station to the Osaka Human Rights Museum (also known as Liberty Osaka). The central Taiko Maker Zone is marked by a series of round metal information kiosks shaped like taiko drumheads. The kiosks not only give directions to sites on the road or to nearby train stations but also contain longer, instructive passages on various taiko-related topics. One kiosk describes the emergence of ensemble taiko drumming as a new performing art; another explains the centrality of Watanabe Village in the history of Japanese taiko production. Other kiosks utilize images to depict the seven stages of the taiko-making process: the transformation of a tree trunk into the body of a drum; the techniques used to convert cowhides into drumheads (notably, the first few steps of this process are described in text only); and the methods involved in fastening the finished skins on the drum shells. At the bottom of all the kiosks are directions to the Osaka Human Rights Museum, written in Japanese, English, Chinese, and Korean.

Perhaps more striking, everyday objects modified to reflect the heritage of drum making in the community are placed strategically along the road. Right outside Ashiharabashi Station, for example, a wheelchair-accessible telephone booth has half a taiko shell jutting out of its top. Farther down the road, flowerpots fashioned in the shape of taiko drum shells decorate the entrance to the Naniwa Human Rights Culture Center. Bus shelters lining the road have benches with armrests that look like the riveted heads of taiko drums. During the day, these shelters announce the imminent arrival of buses with the sound of taiko drumming. The drumming is a recorded performance of Taiko Ikari, reflecting the subtle yet significant recognition of the group's importance to the community that runs through the exhibits along the road. Small posters placed around the bus shelters display images

FIGURE 7. Discrimination against *buraku* communities in Japan has even attracted the attention of foreign organizations like the United Nations. This cartoon from a *Japan Times* newspaper article visually expresses how *buraku* communities have adopted both ensemble taiko and the global discourse of human rights to counter discrimination (Priestly 2009). Illustration by Chris MacKenzie.

of different kinds of taiko, and informative panels located above the benches tell visitors about taiko design and construction, such as the rivets that attach drumheads to drum shells and the carrying handles fastened to the sides of the drum body. One particular panel displays an example of taiko notation used by Taiko Ikari. The taiko score is printed not on paper but on a rectangular piece of dried rawhide, joining together the two *buraku* industries of leatherwork and taiko making.

The terminus of this section of the road opens on the left into Tamahime Park (Jeweled Princess Park). Standing in the center of the park, encircled by a wooden bench, is a tall zelkova tree. The tree's placement at the center of the park is an indication of its symbolic importance: known for its strength and beautiful grain, zelkova is one of the most popular woods for taiko. Just beyond the main entrance to the park stands another important landmark. On top of a series of curved wooden slats, which are designed to appear as if they have sprouted up from the ground, sits a large clock tower. The tower rises to a height that makes the clock visible from some distance, but it does not merely indicate time. At six points in the day, the tower opens up to reveal two wooden puppets placed on opposite sides of a taiko drum. As the recorded sound of drumming emanates from the tower, the puppet drummers move on a rotating platform in a manner that mimics the choreography of the recorded taiko performance. (The recorded drum pattern here as well is played by Taiko Ikari, whose members also served as models for the puppets.) The clock tower is located on a site that used to be the home of the most prosperous taiko maker in the community, Taikoya Matabē. As the monument explains, it was the success of this merchant that brought renown to the Watanabe Village community of drum makers in the past. Reflecting this reverence for heritage, the curved slats supporting the tower are meant to represent the supportive hands of the Naniwa community, joined in the spirit of cooperation and respect for inherited culture.

A walk down the main axis of the Taiko Road thus takes the visitor on an educational journey through the history and industry of the old and new Naniwa community. Rather than obscuring the history of leather production and taiko production, the road opens up this heritage for public consumption. Much like the Asano Taiko Corporation's celebration of its four-hundred-year tradition of taiko production, the past is not bemoaned as a shameful encumbrance but rather embraced as a valued inheritance of skills, knowledge, and culture. The ensemble drumming of Taiko Ikari is featured throughout the road as evidence of a vibrant new performing arts culture that builds on this local inheritance. References to the generations of discrimination that brought the community into being (and contributed to its longevity) are left off signposts, displays, and kiosks. (These are reserved for exhibits in the Osaka Human Rights Museum.) Instead, the road presents Naniwa as a community that is mindful of its past and concerned with the preservation of human rights into the future. One ward poster on the road gestures toward this new direction and to the centrality of respect for human rights in its vision of the future. It proclaims Naniwa Ward to be a community based on "Life, Love, and Human Rights," with tolerance and understanding for those who have different cultures and customs.[10]

Indeed, as one moves from the park through the Taiko Maker Zone toward the Osaka Human Rights Museum, several bronze statues of drummers ground these more abstract notions of human rights within the more accessible context of drum culture. Perhaps predictably, the first statue one encounters is a representation of *wadaiko* (Japanese drumming). Two male drummers stand playing large and small *chū-daiko* while a third sits in front of a *shime-daiko*. Echoing the theme of taiko production as well as performance, the monument explains the process used to make the drums shown. Informants told me that the drummers from Ikari posed as models for this statue, expressing once again the association between the road and Taiko Ikari.[11]

Farther down the street is a statue of three Okinawan *eisa* drummers. Their drums, playing position, and costumes clearly differentiate them from those displayed in the statue of the *wadaiko* drummers. The monument explains that *eisa* is a drum-dance style native to Okinawa. Now a part of Japan, Okinawa was not always so. (An independent kingdom until the seventeenth century, Okinawa was also a U.S. territory from 1952 to 1975.) Possessed of ethnic characteristics that distinguish them from mainland Japanese, Okinawans compose one of Japan's largest minority groups (Taira 1997). Here, the statue stands as a testament not just to the existence of this significant national minority but also to something much closer to home. Not far from Naniwa Ward, the Taishō Ward of Osaka contains one of the largest concentrations of Okinawans on the mainland. The statue explains that the young members of this community took up *eisa* drumming in the mid-1970s as a means of performing ethnic heritage. The statue functions to include the Okinawan minority, ambivalent members of a national Japanese community that has sometimes denigrated them as backwards, as a part of the multiethnic tapestry of modern Osaka.

Just beyond the statue of *eisa* drummers is a statue of four musicians (three women and one man) seated in the playing style of *samul nori*. Utilizing four ethnically Korean percussion instruments—*janggo, jing, kkwaenggwari,* and *buk*—*samul nori* derives from Korean folk music but was converted into a stage art in the 1970s, much like ensemble taiko in Japan (Hesselink 2004). Along with *burakumin* and Okinawans, ethnic Koreans constitute another of Japan's and Osaka's largest minority groups. In fact, one of the largest communities of ethnic Koreans in Japan is located in the Tsuruhashi district just east of Naniwa Ward. The descendants of Korean migrants to Japan before and during World War II, ethnic Koreans like these Osaka residents have suffered from discrimination at the hands of majority Japanese for generations (Chung 2006; Henshall 1999; Lee 2006). Unable to achieve citizenship without giving up their Korean heritage and adopting new surnames, ethnic Koreans commonly feel alienated from Japanese society, even though many do not even speak Korean (Henshall 1999, 62–65). Here, the arrangement of drummers symbolizes the ethnic Korean community of Osaka that, like the community of Okinawans, has taken up *samul nori* as a means of performing ethnic identity.

The Taiko Road ends with another statue of generically "Japanese" drummers. This time, the statue features *hayashi-daiko,* a style of playing that utilizes shoulder-harnessed *okedō-daiko* drums. This style of playing has been associated historically with folk performance in northern Japan. (In its contemporary manifestation, though, this playing style has also been heavily influenced by the Korean style of playing the shoulder-harnessed *janggu*). Here, this "regional" playing style is rendered generically as another form of *wadaiko.* In contrast to the first *wadaiko* statue, however, this one features a woman holding and playing a drum as well as two men, breaking with the masculine orientation of the other statue and perhaps signaling the popularity of taiko drumming among Japanese women.

Across from this final statue lies the entrance to the Osaka Human Rights Museum. Inside the museum is a series of exhibits about the largest minority populations in Japan—the *burakumin,* ethnic Koreans, Okinawans, the Ainu of Hokkaido—and other groups in Japanese society that have suffered from discrimination, such as women, gays and lesbians, the disabled, homeless, HIV/AIDS sufferers, as well as victims of leprosy, Minamata disease, and other forms of industrial pollution. The four statues of drummers thus provide a space of transition from the celebration of taiko production and performance in the Taiko Maker Zone and the concern with human rights in the museum. Japanese, Okinawan, and Korean drumming are not displayed for their intrinsic interest alone but function to demonstrate the commitment of community leaders to move in solidarity with all discriminated communities in Japan, locally in Osaka, and even beyond Japan throughout the world. Knitting these large Japanese minority groups even closer together is their shared use of drumming to perform ethnic identity.[12]

· · ·

Visiting the Taiko Road in the summer of 2008 made me recall an experience I had in 2000 during my fieldwork with the taiko ensemble Kodo. One weekend morning, as I sat working on translations in the Kodo office, Akira, an office manager, came to my desk with an excited look on his usually somber face. He carried in his hand a copy of that morning's *Nikkei* newspaper (a nationally circulating financial newspaper like the *Wall Street Journal* or *Financial Times*). He opened up the front section of the paper and showed me a full-page advertisement that had been taken out by the Asano Taiko Corporation. The advertisement celebrated the company's achievement in having received a Good Design Award for one of its custom-designed drums. This was the first time that a taiko maker had received such an award (the company has gone on to win two more), and it appeared that the Asano Corporation was eager to publicize its achievement. Akira asked what I thought the advertisement meant. I told him that the advertisement probably demonstrated the company's pride in receiving the award, but he seemed unconvinced. Shaking his head slightly, he said, "Well, sure they're proud. But this is more than just pride. I think there's an attempt to compensate for some feelings of inferiority. There's pride, and then there's a full-page ad in the *Nikkei*..." At the time, I found Akira's comment to be a bit harsh. Reflecting on my research since, however, I think that he pinpointed early on the desire for recognition that underlies Asano Taiko's business and cultural activities, Taiko Ikari's mission, and the organization of the Taiko Road.

This chapter began with a description of the major genres of Japanese musical performance and the function of drums within them. As one moves further from the center of "traditional" theatrical performance and closer to peripheral performance styles (literally "peripheral," in the spatial sense of regional or rural places), the use of taiko increases. This peripheral status as well as the informality and flexibility associated with it contributed greatly to the emergence and popularization of ensemble taiko drumming. Ultimately, this led to a shift in the place of taiko from the margins of performance in *gagaku,* Noh, and kabuki to the center of new taiko ensembles.

The emergence of taiko ensembles and the ensuing taiko boom helped bring about a movement from the margins to the mainstream of cultural consciousness for the drum makers as well as the drums. The presence of the Asano Taiko Corporation, the members of Taiko Ikari, and the taiko makers of Naniwa Ward in Osaka at the heart of one of Japan's most vibrant performing arts provides as much evidence of their long commitment to drum making as the surge in the popularity of taiko drumming called the "taiko boom." This new popularity of Japanese drumming, though not actually stimulated by the *burakumin,* has enabled members of this formerly marginalized occupational caste to reappropriate their heritage as yet another Japanese cultural tradition. It has also enabled them to advocate in solidarity with other minority groups that have faced obstacles in Japanese society.

TWO

Genealogies of Taiko I

OSUWA DAIKO, SUKEROKU DAIKO, ONDEKOZA

THE CHARACTER OF CONTEMPORARY JAPANESE TAIKO has been most profoundly shaped by four ensemble groups: Osuwa Daiko, Sukeroku Daiko, Ondekoza, and Kodo. These are not the only influential groups, as regional drum styles have been widely adopted across Japan as well. But only after these four groups started to popularize a new ensemble form of Japanese drumming did rhythmic motifs found in particular folk performances attract broad interest. These innovations remain in the ensembles' performance style, aesthetic sensibility, and repertoire, as well as in those of the groups they have influenced. While these elements permeate contemporary taiko to the extent that only a discerning ear can recognize their influence, members of all four groups strongly maintain that they developed their music in relative isolation from one another. No single person or group, they say, can lay claim to being the singular "origin" of Japanese taiko.

Isolated as these groups were from one another, the character of each is marked significantly by the sociohistorical context in which it evolved. Osuwa Daiko, arguably the first ensemble taiko group, emerged out of the ferment of postwar reconstruction and expanding domestic tourism in the 1950s. Sukeroku Daiko developed in the midst of Tokyo's flourishing festival culture and burgeoning population in the 1960s. Ondekoza arose during the reappraisal of folk culture that took hold of Japan in the 1970s, and the group became one of the most influential Japanese performance ensembles in the world. Kodo, which developed out of Ondekoza, absorbed the increasingly international outlook of Japan as it rose and fell as a global economic superpower in the 1980s and 1990s. Engaging with audiences worldwide clearly figured into the plans of Ondekoza and Kodo early on, but Sukeroku Daiko and Osuwa Daiko were also stimulated in important ways by art forms from out-

48

side Japan. The paths of creativity and innovation traveled by these groups, therefore, do not merely express the creative genius of talented individuals but reflect as well the growing cosmopolitanism of Japan over the last half century.

OSUWA DAIKO:

TRANSLATING THE WEST THROUGH TAIKO

One of the first and most influential styles of ensemble taiko drumming emerged in the early 1950s in Okaya City, a small city near the shores of Lake Suwa in Nagano Prefecture. Oguchi Daihachi, a resident of Okaya City and veteran jazz drummer, is widely credited with inventing the modern style of taiko performance in which taiko of different pitches are combined in a drum set–like setup (see figure 1) and taiko of different sizes, shapes, and pitches are arranged on stage as in an orchestral rhythm section (see figure 2). The latter has come to be called *kumi-daiko,* or "ensemble taiko" (*kumi* is a Japanese word meaning "group"). While the terms *drum set* and *orchestra* are used here only in a descriptive capacity, they are in fact more significant than that might imply. Oguchi has remarked that images of the jazz drum set and the orchestra both influenced the creation of *kumi-daiko.* A brief review of his background will help explain how.

Born in the 1920s in Hirano Village (later incorporated into Okaya City), Oguchi grew up listening to the popular music of the day. After moving to Tokyo to attend university, he studied with a drum teacher and began playing in a band led by a Hawaiian-born Japanese American singer named Haida Haruhiko. Oguchi's brief career as a musician was interrupted when he was drafted and sent to war in China. Not long after he arrived in China, Oguchi was captured and held prisoner for approximately a year. When he returned to Japan after the war, he went back to Okaya City and to his life as a drummer, playing tango and Hawaiian music around town. As he put it to me, "Everyone's mood was gloomy after the war, and playing music helped keep people's spirits up."

A few years later, a relative showed him what seemed to be a musical score of some kind that had been discovered in a miso cellar on the man's property. The score was an assemblage of circles, checks, and dots and appeared to be that of a taiko pattern played in the past during a local festival, O-funa matsuri. Typically, the resident Shinto priest would know how to interpret such a pattern, but the priest serving at that time had been sent from a central office outside the district and was not familiar with the pattern. The relative and his friends wanted to revive the festival and the drum pattern, and they thought that Oguchi might be able to help them decipher it. Oguchi could not read it either, and he began searching for someone to assist in its interpretation. He finally found an older gentleman, a blacksmith, who had studied with the person who had left the drum pattern and remembered how to interpret it.

With this man's help, Oguchi learned that small and large circles on the paper marked short and long drumbeats, respectively, while the small dots indicated a tap on the edge of the drum. The score suggested that, like most ritual performances of taiko, it was a pattern for only one drum. From the elderly blacksmith's explanation, it also appeared to be a rather slow and deliberate pattern. Despite its apparent authenticity, reviving the pattern in its written form did not seem very attractive to Oguchi, who had been raised on a musical diet of jazz, tango, and other contemporary music. He found the rhythm pattern neither interesting to play nor pleasing to the ear, and the more he thought about it, the less enthusiastic he was about reviving it in its original form.

Oguchi began thinking about jazz, especially the ways in which ensemble playing proved stimulating for both performers and audiences. He wondered why Japanese festival taiko were always played by only one person.[1] There were of course festival ensembles, but to the extent of his knowledge, even those ensembles rarely had more than one medium-size *chū-daiko*. He asked several Shinto priests why this was, but none could provide him with anything more than "From a very long time in the past, our ancestors have treated taiko as the abode of Shinto and Buddhist spirits. They were not something that everyone could play, but were reserved for only the highest religious officials."

The answer did not sit well with Oguchi, and he continued to think more about jazz and the structure of the drum set. A drum set has a snare drum, a set of tom-toms, a bass drum, and cymbals—each of which provides a different timbre and pitch, ranging from low to high. In essence, each of these parts represents one unit of an orchestral percussion section. Drawing on his ensemble experience, Oguchi imagined a way of playing taiko that would utilize several people and different taiko drums to create an orchestral array of percussion sounds. As he told me, he wondered, "Aren't there different sized taiko drums in Japan that could mimic the pitch of a snare, a bass, and a tom-

FIGURE 8. Oguchi Daihachi's *kumi-daiko* versus a Western drum set. The appearance of Western-Eastern difference is illusory, as Oguchi's arrangement of taiko is indebted to orchestral and jazz drumming. Photo courtesy of Osuwa Daiko.

tom?" Oguchi chose the small, high-pitched *shime-daiko* drum as the time-keeping "snare" (the "rhythm section"). He selected the medium-size, barrel-shaped *chū-daiko* as a "tom-tom" ("melody") and the large, rope-fastened *okedō-daiko* as the "bass" that would help modulate the high and medium pitches of the *shime-daiko* and the *chū-daiko*. The result was an arrangement of Japanese drums modeled on the Western drum set and orchestral percussion section (figure 8). As Oguchi remarked in a published interview, "For these reasons, contemporary taiko drumming is modeled exactly on the idea of a [jazz] band" (1995, 10).

Oguchi named his ensemble Osuwa Daiko, after his native Suwa region and the Osuwa shrine with which the recovered drum score was associated. In addition to the new arrangement of instruments and multitude of players, Oguchi added *furi* (arm movements) and *kakegoe* (call-and-response vocal gestures) for dramatic effect.[2] He increased the speed of the drumming to "match that of the times" and integrated rhythmic patterns more characteristic of jazz drumming than of festival taiko performance. Combining instruments, rhythm, movement, and voice, Oguchi created the first Osuwa Daiko piece, called "Osuwa Ikazuchi" (Thunder at Suwa).[3] Seeing Oguchi's new ensemble taiko performed, one Shinto priest in the area told him that he did not approve, because taiko were sacred instruments. But the resistance was short-lived. Oguchi told me that the majority of head priests at branches of the Osuwa shrine appreciated how the popularity of Oguchi's performances helped money flow into their coffers, and few resisted his innovations.

In subsequent years, Oguchi and his small ensemble of drummers performed at local schools, festivals and events, hotels, hot springs resorts, and other tourist attractions in the Nagano area. Mass media, especially the new technology of television, helped popularize Oguchi's ensemble taiko beyond Nagano Prefecture. In the late 1950s, after Nippon Hōsō Kyōkai (NHK), a major TV network in Japan, broadcast footage of Osuwa Daiko, requests from individuals seeking instruction poured in, and Oguchi's Osuwa Daiko soon came to be identified as a distinctive performing art of Nagano Prefecture. Oguchi's ensemble drumming got its biggest boost a few years later, when it was included in the opening ceremony of the 1964 Tokyo Olympics.[4] It was only after the 1964 Olympics, which are widely considered to be Japan's symbolic (re)entry into the world as a refreshed and reconstructed country, that Oguchi was able to support himself financially from the performance, instruction, and production of ensemble taiko alone. This fact has led one knowledgeable observer to write that the Tokyo Olympics, along with taiko performances at the Osaka World's Fair in 1970, was one of the most important events in encouraging the spread of ensemble taiko across Japan (Takada 1995, 43).

What makes Oguchi's drumming innovations especially fascinating is that they incorporated Western rhythms and instrumental composition in a manner that appears entirely indigenous. Japanese audiences that attend Osuwa Daiko's performances (and those of other taiko groups that Oguchi has inspired) are unlikely to know that their inspiration is as much American as Japanese. Although it is possible that there were other musicians who experimented with arranging Japanese instruments to mask Western influence through this sort of instrumental "translation," Oguchi's ensemble taiko is likely the first example of this kind of musical innovation in modern Japanese history.

"IKI NO TAIKO": SUKEROKU DAIKO
AND THE ESSENCE OF TOKYO STYLE

Just as Oguchi Daihachi began to expand the performances of Osuwa Daiko throughout Nagano Prefecture, the four teenage boys who would be instrumental in the formation of Sukeroku Daiko, a Tokyo-based taiko group, were beginning to hone their skills as taiko players at the newly revitalized summer festivals held in the "downtown" *(shitamachi)* section of Tokyo. After two decades of war and seven years of American occupation, Japan was gradually starting to recover from the Pacific War and embarking on rapid economic development. Local administrative districts in Tokyo seeking to enrich community life revived summer festivals that had lain dormant for the duration of the conflict and occupation.

Many of these festivals took place around the time in late summer called O-Bon, when the Japanese believe that the spirits of the dead return to their former homes. During O-Bon celebrations, relatives make offerings of food to welcome their ancestors back and to see them off again once they depart. In addition to religious rites held privately in homes or publicly at Buddhist temples, community members often sponsor Bon festivals featuring large *Bon-odori* (Bon-dancing) groups that dance to the accompaniment of recorded folk songs *(minyō)*. In the past, my informants told me, a group of live musicians used to provide background music for the dancers. In postwar Tokyo, however, background musical accompaniment was usually limited to recordings of folk songs from various regions in Japan. As was the case then and still is now, the only live musical accompaniment is supplied by a single taiko drummer who stands on a raised platform *(yagura)* in the middle of the circle of dancers and plays a standard rhythmic pattern along with the recordings on a medium-size *chū-daiko*. Paper lanterns often hang from the edges of the raised platform to help guide the returning spirits home.

I asked several informants why the taiko is the only instrument played live. No one could give me an answer with confidence, although some speculated that it was related to the fact that singing and playing *shamisen* (three-stringed Japanese lute) and *fue* (high-pitched Japanese flute) could no longer be performed proficiently in all areas. While this may be the case, it still does not explain why the taiko is played live, since it is possible to rely entirely on recorded music without live accompaniment.

In the 1950s, local Bon celebrations as well as other locally held Shinto festivals were popular social events, drawing hundreds of individuals from surrounding communities. Informants attributed the popularity of these events to the fact that there were few other things for children to do in Tokyo in the days before television, video arcades, and the like. The opportunity to play taiko—*Bon-daiko*—at these festivals also proved attractive to young men living around the city center. Informants described the atmosphere at these Bon celebrations as relaxed and informal, in contrast to the shrine processions associated with Shinto festivals, where participation is more strictly regulated and often restricted to individuals living in a circumscribed area. Although the men of the sponsoring locality usually handled the task of playing *Bon-daiko,* young individuals from other communities were often granted the opportunity to trade in for a few songs if they asked.[5] In this way, the four future performing members of Sukeroku Daiko—Kobayashi Seidō, Onozato Motoe, Ishizuka Yutaka, and Ishikura Yoshihisa—were able to play *Bon-daiko* in Tokyo's *shitamachi* area for several months in the summertime.

The context of this participation by outsiders thus differs in several respects from festival experiences in regional communities and has important implications. First, in contrast to the strict hierarchy of participation in regional communities by which elders instruct younger individuals in proper performance technique, the lack of any parental involvement in the early stages of *Bon-daiko* learning contributed to the development of an ad hoc playing technique and fostered an atmosphere of innovation. The latter was accentuated by competition for the attention and adoration of the sizable crowds, including the many young women who attended Bon festivals. This led innovation and experimentation in the direction of flash and popular appeal and contributed to a sense that one could "stand out" by playing *Bon-daiko.* These motivations contrast starkly with the strict and precise replication of inherited forms common to most festival music. Finally, the diverse selection of recorded folk songs "from all parts of Japan" accompanying these Bon celebrations severed the connection between music and place so emblematic of folk music, while also fostering a conception of folk songs as transportable and transformable. Without the dictates of local custom casting a shadow of authority over their performance, young taiko players in Tokyo were able to experiment and innovate in a manner that reflected the dynamism and cosmopolitanism of their city. In fact, they were compelled to do so, given that Bon celebrations in Tokyo had by this time become popular events where spectacle trumped the serenity of ritual.

While the future members of Sukeroku Daiko each came from different communities within the *shitamachi* area, they became acquainted through visits to various local festivals, especially the large Bon festival at Shinobazu Pond near Ueno (see map). They had also begun to compete against one another at a *Bon-daiko* contest held locally at the Yushima Tenjin shrine near the main campus of Tokyo University. The contest started in the early 1960s as one of a series of efforts to provide enjoyable activities for the many children who gathered at the shrine's summer festival and was probably the first

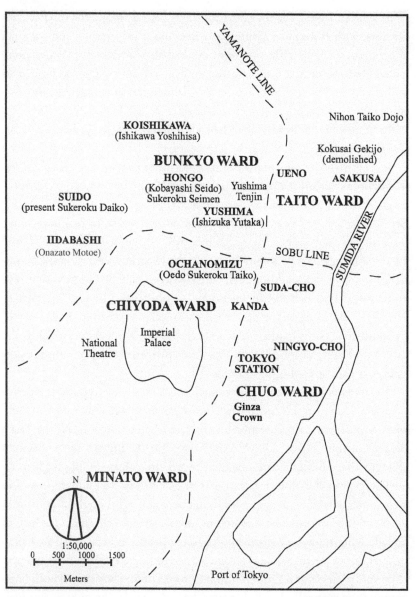

Tokyo's *shitamachi* area showing areas important to the development of Sukeroku Daiko.
Adapted from Endo (1999, 83).

of its kind in Japan. The four boys routinely placed among the top five contestants, with Kobayashi winning the first and third contests and Ishizuka the fourth. Concurrently, the four boys had also joined a *Bon-daiko* group called Oedo Sukeroku Kai (hereafter, Sukeroku Kai), which was headed by Kobayashi Seidō's older brother Seikō. The first part of this group's name—Sukeroku—recalls the name of a character in the kabuki play *Sukeroku Yukari Edo-zakura*. But in fact it had a less literary origin: Kobayashi's family ran a noodle shop called Sukeroku Seimen in the Hongō area of Tokyo.

Joining Seikō's group gave the four young men an opportunity to play *Bon-daiko* more than once a year and they learned from Seikō much of the technique that helped them win the annual contests at Yushima Tenjin shrine. Seikō, who was in his early thirties, had refined his taiko technique after learning the *Bon-daiko* style of his relatives' village in Niigata Prefecture. Like the teenagers who joined his group, he experimented with and modified these techniques, adding performative elements of his own creation. The emphasis of the group was on what these members described as "free solo" or "freestyle": building on the basic rhythm common to all kinds of *Bon-daiko* by adding one's own mallet twirls and acrobatic movements. As much as the Sukeroku Kai was a collection of *Bon-daiko* players, group performance provided a backdrop for highly individual display.

The transformation from an early collective of individual players to a group of ensemble performers began when one of the members answered a newspaper advertisement soliciting members for a taiko club called the Nihon Taiko Seinen Gurūpu (Japan Taiko Youth Group) (Mogi 2010, 35). The young man thought that joining a club outside the Sukeroku Kai would give him an advantage over the other members. As he put it to me in an interview, "We were 'rivals' all trying to get better than one another. I thought that I would get an edge by doing some study on my own." The advertisement led him to Sanada Minoru, a dancer and choreographer at a high-class club in Tokyo called Ginza Crown. Sanada introduced the young festival drummer to new rhythmic patterns and showed him how to play taiko positioned both horizontally and vertically. Until that time, he had played taiko only on the diagonal stand adopted by the Sukeroku Kai and several other *Bon-daiko* drummers in Tokyo, so these placements were something new.

Sanada soon invited his new protégé to accompany him on a weeklong dance performance at the Crown. The performances were a success, and the two became more relaxed around each other. One day Sanada asked the drummer if he had any friends who were familiar with *Bon-daiko*. After some hesitation—he had enjoyed showing off on stage and receiving applause—the young man introduced the rest of the Sukeroku Kai. The new taiko "club" that emerged eventually took the name Shin-On Taiko (New Sound Taiko), a moniker that befitted its members' new status as taiko innovators.

Even before Sanada Minoru had met any of the young drummers, he had come upon the idea of forming a taiko group. The thought had struck him years earlier on a visit to Brazil with the Masuda Takashi Dance Troupe (Masuda Takashi Buyōdan), of which he was a member. Sanada was impressed by the intricate rhythms and sensuous movements of Brazilian samba, and he wondered if there might be a way to create a performing arts group featuring Japanese drums that would be as rousing for contemporary audiences. Much like the members of Ondekoza, Sanada dreamed of taking his group around the world to show off the artistry of Japanese folk performance (Mogi 2010, 35). Thus, even though it was not conceived by the drummers themselves, the eventual emergence of Sukeroku Daiko as a Tokyo-based taiko group was in fact first inspired by a foreign model, much like Oguchi's Osuwa Daiko.

Unfortunately, the newly formed Shin-On Taiko did not last long enough to see Sanada's dream realized. After a few weeks of rehearsal, the group performed at several shows arranged by Sanada at the Ginza Crown. The shows featured twelve minutes of folk songs, dance, *shamisen,* and taiko (*ōdaiko* and *shime-daiko*) playing. The group was well received, and soon requests for performances at other locations started coming in from the numerous corporate bosses in the audience. Sanada saw the potential profits and began taking the group of musicians to performances outside the Ginza Crown. The new performance schedule and Sanada's apparent desire to turn the club into a professional group did not sit well with the young men he had recruited, some of whom were still in high school. As one former member told me, "We weren't 'pros,' and while it was fun to perform when we were into it, going to perform daily got to be a pain. We weren't able to do our schoolwork and our parents started getting angry at us. So we all quit."[6]

When they quit, Kowase Susumu, the *shamisen* player in the group Sanada had created, approached them about forming a new taiko group on the model of Shin-On Taiko. Ishizuka told him that he wanted to wait until after high school, and Kobayashi's brother forbade him from participating at first, but the other two performers, Onozato Motoe and Ishikura Yoshihisa, quit their jobs and joined immediately. Kowase was the son of Kineya Sasazō, Sanada Minoru's taiko teacher and a performer at Tokyo's International Theater (Kokusai Gekijō). Having broken ties with Sanada at the Ginza Crown, the group used the theater as its new practice space. Needing a new name to detach themselves from their association with Sanada, the group members reached back into their collective history and settled on Sukeroku Daiko.

Former members of the group told me that they chose the name Sukeroku not only out of a feeling of nostalgia for the former *Bon-daiko* group. Sukeroku is also the name of a character in the aforementioned kabuki play. Group members regularly called him an Edo "dandy" and told me that he epitomized the spirit of old Edo. Pushed to elaborate further, they would typically make use of the Japanese word *iki,* a term that is difficult to translate into English. The people of *shitamachi,* which formerly composed most of urban Edo, like to think that their men possess this quality of effortless sophistication. The term *iki* also connotes someone who is vivacious and energetic. In this sense, the style of taiko that they played was not the slow, languid type one would find at a Bon dance, but an upbeat and fast-paced variety. For Sukeroku Daiko, the quality of *iki* embodied by the character of Sukeroku defined their approach to performance. As a professional group centered on the ensemble playing of an assortment of taiko drums and *shamisen,* Sukeroku Daiko inherited the spirit of Shin-On Taiko as much as it broke with the individual showmanship and festival milieu characteristic of the Sukeroku Kai and *Bon-daiko* (figure 9).

After its formation, the group conserved much of the repertoire of Shin-On Taiko and began to compose additional pieces for shows at hotels, cabarets, and clubs around Tokyo. The ensemble consisted of one *ōdaiko,* two *chū-daiko* and one *shime-daiko.* In the beginning, they performed with *shamisen* accompaniment. Over time, though, the *shamisen* accompaniment receded and the role of the *shime-daiko* expanded to provide a harmonic contrast to the low-pitched *chū-daiko* and *ōdaiko.* It is not clear to what degree the new group continued to use the original playing techniques that Kobayashi Seikō had shown them, since these were never set down in any independent form, but from the account of the group's history it appears very likely that significant modifications and additions were made. The players incorporated aspects of *kabuki hayashi,* particularly the verbal cues that kabuki musicians use to maintain consistent ensemble performance. They also created new pieces, like "Nidan-uchi" and "Yodan-uchi." Inspired in part by the television broadcast of a Korean female drum troupe, these pieces mixed acrobatic spins and jumps with successive solo displays of taiko prowess by individual drummers.[7] As such, they represent a cross between the group's inheritance of *Bon-daiko* technique and the back-and-forth improvisation of jazz. Along with high-

FIGURE 9. The four original members of Sukeroku Daiko, Tokyo's first professional ensemble taiko group. Photo courtesy of Oedo Sukeroku Taiko.

lighting solo performance and acrobatics, the diagonal angle at which they positioned their drums, another vestige of *Bon-daiko,* came to distinguish them from ensemble taiko groups like Osuwa Daiko that placed their drums either vertically or horizontally (and also avoided flashy acrobatics).

In the late 1970s and early 1980s, three of the original members of Sukeroku Daiko left the group. Two went on to pursue careers playing *ko-tsuzumi,* the small, handheld drum used mainly in classical Japanese stage music. The third went on to form another taiko group in a different part of Tokyo. Later, a dispute over money and the direction of the group drove Imaizumi Yūtaka, a featured taiko player who had joined in the early 1970s, and Kobayashi Seidō apart. Imaizumi went on to form Sukeroku Daiko (where I studied), while Kobayashi, perhaps attempting to recapture the feeling of the group's earliest days, founded Oedo Sukeroku Taiko. As of this writing, both continue to perform in these groups.

Sukeroku Daiko's flashy style has had considerable influence on taiko groups throughout Japan, especially in the Tokyo area. The group also had a significant effect on the development of taiko drumming in North America; a trip to the United States early on and the group's instruction of a major North American ensemble taiko drummer, Tanaka Seiichi, led a number of American groups to adopt Sukeroku's performance style. The light, bouncy rhythms and acrobatic movements found in original Sukeroku Daiko pieces like "Matsuri Daiko," "Yodan-uchi," "Midare-uchi," and "Oi-uchi Daiko" have also been integrated into the repertoires of many ensemble taiko groups in Japan.

ONDEKOZA AND KODO:
MUSIC OF THE FOLK, MUSCLE OF THE ARTISAN

In contrast to Osuwa Daiko, which developed out of a desire to reinvigorate a local festival and performed mostly in regional events and at inns and hotels, Sukeroku Daiko's performances at Tokyo bars and cabarets represented new venues for taiko performance. What these two groups shared in common, however, was that they were "hired out" for their performances, regardless of whether those performances took place at festivals, inns, bars, or cabarets. In contrast to both Osuwa Daiko and Sukeroku Daiko, the first group to elevate taiko drumming from community festivity and small venues to the central focus of an artistically inspired stage performance emerged in 1971 in the provincial setting of Sado Island, an island located off the coast of Niigata Prefecture in northern Japan. The group was named Ondekoza, and it was established with the primary aim of reinvesting desiccated regional folk entertainments with youthful vigor and style. With stage performance as its goal, the group hoped to perform around the world to amass the funds necessary to found an "artisan academy" *(shokunin daigaku)* dedicated to carrying out the group's mission on Sado Island. Having accomplished its objective, the group would then cease performing.

Although the group never founded such an academy, Ondekoza did become the world's ambassador of Japanese drumming. This role was inherited by Kodo, which was established on Sado in 1981 when Ondekoza's performing members split with Den Tagayasu, the group's manager. The combined artistic influence of both groups is enormous. Several of their pieces, like those of Osuwa Daiko and Sukeroku Daiko, have become taiko standards, and the unique style of playing the large *ōdaiko* drum that developed in Ondekoza has become perhaps the representative symbol of Japanese drumming worldwide. While this immense musical influence alone warrants an extended review of Ondekoza and Kodo, their paradigmatic expression of what I have called "new folk" performance earns them an especially significant place in this study. Ondekoza began both as an experiment in a new kind of music making and as a new kind of community-making project based around the folk performing arts. In this sense, it is a model of the communities that engendered the Japanese "taiko boom."

Tajiri Kōzō to Den Tagayasu

While Ondekoza's ideology bears the stamp of the postwar social milieu in which it emerged, much of the group's vision reflects the beliefs and desires of its founder, Den Tagayasu. Admittedly, identifying the origins of a group with an individual can be risky. The wide range of social, economic, and cultural forces that act on and guide behavior tend to be minimized when analysis is distilled to the level of the individual person. This is particularly the case when dealing with artists, whose sense of self is closely tied to the possession of unique talents and abilities. While acknowledging these complications, it is nevertheless easiest to understand the ideology of Ondekoza by reviewing some of Den's formative experiences.[8]

Tajiri Kōzō (who would later change his name to Den Tagayasu) was born in 1931 in the Asakusa district of Tokyo.[9] (Asakusa is located in the same *shitamachi* section of Tokyo where Sukeroku Daiko would emerge thirty years later.) Asakusa, now famous as a nostalgic tourist site, was in Den's day a bustling community of merchants, artisans, and upper-crust café society, a position it would later yield to the suburban communities sprouting along the Yamanote train line in western Tokyo. Den lived there until March 1945, when he moved to his mother's family's home in Kagoshima on the southern tip of Kyushu. The timing proved fortuitous; a week after Den's departure, nearly all of his elementary school classmates perished in a nighttime bombing raid by American forces.

Den returned to Tokyo after the war to attend high school. After graduating in 1952, he entered the literature department at Waseda University to study Chinese literature, and not on academic merit alone. As he put it to an interviewer, there were only two reasons why he was able to enter Waseda University: first, no one else was interested in studying Chinese literature, and second, he was "scouted" by the school's left-leaning self-governing association, which had heard of his abilities as an organizer. In high school, Den had led a strike that resulted in the ousting of the school's principal (Mitsuya 1994, 60). His strengths as an organizer were thus evident early on.

No more than three months into his tenure at university, his involvement in a series of violent student demonstrations resulted in his dismissal. Fearing arrest, Den fled Tokyo for Kobe. Once there, he moved into a hostel for laborers and began working on the city's busy port unloading cargo from Hong Kong freighters. After working at the port for about six months, he stole away on a steamer bound for Germany. Informants who knew Den told me that he was not only unimpressed by Germany but that, during the trip there, his German shipmates racially insulted him and made him feel that he, as a Japanese man, was inferior. It is difficult to know the significance of this experience, but it seems to have made enough of an impression on him that he remembered to tell his future underlings about it. Quite likely, they reasoned, his visit to Germany made him conscious of his identity as a Japanese person in a way he had not been before. Indeed, not long after returning to Japan, Den discovered an interest in the work of Japanese folklorists and the folk culture about which they wrote.

While browsing in a bookstore, Den stumbled on a book entitled *Umi ni ikiru hitobito* (The people who live on the sea), which was written by the acclaimed folklorist Miyamoto Tsuneichi. The book describes the life and culture of a rural Japanese fishing village, and it appears to have had a profound impact on young Den's conception of Japanese culture. In an interview, Den remarked:

> In the messy confusion of postwar Japan, [Miyamoto's] book gently suggested that we should not just borrow democracy from the United States but instead recognize that democracy has existed in Japan since ancient times. . . . Ancient Japanese fishing villages exemplify this. Neither men nor women used polite language *[keigō]*.[10] There were no borders [and, consequently, no fences] in the sea. . . . Now, commercial fishing boats come with their nets to catch huge amounts of fish, but the local fishermen of Japan take only enough to provide sufficient income to support their families. (Mitsuya 1994, 62)

Den was so moved by the book that he immediately phoned the author. Miyamoto, impressed by the excitement and idealism in the young man's voice, invited him to his home. Den soon found himself sitting with Miyamoto at the Tokyo home of Shibusawa Keizo, Miyamoto's benefactor and a folklore scholar affiliated with the Center for the Study of Folk Culture in neighboring Kanagawa Prefecture. Although Miyamoto's and Shibusawa's discipline, *minzokugaku,* is often translated as "folklore studies," the aims and techniques of their brand of scholarship might better be rendered as "native ethnology" (Harootunian 1998). The foundations of this discipline had been laid in the early twentieth century by such scholars as Yanagita Kunio and Orikuchi Shinobu, who borrowed techniques from German folklore studies and began to record the stories of the "common people," a neologism Yanagita created to refer to the people living in the Japanese countryside. Despite its debt to the work of European scholars, native ethnology in Japan has been marked by Yanagita's nativist assertion that Japanese ethnology should be conducted only by Japanese.

Even though onsite fieldwork in local communities was not rare among these scholars, Miyamoto and Shibusawa were both regarded as exceptionally intrepid fieldworkers. Of the two, Miyamoto was the more impressive. By the end of his career, he had covered a total of 160,000 kilometers, mostly on foot, and had been put up at over a thousand different homes. Shibusawa joked that "if one were to make a red mark on a map of Japan for every place that Miyamoto had visited, the map would end up solid red" (Sano 2000, introduction). Although no record remains of what transpired between Den and Miyamoto at that first meeting, it is clear that Miyamoto's writing, itinerancy, and life experience deeply impressed Den. In fact, Den later attributed his decision to travel around Japan directly to Miyamoto's example (Sano 2000, 146).[11] The fortuitous meeting between Den and Miyamoto thus draws a direct line of influence from the native ethnologists, starting with Yanagita Kunio and continuing through Miyamoto Tsuneichi, to Ondekoza and later Kodo, who attempted to reinvigorate the very folk culture these scholars first imagined.[12]

Not long after meeting Miyamoto, Den left Tokyo and traveled south toward his former temporary home of Kagoshima. Stopping in various villages along the way through southwestern Japan and the southern tip of Kyushu, Den came to rest on Yonaguni-jima, one of the Okinawan islands and the westernmost point of Japan (seventy-eight miles from Taiwan), where he worked for two years as a substitute teacher at a junior high school. Those who knew of Den's interest in revitalizing the folk performing arts, particularly the taiko, recalled that it was on this island that he first encountered both the power of the folk performing arts to impress and the pitiful state of their decline. During his stay on the island, Den was captivated by the performance of an older villager who "brought a taiko drum to the beach in the evening and played it until the sun came up" (Shinoda 1994, 32). Unfortunately, there is no record of what kind of taiko Den heard or what else happened to him during this period.[13] What is clear is that Den left Yonaguni-jima to visit Sado Island in the spring of 1958.

Following Miyamoto's suggestion, Den sought out Masahiko Honma, a local historian and teacher affiliated with the Sado Agricultural High School. The two discussed Den's recent travels, and Honma offered Den a room at his home in exchange for help with Honma's research activities. Thinking that Den would be impressed by a demonstration of Sado's taiko just as he had been by the taiko on Yonaguni-jima, Honma took Den to see a folk performance at a nearby hotel. At the hotel, a travel agency was sponsoring performances of Sado's *ondeko* (which means "demon drumming," in Sado dialect), a kind of drum dance performed annually at the start of the planting season to ensure a good harvest and good health. To Honma's surprise, after the performance concluded, Den exploded in scathing invective at what he had just seen. Honma paraphrases:

> *Ondeko* is becoming nothing more than a showpiece lacking in vitality. The drummers use only the strength of their hands to strike the drum, dulling the sound and exciting no passion in the listener. Taiko used to have a contagious, spiritual power, like that of a shaman—it could *infect* people. Traces of this remain in Shinto ritual, but *ondeko* is losing this infectious power. If there is no return to its original inspiration, no attempt to recoup that original vitality, *ondeko* will devolve into nothing more than a meaningless dance.

Den then pulled out of his pocket a worn and tattered little book that he claimed was his "bible," the title of which Honma could not recall but which he believes was a collection of sayings by Mao Zedong on the arts and literature of peasants.[14] Reading out of the book, Den announced resolutely, "The energy of literature and the arts has its source in the farming communities of the peasants!" (Honma 1994, 11).

Honma's anecdote captures well how Den's interest in the folk performing arts and his activities as a Marxist-Maoist agitator worked together to focus his attention on reviving regional communities through the reinvigoration of folk performing arts. Den's reference to a connection between folk labor and folk performance also presages the conflation of craftsmanship and music making in the future Ondekoza. His belief in this connection was further confirmed by two additional experiences with *ondeko* on Sado Island. On the southeastern end of Sado, Den met an elderly man who told him that the sound of *ondeko* used to be heard in villages seven or eight kilometers away but now did not resound with anything close to the power it had in the old days. Den then set out to find a particular *ondeko* player on the island who was known for the dynamism of his performance. Den learned that the man's strong arms were largely the result of his daily labor as a sawyer, affirming his conviction that the taiko could not be sounded impressively without a powerful body.

Den soon encountered a group that also took seriously the connection between proletarian labor and the folk arts. Six months after stopping on Sado, he abruptly pulled up roots to begin traveling once again. During this time, Den spent approximately one year as a guest of Warabiza, a troupe of theatrical performers based in northeastern Japan. Warabiza had been founded several years earlier, in 1953, by Hara Tarō, a former member of a Tokyo-based theatrical group made up of young communist sympathizers. Hara and the members of another group he had started in Tokyo (Gakudan Umi-tsubame) set up a commune near Tazawako Town in Akita Prefecture. Much like Ondekoza, which would be formed several years later, Warabiza endeavored to breathe new life into the folk performing arts, particularly dance and theater, and the group members' move to Akita Prefecture was likely an attempt to get closer to the source of their artistic inspiration.

Current members of Kodo who knew Den are circumspect with regard to the influence Warabiza had on him. The inspiration behind Warabiza's activities as well as the group's communal organization, however, are so strikingly similar to the early Ondekoza that it is hard not to assume that they influenced his thinking in a significant way. This is particularly the case in the latter's use of taiko, as Warabiza likely anticipated Ondekoza's integration of taiko drums into a theatrical performance based on the folk performing arts.

After leaving Warabiza, Den returned to Tokyo. He published a series of articles in a newspaper called the *Nihon Dokusho Shinbun* under the title "Hōrōsha no techō" (From a vagabond's notebook) along the way. Elements of this series were used in an NHK television series about puppet theater, and it was through this connection that Den first came in contact with the celebrities and broadcasters who would be integral to the establishment of Ondekoza. Den also remained active as a protestor. He supported the famous labor strike at coal mines owned by the Mitsui Company in Miike by entertaining other protesters and laborers with puppet theater. Like many disaffected Japanese citizens, he also took part in the massive demonstrations against the ratification of the U.S.-Japan security treaty that rocked Tokyo in 1960.

Eight years later, in 1968, Den arrived again on Sado Island, this time with a wife and son in tow and the intention to stay permanently. By now, Masahiko Honma had taken up Den's suggestion to try to recover the former vitality of *ondeko* and had started an after-school *ondeko* club at the Sado Agricultural High School, where he worked. Honma brought Den in after his return to the island to help with the instruction of the group.[15] Den moved his family out of the white van that had been both their home and their transport into a tiny old house on the island. They soon left this house and settled into a building that had formerly been a small clinic, in preparation for the communal living that would be a part of Den's next big project. Other than financing, the necessary foundation had been laid for the creation of Ondekoza.

At some point during his journeys through Japan, Den changed his name from Tajiri Kōzō to Den Tagayasu. The name change indicates a significant transformation of self-identity. To create the two-character name Den Tagayasu, Den combined the first Chinese character of his last name, which means "rice field," and the first Chinese character of his first name, which means "to cultivate," to create a new personal name that reads as an activity: Den Tagayasu, "the one who cultivates rice." This nominal reinvention not only expresses Den's enchantment with Japan's rice-growing peasantry, but also gestures toward the contribution that folkloric imagery would make in the accomplishment of his future objectives.

Creating Ondekoza

Den soon put this image to the test. In the fall of 1969, he phoned Miyamoto Tsuneichi to announce that he had settled on Sado and, in the ten years since the two had last been in contact, had been preparing for the creation of Ondekoza. Den explained that Ondekoza was to be a group of young people based on Sado Island who were dedicated to restoring the spirit and self-confidence of local youth by "revitalizing [their] traditional arts" (Sano 2000, 146).[16] Miyamoto had also considered encouraging tourism to the island by showcasing its folk performing arts, so it is not surprising that he greeted Den's phone call with great interest. Den asked Miyamoto to contribute some money and introduce him to three other potential contributors. Following this fundraising strategy for a year, Den, a gifted salesman, raised a considerable sum.

Having secured the initial funding, Den organized an Ondekoza summer school in 1970. The workshop brought together public intellectuals— including Miyamoto Tsuneichi, Shimazaki Makoto, the radio personality Ei Rokusuke, and several other influential artists and designers—with approximately forty-seven young people, the majority of whom were university students from outside Sado Island. During the weeklong "school," participants listened to informal lectures and traveled around Sado visiting cultural sites and taking in displays of local performing arts. On the final day of the workshop, Den, who had stayed behind the scenes during the workshop, asked the young attendees, many of whom were veterans of university riots, how serious they were about wanting to "dismantle" their universities. If they were serious, he said sternly, they should consider staying with him on Sado to form a taiko and puppet theater troupe that would travel around the world and raise enough money to start their own "university" on Sado—an "artisan academy" where members would have exclusive control over faculty and curriculum. After seven years, the group would disband and the participants would be free to do as they wished.[17]

After hearing Den's request, a few young participants remained, on the assumption that the group would be in existence for at most seven years.[18] Ondekoza next opened an office in Tokyo. Although Den had accumulated enough seed money to get the group started, founding members of the early Ondekoza began traveling to different parts of Japan to gather local merchandise to sell at department stores in Tokyo. Toward the end of the year, the core group of about six members had become close, and they returned to Sado the following spring to begin living communally in pursuit of their future objectives.

At first living communally was a relaxed affair. Having no musical instruments, there was nothing to play; having no teachers, there was nothing to practice. Male members filled their time making little things that the group needed, like a shelf to store shoes or a table for the communal dining room. Partly done out of economic necessity, this work also accorded with the craftsman ethic that came to dominate the thinking of the group: whatever they needed, they would make for themselves. This included food, and in the first few months food preparation was handled by female members of the group and by Den's wife.[19] The group bought only the bare minimum from nearby markets and tried to grow whatever else they needed. For boys and girls fresh out of high school and used to the comforts of the city, this must have required some adjustment. While the ideal of self-sufficiency is appealing, it can often be challenging in practice.[20]

In addition to taking care of daily chores and readying the material objects necessary for self-sufficiency, group members began the physical conditioning needed to withstand the demands of a stage performance based around drumming, dancing, and long international tours. There was general agreement among the group members that Ondekoza would be primarily a taiko and puppet theater troupe. Yet in practice, it was difficult to tell whether they were a troupe of musicians or a band of marathon runners. What began as light, daily jogs of three or four kilometers turned in subsequent months into endurance runs ten times longer.

The intensity of Ondekoza's training program is the stuff of legend, but exactly who was responsible for implementing the program of long-distance running and how it came to reflect, or to some extent produce, a philosophical approach to artistic production and performance is a matter of dispute. Den has claimed that the casual atmosphere of the group changed one day when he became fed up with their lack of progress and ungrateful dependence on the generous housekeeping efforts of his wife. Two former members of the group recalled differently that the strict lifestyle and training regimen came about partly as a result of Den's demands and partly as a consequence of a shift in the attitudes of the group members themselves. A kind of self-imposed isolationist monasticism took over the group. They swore off alcohol and cigarettes and cut off access to television, radio, newspapers, and magazines. Free time, romantic encounters, and risqué chatter were also forbidden.

Regardless of whose version is correct, the decision to raise the intensity of group training clearly resulted from a combination of impending future obligations and internal demands, not merely Den's ideological leanings. Nevertheless, in his contacts with press people outside the group and in his statements within the group itself, Den emphasized the merits and philosophical importance of the group's newfound practice of running. The act of marathon running was compared to a stage: "Marathon running is like being on a forty-two-kilometer stage where only you are the performer. There is no other venue that can compare. There is nothing more creative; nothing that better exposes the successes or failure of one's physical conditioning, one's lifestyle, and one's dedication to practice. For young people deeply frustrated by the illusion of a prosperous society, the experience of running, of sweating day after day, is of extreme importance" (Den Tagayasu, quoted in Sato 1994, 20). By "illusion of a prosperous society," Den likely had in mind both a critique of affluent Japan and the cadre of disillusioned dropouts and frustrated students who made up the bulk of his group. For students who had grown weak from studying or battling authority, running served the important purpose of reinvigorating body and mind. Den sardonically dubbed the

unique performance that resulted from Ondekoza's intense emphasis on running *sōgaku*, which literally means "running music" (Kashiwagi 1994, 26).

Shinoda Masahiro, Den's close friend, director of the first documentary
about Ondekoza, and a marathon runner himself, has written perhaps the
most eloquent exposition of Ondekoza's integration of long-distance running, the craftsman ethic, and the folk performing arts. In an essay for a
Japanese magazine, Shinoda connects Den's philosophy of running and his
dream of recuperating the culture of the craftsman class.[21]

> Ondekoza first began running as a result of their flight from the outside world.
> They rehabilitated their wounded spirits and flesh, as if they were reborn, and
> developed a new sensibility and sensitivity toward their artistic endeavors....
> [To do this], they had to build the physical power required by the folk per-
> forming arts, which in previous epochs were supported by the arm and leg
> strength forged in the practice of hard manual labor....
>
> These days the agricultural skills and technology of old have been discarded.
> Foot-worn paths between rice fields have been paved with concrete, and the
> spades and hoes of the past have been replaced with combines and tractors.
> The spirits of the rice fields have been driven from their lairs, and the folk arts
> that were once performed in service to them have been reduced to nothing
> more than community festivities. The strong arms and legs that once sup-
> ported these folk arts have long since vanished from the face of the earth....
>
> In the past, the people who created these folk performances had to inspire
> people struggling with the weight and brutality of an everyday life from
> which there was no salvation. They needed performances that were powerful.
> If the display lacked power and physical drama, it would never rouse them
> from their toil.
>
> As the agricultural society that both produced and thirsted for this power
> has disappeared, the opportunity has come for Den's method [of training] to
> produce the physical strength and sensitivity necessary to perform convinc-
> ingly. The hands that plucked the *shamisen* and the hands that struck the
> taiko were once wrought through the labor of the farmer and the blacksmith.
> With the advance of "civilization," these hands have been rendered weak.
> Ondekoza's goal is to overcome at once this debilitation and decay to return
> to the fundamental wellspring of the performing arts. (1994, 33–34)

In naming the group Ondekoza, Den had already conflated the relationship between artisan and folk performance at the root of Shinoda's missive,
as he believed that historically *oni* were both "carpenters" and "demon dancers."[22] Although the Chinese character for *-za* typically means "seat," the
character is also used in contemporary Japan to refer to a troupe of actors or
musicians. The suffix *-za* also was used formerly to refer to both trade and

merchant guilds in feudal Japan. Den was well aware that the suffix possessed this dual sense of performing troupe and trade guild, and he traced this usage to the similar class position of artisans and performers in feudal Japan: "The 'fictional work' of the artist should be combined with some kind of 'real world' labor. The ideal is to be a *shokunin* [artisan] who is also an entertainer. It is especially important for taiko players to combine an occupation with their performance activities since they will inevitably face physical limitations in their later years" (quoted in Honma 1994, 13).

Given Den's understanding of the connection between artists and artisans, Ondekoza's professed desire to build an artisan academy on Sado appears less capricious. Institutionalizing the study of a trade not only makes available an alternative supporting occupation for the aging taiko player but also ensures that the physical foundation of vibrant folk performing arts in the well-developed bodies of artisan-drummers will continue into the future. From early on, group members visited Tokyo to study elementary woodworking with the renowned industrial designer Akioka Yoshio. Utilizing the skills they learned, members fashioned their own drum mallets and other everyday items.

Along with greater respect for the work of artisans came an appreciation of high-quality craftsmanship. Visitors to the group's spartan headquarters were astounded by the fine works of lacquerware they possessed. For Den, the investment in such works of art was well worth the expense, since in his opinion only exposure to the finest *objets* could cultivate the refined artistic sense needed to present a convincing stage performance: "Cheap imitations only cause distractions; only through daily contact with authentic objects can a pure sense of beauty arise" (Den Tagayasu, quoted in Honma 1994, 13).

Den adopted a similar approach with regard to training in musical technique. In the second year of their training, the young players began to receive professional instruction in the classical performing arts. They studied *shime-daiko* from the grand master *(iemoto)* of Tanaka Densaemon, the Tanaka school of *kabuki hayashi* accompaniment.[23] They also began to receive training in *fue* from Tōsha Suihei, in *shakuhachi* (Japanese long bamboo flute) from Sakai Chikuhō, and in the *tsuzumi* from Tōsha Roetsu. In general, they learned only playing technique from these teachers, although it appears that a *shakuhachi* piece may have been written for them by one of their teachers. For actual content, the players instead used pieces derived from the folk performing arts they learned in their trips to the many regions of Japan.[24]

This combination of classical technique and folkloric content presents one of the most intriguing aspects of the early Ondekoza. Although the group's members developed little in the way of a repertoire from the classical performing arts, they applied these techniques to playing the repertoire they constructed out of a basis in the folk performing arts. They knew that they could never become professional practitioners of the classical performing arts, for this was too difficult and would take too long given their time constraints. But there was an additional reason why they did not integrate significantly the music of the classical performing arts. Even though Den wanted to expose them to classical performance techniques, his Marxist roots and veneration of the folk implied an element of resistance to the status of the classical performing arts, which he considered to be the effete entertainment of upper-class Japanese society. As a former member of Ondekoza recounted to me in an interview:

> [Den] had great admiration for Mao Zedong. For Mao, the most impressive performing arts came from the lowest classes, not the upper classes. Den would often quote Mao by saying that there were three secrets to success: youth, poverty, and anonymity....
>
> Nevertheless, he did not think that the folk performing arts of the lower classes alone were sufficient, since, artistically, in our performances we were aiming to perform at the highest level. So, while we had elderly taiko players from the countryside come teach us their folk dances and rhythms, we also had "top-class" *kabuki hayashi, fue,* and *koto* teachers instruct us in technique.

Presumably, though, the group could have become proficient musicians by concentrating only on the folk performing arts. Den probably considered classically trained musicians to be artisans of a different kind in their continuous attention to refining their technique. In this respect, Ondekoza was very likely the first group in Japan to apply techniques taken from the classical performing arts to the folk performing arts. Moreover, in contrast to contemporaneous forms of the Japanese performing arts, Ondekoza did not attempt to combine Western and Japanese musical forms, emphasizing instead the purely Japanese combination of classical techniques and folk motifs.[25] With this unique combination of musical influences and communal living, Ondekoza set upon creating what would become perhaps the most influential repertory in Japanese taiko.

. . .

The lack of visibly foreign instrumentation in the early Ondekoza recalls its absence in both Osuwa Daiko and Sukeroku Daiko. Although these three groups differ in their performance goals and sites, they all share an aversion to the combination of Western and Japanese instruments on stage. This is surprising given that foreign models of musical organization figured so significantly in the development of Osuwa Daiko and Sukeroku Daiko. In addition, all three groups demonstrate a fierce attachment to particular places. For Osuwa Daiko, it was the Suwa region of Nagano Prefecture; for Sukeroku Daiko, it was the uniquely Edo spirit embodied by Tokyo's *shitamachi*; for Ondekoza, it was the folk culture of Sado Island. However, the expression of these attachments to local places was dependent on influences from and travel to regions beyond. Ondekoza's collection of nonlocals attempting to establish a new drumming community in an isolated outlying region most starkly demonstrates this admixture of local and nonlocal. Beyond personnel and ideology, Ondekoza's developing performance techniques and repertoire also emerged out of considerable movement of people and ideas to and from Sado. The next chapter examines in more detail how this oscillation between movement and place contributed to the creation of Ondekoza's widely emulated repertoire and the most influential group in Japanese taiko, Kodo.

THREE

Genealogies of Taiko II

ONDEKOZA TO KODO

GIVEN THE ORIGINALITY OF ONDEKOZA'S REPERTOIRE and the influence the group has had on taiko ensembles throughout the world, it is worth analyzing in detail how three of its most emulated pieces were created. The analysis of these three pieces demonstrates how Ondekoza put into motion regional culture in the process of preparing a repertoire to take around the world. In some cases, inheritors of the folk performing arts were able to visit Ondekoza in Sado to instruct the group in their local performing art. This was the case for Shimomura Keiichi, who taught the group the *hi no taiko* of his native Fukui Prefecture. Like those in the many amateur taiko ensembles that would follow Ondekoza, though, in most cases group members traveled to the region in which the performing art originated. Travel of individuals to and from Sado Island was thus instrumental in generating Ondekoza's repertoire and establishing its presence on the island.

"YATAI-BAYASHI"

The first ensemble piece the group mastered is based on a kind of festival music native to Chichibu City in Saitama Prefecture, about two hours by train from Tokyo. In the first few days of December, the community buzzes with anticipation for its popular winter festival. The festival lasts two to three days and features a procession of giant wooden floats, or *yatai,* that are pulled through the community's main thoroughfares. As in most Shinto festivals in Japan, the *yatai* are pulled through the town as part of a ritual to rid the community of malicious spirits and forces after being ritually infused with the spirit of the local shrine. Shrouded by hanging carpets inside the *yatai* is a small ensemble *(hayashi)* composed of two *shime-daiko* players, one *chū-daiko* player, one *fue* player, and one *kane* (small brass gong) player.[1] The ensemble plays a supporting cadence for the group of young people pulling the heavy *yatai*. The young man playing the *chū-daiko* sits with his legs underneath the length of the horizontally mounted drum, forcing him to lean backward while striking it. Several individuals switch off playing in this position as the complex *chū-daiko* drum pattern is repeated continuously.

Den decided that he wanted the group to learn *Chichibu yatai-bayashi*, since they had learned some basic drumming techniques but had no piece to play on stage.[2] The group invited a member of one *yatai-bayashi* group to teach them on Sado, but the workshop failed, largely because the Ondekoza members had not yet acquired the technical proficiency needed to master the rhythmic pattern. Toward the end of 1972, three members of Ondekoza traveled to Chichibu to spend a week observing the members of Chichibu's Shitagō Ward practice *yatai-bayashi* in preparation for the upcoming festival. It was at this point that the members of Ondekoza, as outsiders, met with a difficulty posed by the customary transmission of the folk performing arts. As one former member of Ondekoza, Hayashi Eitetsu, remarked:

> Japanese folk music was originally not conceived on a structure of specific beats per measure, nor was it written down on a score. Pieces were usually learned by memorizing a series of *kuchi-shōga* [rhythms and sounds represented by onomatopoeic patterns]. . . . In addition to the fact that each player's method of playing the assigned part differed slightly and often featured an element of improvisation, it was extremely difficult for people like us, who did not have the benefit of practicing as children, to pick it up in such a short time. (1992, 59)

To assist in the memorization of this "traditional" piece, the group had to utilize "modern" technology by recording practice sessions on reel-to-reel tape. This gave them the ability to analyze the piece as needed and to take the sound of the pattern back with them to Sado. Hayashi, who had some experience playing a drum set as a junior high school student, took it upon himself to transform the original *Chichibu yatai-bayashi* into a piece that the group could use in stage performance. Den suggested that they adapt the pattern to use three *chū-daiko* instead of the single *chū-daiko* in the original. This left Hayashi and the other members of the group with the task of adapting a rhythm pattern they could barely play onto an arrangement of instruments for which they had no model.

As a means of working toward this goal, Hayashi first used the recording to transcribe the entire rhythmic pattern onto a four-beat measure in order to study how the parts of the pattern fit together. Hayashi had learned how to write some basic rhythmic patterns in his brief time playing a drum set and had managed to figure out that *Chichibu yatai-bayashi* utilized one main rhythmic motif that repeated. As he came to understand the structure of the piece, he realized that it would be impossible to simply play it on three *chū-daiko* drums as it was. After practicing the piece a number of times, the group devised a system by which they repeated an arrangement of the original Chichibu rhythmic pattern on the three drums as in a choral round. With background accompaniment provided by two *shime-daiko* players, one *chū-daiko* drummer starts playing the pattern. After he repeats it twice, the next *chū-daiko* drummer joins. The first drummer then gradually decreases his playing volume and stops. The second and third *chū-daiko* drummers repeat the process. When the third drummer finishes, the second and third drummers stop playing as the first (lead) *chū-daiko* drummer turns to a *shime-daiko* for a solo. (Later, they would have the first and second drummers turn and play together.) After completing the solo, the lead drummer returns to his drum, at which time the three drummers play in unison and conclude.

Ondekoza's creation of this piece exemplified many of its arrangements of folk taiko. Because many of the folk drumming patterns that they borrowed were short, irregular, repetitive, and used to mark time or punctuate dance, they had to rearrange the original pattern—by staggering beginnings and endings, making irregular rhythms regular, and distributing one drum part over several—in order to produce something of interest to contemporary audiences. In this sense, while Ondekoza's style developed independently of Oguchi's Osuwa Daiko, the process of arranging folk rhythms for contemporary performance was remarkably similar.

For Hayashi, the lead drummer's *shime-daiko* solo was the most difficult part of the sequence to master. All he had to work from was an audio recording, so he slowed down the tape, listened to it over and over, and transcribed it without even understanding exactly how the original part was played. Having no video recording on which to rely, Hayashi devised a sticking pattern, new rhythmic phrasing, and playing position that suited him. He also modified its rhythmic "feel." The original Chichibu festival rhythm has a slight shuffle to it, wherein each drumbeat is placed slightly ahead of or behind the underlying pulse, as if the drummer is abruptly speeding up

FIGURE 10. Kodo's "Yatai-bayashi" increases the number of drummers and dramatizes the strain of performance. Photo by Tanaka Buntarō.

and slowing down. The members of Ondekoza could not duplicate this local technique, so Hayashi took it out entirely, giving the piece a steadier, more mechanical feel.[3] The group also decided to increase the tempo. As Hayashi explained to me, "We were really bad drummers and we knew that the only way we could show that we were trying our best was to speed the piece up." To heighten visual presentation and dramatize the strain of playing, they put their legs even farther underneath the drum and leaned back even more than in the original, dramatizing the strain of playing (figure 10). They introduced a decrescendo-crescendo into the middle of the piece and left the *fue* part as it was in the original. To help his fellow members learn all the rhythm patterns, Hayashi transcribed the piece yet again, writing out *kuchi-shōga* and a series of pattern and accent marks on a large poster.

The process by which Ondekoza created "Yatai-bayashi" exemplifies the movement of people and musical cultures across localities at the heart of Ondekoza's performing mission. This probably marks one of the first times that a Japanese group visited an area with the express purpose of taking a festival drum pattern out of its original local context to adapt it for stage performance. Using audiotape, Ondekoza "delocalized" the Chichibu rhythms. The group transported them, slowed them down, transcribed them, analyzed them, and stripped out the intricacies of local nuance. Once complete, they arranged these now-abstract units for their own use, reincorporating them to best approximate the original. Ondekoza did not just extract the "essence" of the piece; they sped it up, smoothed out its rhythmic irregularities, arranged it for multiple drums, introduced a sequence of parts for multiple players, and created something new. This process, ironically, disrupted all that was "traditional" about the transmission of *yatai-bayashi* in Chichibu in order to represent elements of it as stage performance.

The contradictions inherent in the tension between transmission and interruption continue to mark the way in which Ondekoza, Kodo, and other taiko groups negotiate their relationship to local folk performing arts. In Hayashi's opinion, the struggle to create Ondekoza's "Yatai-bayashi" through trial and error reflects the unique character of the "local" society (that is, Ondekoza) in which it was arranged, not the original local context of Chichibu.

> ["Yatai-bayashi"] was, therefore, not my own arrangement but instead resulted from cooperation among all the members of Ondekoza. . . . At the time, we had no idea that we were intentionally arranging the piece—we hadn't even heard of this word! For better or worse, the "Yatai-bayashi" that resulted was our own creation. Its high tension owes more to the harshness of our communal lifestyle and training regimen than to the carefree, festival spirit of the original. In my opinion, the sheer effort involved in our performance was undoubtedly one reason for its enthusiastic audience reception. (1992, 63)

What Hayashi feels is authentic about Ondekoza's "Yatai-bayashi" has little to do with the representation of a locally transmitted folk performing art. Yet, in framing his statement, he embraces the discourse of localism to explain how Ondekoza succeeds in substituting an authentic presentation of its own local culture for a re-presentation of folk culture by accident more than intention. Moreover, the wide adoption of Ondekoza's "Yatai-bayashi" by groups in Japan has made this physically spectacular version, rather than the original, a part of contemporary ensemble taiko performance in Japan. Processes of transformation and emulation continue in the creation of the next, and perhaps most distinctive, Ondekoza piece, "Ōdaiko."

"ŌDAIKO"

Den's project of the future—his desire to restore through Ondekoza the vitality of folk culture and the values of the artisan class—was predicated upon specific representations of the Japanese past. In some cases, these came from the firsthand accounts of the elderly villagers Den encountered in his years traveling around the country. In other cases, they came from secondary accounts in the work of Mao Zedong or the Japanese folklore scholars, such as Miyamoto Tsuneichi and Shibusawa Keizō, whom Den idolized. None of these sources of influence, however, suggests exactly why Den chose the Japanese drum to be at the heart of Ondekoza's activities, especially since the group never developed Sado's *ondeko* as a performance piece. Presumably, other instruments could have been selected instead. Why is it that Den was so strongly attached to the taiko?

The evidence suggests that Den's interest in the Japanese drum was inspired not by local remembrances but rather by a fictional story. The association between the taiko and the central elements of Den's philosophy are fused in the character of Muhōmatsu in the film *The Rickshaw Man* (Muhōmatsu no issho).[4] Although it may seem an exaggeration to consider so seriously the effect that this film had on Den, there are several anecdotal reports about how profoundly he was influenced by *The Rickshaw Man*. Several members of Ondekoza recalled how Den had them watch this film repeatedly to illustrate what he described as the ideal taiko performer. Some even speculated that Den's desire to start Ondekoza derived from this film's effect on him as a young man. One critic reported that this is exactly what Den told him in conversation (Shirai 1996, 12). Of course, reducing one person's decision to create a performing arts troupe to this level runs the risk of oversimplification, not to mention the attribution of excessive causal power to fiction, especially considering Den's many years of travel across Japan. But it may have been precisely because Muhōmatsu's energetic display of folk culture existed only in the realm of fiction and not in reality, as Den's experiences in local areas affirmed, that he was so passionate in his attempt to re-create it. Or perhaps, as one former member of Ondekoza has suggested, Den formed the group not to reinvigorate the folk performing arts but, in striking circularity, to put his own version of Muhōmatsu on screen. Whatever Den's ultimate objectives, the apparent influence of this film on the ideology of the group he started and on the content of their performance repertoire warrants consideration in an account of the group's origin and development.

The Story of Muhōmatsu

The Rickshaw Man is based on the novel *Tomishima Matsugorō-den* (The story of Tomishima Matsugorō) written by Kyushu native Iwashita Shunsaku in 1939. In 1941, the story was adapted for dramatic use by the theater troupe Bungakuza. Two years later, the director Inagaki Hiroshi and screenwriter Itami Mansaku turned it into a black-and-white film called *The Rickshaw Man*, which they remade in color in 1958.[5] Bandō Tsumasaburō and Mifune Toshirō, each the leading man of his day, were featured successively in the role of Muhōmatsu. The 1958 version starring Mifune, a veteran of such classic Akira Kurosawa films as *The Seven Samurai* and *Rashomon*, was internationally successful, winning the prestigious Golden Lion award at the Venice Film Festival that year. In 1963 and 1965, the film was again remade by two different directors, making a grand total of four cinematic productions of the story over a twenty-year period. Its popularity with film and theater audiences in Japan appears without question.

One likely reason for the successive productions of the film is the richness of the story: it is at once a tale of unrequited love, a portrait of the class society of early modern Japan, and a critique of Japan's rush toward modernization. The film opens in Kokura, Kyushu, in 1898, the thirtieth year of Emperor Meiji's reign.[6] The protagonist, Matsugorō Tomishima, is a local rickshaw driver whose raffish pugnacity has earned him the nickname Muhōmatsu ("the untamed").[7] One day while driving his rickshaw, Muhōmatsu happens upon a young child with an injured leg. Revealing a tender side, Muhōmatsu picks up the child and takes him home to his parents, and then later, at the mother's request, to the hospital. The child, Toshio, turns out to be the only son of a high-ranking officer in the Japanese army named Yoshioka. Muhōmatsu refuses to take anything in return for his generosity. Upon hearing of the helpful stranger from his wife, Yoshioka quickly realizes that the strange man is the Muhōmatsu of whom he has often heard. Perhaps as a show of appreciation for his good deed or merely out of curiosity, the officer invites Muhōmatsu to his home and has the rickshaw driver entertain him with song.

The officer soon dies from pneumonia contracted while leading military exercises in the rain. Left with the burden of rearing the young boy on her own, the officer's widow asks Muhōmatsu to help show the boy how to "be a man."[8] Muhōmatsu obliges, and in the course of helping to raise young Toshio, he gradually falls in love with the boy's mother. As Toshio grows older and more self-consciously embarks on the elite track befitting his social status, he grows apart from Muhōmatsu. Muhōmatsu's feelings for the widow grow stronger, but his respect for the deceased officer, along with his recognition of the unbridgeable gap in social standing between himself and the widow, ultimately prevents him from expressing his true feelings to her. In a moment of high drama, he tells her that he can never see her or Toshio again. Now estranged from his beloved companions, Muhōmatsu stumbles home drunk and alone on a winter day and dies in the street of a heart attack. After his death, two bankers tell the widow that, despite his limited means, Muhōmatsu had set up an account for her and her son in which he had left a considerable sum.

The film is melodramatic and, in the end, tragic, but this alone is not why it held such interest for Den and other taiko enthusiasts. Much of the film's appeal has to do with a scene in which Muhōmatsu demonstrates the playing techniques of *Kokura gion daiko*, a type of drumming performed annually at the Kokura Gion Festival, for one of Toshio's teachers. The scene opens as Muhōmatsu, Toshio, and Toshio's teacher approach the festival procession through a crowd. In the distance, two drummers stand atop a mobile drum platform, or *yagura*, on either side of a medium-size *chū-daiko*, which has been placed horizontally on a drum riser. In the front of the *yagura*, which is ringed by small Japanese lanterns, two people play *chappa* (small hand cymbals). The three observers begin to converse:

> HIGH SCHOOL TEACHER: *(Surveying the drummers)* People say that this isn't the real way to play *gion daiko*.
>
> MUHŌMATSU: Yeah, that's right. There aren't many people left around here who know how to play it the right way anymore.
>
> HIGH SCHOOL TEACHER: *(Disappointed)* So, there's no way to see the *real* thing then. That's too bad....
>
> MUHŌMATSU: *(Humbly)* Well...I guess I could give it a try.
>
> TOSHIO: *(Surprised)* You can play *gion daiko*?

As Toshio speaks, Muhōmatsu steps onto the drum platform and asks the young drummer if he can trade in. Muhōmatsu takes the drummer's mallets, bows respectfully to the teacher, then turns to face the drum and begins playing lightly, shouting, "This is called *kaeru-uchi!*" Gradually picking up the tempo, Muhōmatsu calls out the name of the next pattern, "This is called *gion daiko nagare-uchi!*" He starts to dance and sing as the crowd cheers him on. The two young *chappa* players forget their parts and look over at him in bewilderment. Muhōmatsu then shifts into another rhythmic pattern and yells, "Next...*isami-goma!*" He pulls his right arm out of his kimono sleeve and begins twirling his sticks and playing to the crowd.

At this moment, the camera cuts to a scene of an older man rushing out into the street with a look of astonishment on his face. Cocking his head in the direction of the music, the old man asks excitedly, "Who is that playing *isami-goma?*"

"I'm not sure, but I heard that somebody just jumped in," one of two young men rushing out after him answers.

Somewhat puzzled, the old man mumbles, "I didn't think that there was anybody left in Kokura who could play this kind of taiko . . ."

Another young man nearby asks, "Is this the *isami-goma* you keep telling us about?"

The man answers with a slight smile, "That's right. This is the real *gion daiko,* so listen up!" He perks his ear again toward the source of the rhythm.

The camera swings back to Muhōmatsu, who shouts, "Now, *abare-uchi!*" He takes out the other arm from his kimono, leaving his chest and shoulders bare, and begins playing the taiko furiously. The tempo gets faster. The sound of the drum gets louder, and the camera starts to swirl back and forth across the crowd. Scenes of huge waves crashing into rocks and billowing clouds rolling across the sky are interlaced with shots of Muhōmatsu's flailing arms until finally the sequence fades into a series of dreamlike images.

The Meaning of Muhōmatsu

As no other film had before, *The Rickshaw Man,* with its depiction of Muhō-matsu's performance, made the playing of taiko seem "cool." This had a demonstrable impact on Den, and on many others in Japan as well, but this is very likely not the only level on which the movie struck him. Beyond the story of unrequited love on which much of its drama depends, the film is also a provocative analysis of the dynamics of class relations and the effects of modernization in wartime Japan.

In an interview about the film, the professor and film critic Yomota Inuhiko has pointed out that the seemingly assertive Muhōmatsu is remarkably passive throughout the film, except at three significant points (1996, 18–19). The first takes place near the beginning of the film, when Muhōmatsu is refused entry to a theater that he previously had no difficulty entering. Incensed, Muhōmatsu later returns to the theater with a friend, slams down his payment at the door, and goes inside. The two sit down on the floor of the theater on either side of a small barbecue and quickly begin roasting pieces of garlic and other pungent vegetables. The smell soon becomes overwhelming, and fellow theatergoers, including the distinguished visitors in the upper boxes of the theater, start to react. Fighting breaks out and continues until police arrive to take Muhōmatsu and his companion in for questioning.

What offends Muhōmatsu so much that he behaves in this manner? The interpretation of his behavior depends on an understanding of the symbolic loading of the theater and the significance of the transaction between Muhōmatsu and the box office official. By virtue of his status as a rickshaw driver, Muhōmatsu should have been entitled to the customary fraternity of other members of the lowliest classes. In the Japan of that time, this included itinerant actors. The box office official's refusal to allow him free entry indicated a change in this custom, for the theater was now "new" and professional. The man in the box office chastises him, "This is not the kind of thing you guys always watch down around the castle!" Access is granted not by status but by the payment of money, a substitution of economic exchange for the prerogatives of social class. The box office official thus functions doubly as a symbol of the modern economic system of market exchange and capital accumulation that is reconfiguring Muhōmatsu's social world. The official's contempt for the antiquated customs that ground Muhōmatsu's sense of entitlement evokes the attitude of the Meiji elite, whose drive to modernize Japan was founded upon the denigration of the older socioeconomic system. It is to this condescension that Muhōmatsu reacts.

In this sense, the film portrays allegorically how economic and social relationships were changing during the period of Japan's incipient modernization and imperialist expansion. The view toward each of these policies is a cautious one. The film inverts the commonplace understanding that modern Japan was an improvement on premodern Japan by expressing through Muhōmatsu's actions what is and what has been lost in this process. While Muhōmatsu's behavior in the theater can be taken to indicate merely a neutral change in social relations, the protagonist's wrath compels our—the viewer's—identification. The following two examples of Muhōmatsu's initiative further demonstrate the film's point of view.

In one scene, Yoshioka's widow asks Muhōmatsu to accompany her and Toshio to a track meet. Muhōmatsu agrees and the three attend the event. As they watch, pamphlets soliciting participants for the final marathon race of the day circulate through the crowd. Muhōmatsu, who did not complete compulsory education and is illiterate, cannot read the pamphlet. He gives it to the widow, who tells him that it says that anyone can participate in the race and the winner will receive a prize. Toshio urges Muhōmatsu to compete. Muhōmatsu hops out of the crowd and lines up with the other runners, still dressed in his occupational uniform—carpenter's apron (*haragake*) and snug-fitting pants (*pacchi*). The runners take off. Muhōmatsu jogs leisurely at the back of the group. The camera pans down to show that Muhōmatsu's form is the laughably nonathletic wide-stepping hop he uses to drive along his rickshaw. The race continues and, as the other runners tire, Muhōmatsu gradually edges ahead. In the end, he wins decisively, completely outshining the competition, and gets the prize. Toshio is elated, and the widow swoons.

As with the scene in the theater, the race is more than just a race; it is a clash of social worlds. As an event, the track meet betrays all the trappings of modern society. Training for it, tied as it is to the recreational activities of the educational system, is systematic. Its aim is organized competition among equals, and its goal is to teach the value of competition, to encourage the development of physically powerful bodies, and, in a more abstract sense, to simulate military exercises.[9] Into the fray jumps Muhōmatsu, who wins running in the form characteristic of his vocation and on the basis of the physical strength he has derived from it. How could a man of such lowly status and meager means defeat more affluent, better-educated, and presumably better-trained competitors? The juxtaposition is meant to question the pursuit of power through modern means. Muhōmatsu's strength has been forged not in the systematic, rationalized milieu of athletic training but through the occupational demands of premodern Japan. His victory demonstrates that, for all the strength and power industrial development brings, the vitality and stamina inculcated through the demands of life in premodern Japan concomitantly disappear.

A similar point can be made with regard to Muhōmatsu's taiko display. As is evident in his conversation with the visiting teacher and in the surprise of the elderly listener, there are few residents of Kokura who can play the "real" *gion daiko*. By this, Muhōmatsu and the elderly man have in mind a kind of taiko that is rooted in the community of Kokura residents and can be learned only within that community. However, the continuity of direct (male) inheritance of social customs and mores has been interrupted by the factory, public education, and the military. As more children are incorporated into these institutions (two of which are local), their ties to the "traditional" system of knowledge transmission within the community wither, and the "real" way of teaching—that is, one grounded in the direct transmission of folk culture—gradually disappears. In this way, Muhōmatsu again demonstrates what is lost in this shift toward institutionalized education. As Yomota remarks succinctly: "It's not just that Muhōmatsu played the taiko well. In a sense, the very fact that he was unsuccessful within the world of public education and had to drop out put him in a position where he could stay in contact with the knowledge, movements, music, and dance of a world that was gradually being replaced [by modern society]. As we all of course know, taiko is something you have to learn from the time you are a child" (1996, 19). These three events bring into relief important structural oppositions—old/new (economy), high/low (class), modern/premodern (education)—on which the dramatic tension of the film depends.

In addition to its critical view of modernization, the film also interrogates the nationalistic militarism of wartime Japan, again through the character of Muhōmatsu. In two distinct places in the film, Muhōmatsu flaunts the authority of military and police officials. The first instance is subtler and occurs at the beginning of the film, when Muhōmatsu gets in a scrape with a local police officer. The fight occurs because of a disagreement that happens between the two as they pass each other on the road at night. Muhōmatsu has no regard for the officer's authority and goes after him as he would any other man who insults him. The officer, we find out later, is a *kendō* (Japanese sword-fighting) master, and he defeats Muhōmatsu soundly by cracking him on the head with his walking stick.

The second example occurs when Muhōmatsu challenges official authority not through physical confrontation but, rather, by making a solecistic gaffe. When his wife informs him of the "strange man" who so kindly brought home their injured son, Officer Yoshioka realizes at once that she is talking about Muhōmatsu and recalls with a chuckle a story he has heard about the man. The film flashes back as the officer tells of the time an army general from Kokura returned to the city to give a speech at a local school. Muhōmatsu rushes through the crowd greeting the general and invites him into his rickshaw. Instead of switching politeness levels as would be appropriate when addressing a man of the general's status, Muhōmatsu talks with him in the same way that he would with a person of his own class. The army general reacts with more bemusement than irritation, and given the wry tones in which Officer Yoshioka relates the story to his wife, it becomes clear that Muhōmatsu is perceived as innocently vulgar, not intentionally defiant.

Each of these scenes can be taken as a subtle challenge to the authority and power of the military elite. Despite pervasive military control, there are individuals like Muhōmatsu who are so far on the margins of society that they do not submit to its assumptions or social distinctions and, hence, threaten its legitimacy. Yet, even though these individuals do not adhere to this new system of status distinctions, they embody the very Japanese spirit and culture elite military officers purport to represent and swear to defend. Whereas Officer Yoshioka dies after a brief bout with pneumonia, Muhōmatsu recovers from a beating about the head in a matter of days. Who is the stronger: a lowly rickshaw driver who recovers from his head injury in a matter of days or an elite military officer who gets caught in the rain and dies from acute pneumonia? *The Rickshaw Man* suggests the former. But in the end, it is the society of militarism and capitalism that wins. Muhōmatsu is never able to bridge the social-structural inequities that define his existence, and he dies alone, fittingly, below the local schoolhouse—the very institution that cast him out and now replaces him and others like him with its own progeny. The eventual discovery of Muhōmatsu's body by these students, shocked by what they see lying before them, elegantly encapsulates the tragic outcome of the social conflicts that inflect Muhōmatsu's life—the society of the modern, innocent, and fresh-faced, looking back in horror at the destruction it has wrought.

Muhōmatsu and Folklore Studies

The interchange referenced earlier between the teacher, Toshio, and Muhōmatsu does not function only as a demonstration of *gion daiko*. One important aspect of the conversation between the teacher and Muhōmatsu, left out of the film's screenplay, is made clearer in the book of the same name on which the film is based. In the book, we learn that the teacher visits Kokura to observe the *gion daiko* performance as part of his more general research into the folk performing arts. The teacher and Muhōmatsu discuss this while they work their way through the crowd, but the teacher never says explicitly that he is a folklore scholar. Instead, he explains that his research involves traveling to different parts of Japan in order to observe the performing arts of local communities, and that he heard about Kokura's *gion daiko* at home in Hiroshima and wanted to see it. Given that he is a scholar, it is understandable why the teacher asks Muhōmatsu whether he is seeing the "real" *gion daiko* or not, since disciplinary standards dictate that his research be based only on the observation of authentic folk performance.

There are two inferences to be drawn from this. Around the time Iwashita had completed his manuscript in the 1930s, the field of Japanese folklore studies was in the midst of taking shape around the work of such figures as Yanagita Kunio and Orikuchi Shinobu (Harootunian 1998), so Muhōmatsu would probably not have heard of someone like Toshio's teacher going around observing folk customs in different parts of his native country. Second, one can infer further that the integrity of the folk performing arts had deteriorated to such an extent by the time Iwashita wrote his manuscript that he has the amateur folklore scholar-teacher casually inquire into the legitimacy of the folk art being performed. As numerous scholars have observed, these two processes—the establishment of the field of folklore studies and the accelerated disappearance of its object of study—are contemporaneous, and *The Rickshaw Man* may be perhaps the first cinematic representation of this relationship in Japan. In the film at least, the teacher is able to get what he wants: he is able to see an authentic performance of *gion daiko* as a result, of course, of Muhōmatsu's generosity.

Having made this context clear, it is perhaps the film's greatest irony that the "real" *gion daiko* Muhōmatsu performed on camera is *not* the taiko performed annually at the Kokura Gion Festival, a fact that has been confirmed by countless Kokura locals and folklore scholars alike. The drum pattern was created by Tanaka Denji, a disciple of the kabuki drummer Tanaka Densaemon.[10] The director of the film sent Tanaka, a Kokura native and kabuki musician, back to his hometown to do research into the performance of *Kokura gion daiko*. Tanaka evidently did not think that the real *Kokura gion daiko* had enough impact to make it into the film. While preserving the rather unusual position of drummers on opposite sides of the taiko, Tanaka set about creating new rhythms for the rugged Muhōmatsu to play (Mogi 2003, 144–145).

Otsuki Takahiro, a folklore scholar and the author of *Muhōmatsu no kage* (Muhōmatsu's shadow), has taken this detail and pushed the interpretation of the festival scene even further. In the excerpt below, which is taken from an interview, Otsuki discusses how such a presentation made it into a film at this point in Japanese history.

As you know, [in the 1943 version of the film, the actor] Bantsuma gets up on the *yagura* and plays, right? Then there are the cascading layers of images. . . . In my opinion, the narrative logic dictating the way in which taiko was presented in that scene had already become ordinary for people who were watching it in 1943. By this I mean that the experience of seeing in a film the performance of taiko whose actual origin is indistinct but which effectively conjures up the feeling of some anonymous festival was not at all unusual. In the Bungaku-za [theatrical] version of the story, for example, the troupe just made up some drum pattern to create the atmosphere of a village festival. The very fact that these are such roughly hewn collages in each case makes it possible for them to create the ambience of an imaginary festival. . . . Furthermore, the creation of such a collage had become feasible only in the context of modern society, where all things can be torn out of their native context and inserted into a novel one. (1996, 25)

For Otsuki, then, the fact that the taiko performance used in the film deviated from the original is an important indicator of the extent to which Japanese people had become unfamiliar with local folk culture.[11] For the present discussion, it suffices to say that the juxtaposition of the film's narrative, which reveres the power of Muhōmatsu's authentic taiko, and the film creator's rejection of the real pattern on which it is ostensibly based represents a striking irony that says much about the state of folk culture at this time in Japanese history.

Of course, what is most important for the developing argument here is the extent to which this film influenced Den's conceptions of taiko and of the ideal taiko player. As the discussion up to this point has suggested, this effect was quite pronounced. Considering Den's own humble circumstances as a child, his interest in the folk performing arts, his passionate concern for the disappearing culture of the artisan, and his discontent with industrialized Japanese society, it is not difficult to comprehend why he may have found in the vigorous, proudly working-class, and locally grounded Muhōmatsu the ideal taiko performer, or even the ideal Japanese man. The repeated presentations of this film to the members of Ondekoza make this interpretation all the more likely.

Even though it is difficult to trace its impact with certainty, there are indications that *The Rickshaw Man* affected the development of taiko in other parts of Japan as well. One author has suggested that the carpenter's apron that is common to many taiko groups originated from the figure of Muhōmatsu (Yomota 1996, 17).[12] The film profoundly influenced Oguchi Daihachi, the founder of Osuwa Daiko; one of his group's first pieces was even called "Isami-goma"—the name of the third rhythmic pattern that Muhōmatsu shouts to the teacher during his performance.[13] Taiko enthusiasts elsewhere in Japan seem to have been similarly affected. After seeing the film, I was surprised to find that one of the first pieces to be taught to new members of the amateur taiko group that I joined during my fieldwork was taken, with slight modification, from the rhythms used in the film.[14] Although the emergence of taiko groups in postwar Japan was not foreshadowed by Muhōmatsu's individual taiko display, the image of the ideal taiko player in the 1950s and 1960s is clearly rooted in his cinematic presence.[15]

The Creation of "Ōdaiko"

The effect of the film on Den and the group he created was not limited to ideology; it also found tangible expression in a piece called "Ōdaiko." "Ōdaiko" has become one of Ondekoza's most famous and widely emulated pieces, and it features two drummers playing on a large Japanese drum, or *ōdaiko*. Of course, the development of this piece could not begin until the group acquired such a drum. Prior to the eventual attainment of an *ōdaiko,* they had been practicing a drum pattern that they had learned from an elderly resident of Mikuni Town in Fukui Prefecture. The pattern was called *hi no taiko* and is based on an agricultural ritual held in this community in the summertime.[16] In its ritual form, two drummers stand on opposite sides of an *okedō-daiko* positioned horizontally and secured to a small *x*-shaped drum riser with large ropes. While one drummer (the *ko-bai*) maintains a steady supporting rhythm, another drummer (the *ō-bai*) plays accented rhythmic patterns over it, twirling his mallets and performing dance-like arm and body movements *(furi)* to heighten the visual effect of the performance. Each drummer hits the drum at a diagonal angle in a playing style called *naname-uchi.*

In the winter of 1971, the group received a six-*shaku ōdaiko* (a drum nearly six feet in diameter) from a corporate supporter.[17] Shortly after the large drum arrived, Den directed his performers to work up a piece to play on it. They immediately set about applying the rhythms they had been practicing on the drum. The several modifications that were made to it after this point, however, severed the piece from its roots in *hi no taiko* and transformed it into something remarkably similar to the kind of taiko performed in *The Rickshaw Man.*

First, after building a more robust horizontal drum platform, or *dai,* on which to place the drum and which, in a slight departure from the depiction of drumming in the film, raised the drum above the heads of the drummers, Den suggested that they shift the positions of the players so that the *ko-bai* and *ō-bai* play on the front and back of the drum, leaving the rhythmic pattern and diagonal playing style unchanged. Second, he had the drummers position the drum so that its side, not its front, faced the audience, thus highlighting the movements of the drummers and their drum mallets and mimicking the camera angle in the 1958 version of the film (figures 11 and 12).

FIGURE 11. *(Top)* Still from a scene in *The Rickshaw Man* (1958), in which the main character, Muhōmatsu, plays *Kokura gion daiko*.

FIGURE 12. *(Bottom)* Ondekoza debuts "Ōdaiko" in 1975, soon after completing the Boston Marathon. Note the similarity to the positioning of the drum and drummers shown in figure 11. Photo courtesy of Kodo.

Finally, to facilitate the quick entrance and exit of the *ōdaiko* on stage, Den instructed the drummers to build a mobile drum platform virtually identical to the one used in the film, complete with a ring of lanterns on which the group painted their name in Chinese characters.[18]

In another move reminiscent of Muhōmatsu's performance, Den also emphasized that the drummer playing the lead part should execute various amusing *furi* movements to accentuate his performance. At this point, however, the practical constraints of performing on such a large drum began to override Den's artistic vision. Although various members of Ondekoza played the supporting part during this formative period, Hayashi Eitetsu, the most proficient drummer in the group, became chiefly responsible for the lead part, and it was around his strengths and limitations that the piece came to be developed.

A man of small stature, Hayashi found it difficult enough to reach the head of the drum on its raised platform, much less to put energy into his playing. Hayashi built a small platform to raise himself up higher, but this failed to solve the central problem; striking the thick head of the large drum obliquely sent strong reverberations through him, making it hard for him to hit the drum with any strength. Inevitably, Hayashi would work harder to overcome the vibrations of the drum than he would to play expressively. He experimented with various stances and ultimately moved around from the side of the drum to face it directly. By bending his legs, lowering his body, facing the drum, and planting one foot firmly behind him for balance, Hayashi was able to summon all his strength to strike the drum, with much more speed and facility than before.

Even though this greatly improved the musical quality of his performance, it did not sit well with Den, who liked the way in which playing the *ōdaiko* obliquely enabled the audience to watch the drummer's entertaining *furi,* just as in the film. Hayashi, however, felt that he would never be able to carry off these kinds of movements convincingly, and, as he told me in an interview, "adding such *furi* made me feel like I was trying to curry favor artificially with the audience. Frankly, it was embarrassing." For Hayashi, the piece was not meant to be a contrived presentation of theatrical flash; even with the presence of an accompanying drummer, he felt it was fundamentally a solo performance on the drum. To communicate this focus on the lead drummer even more vividly, Hayashi suggested repositioning the drum in such a way that the back of the lead drummer directly faced the audience, thus focusing attention on the physical movements involved in the drummer's performance.

Den initially resisted this change, but he finally relented after seeing how well audiences reacted. Over the next few years, Ondekoza continued to modify the structure of the piece, so much so that references to the original inspiration for the piece—*hi no taiko*—no longer appeared in concert programs.[19] With the benefit of hindsight, it becomes clear that Hayashi's subtle modification was both unprecedented and ironic. It was unprecedented because nowhere in Japanese festival or theatrical drumming did performers strike the *ōdaiko* with two drum mallets head on (in a playing style that has come to be called *shōmen-uchi*). Every contemporary presentation of Japanese taiko that involves a drummer striking an *ōdaiko* while directly facing the drum (unless, improbably, they came on this innovation on their own), therefore, has its roots not in the rich folk culture of Japan but in the famous "Ōdaiko" of Ondekoza. It was ironic because, while Hayashi shifted his position from the side to the front of the drum in order to make up for his own physical limitations, this manner of performance has become the ultimate display of physical power in taiko performance. As such, although its presentation deviates slightly from its cinematic antecedent, "Ōdaiko" can be considered a near-perfect artistic manifestation of the power and, of course, taiko prowess that Den's ideal drummer, Muhōmatsu, represented.

The European Gaze and the Japanese Fundoshi

Any discussion of Ondekoza's "Ōdaiko" is incomplete without detailing a modification that was made to Hayashi's costume not long after the piece was created. In the spring of 1975, four years after Ondekoza gathered together on Sado Island, the group journeyed to France to play a series of concerts at the fashion designer Pierre Cardin's theater in Paris, the Espace Pierre Cardin. Aside from marking Ondekoza's European debut, the concerts in Paris also marked the first time that the *ōdaiko* was played in a theater with the drummers clad only in *fundoshi*, or Japanese loincloths. Although there is no record of taiko being played this way in Japan, informants told me that *fundoshi* were traditionally worn by fishermen, who, the story goes, used to use them as a survival aid in case they accidentally fell into rough water.[20]

It is also not uncommon to see loincloths worn by men at religious festivals in Japan. The most famous example of this is probably the "Naked Festival" (Hadaka Matsuri), which takes place annually on the grounds of Saidaiji Temple in Okayama. At this night festival, thousands of men dressed only in loincloths throng together as they jockey for sacred sticks hurled into the crowd by priests. Ondekoza performed at this festival one year before their trip to Paris, and the drummers donned *fundoshi* at Den's request to keep with the atmosphere of the festival. A photograph from this performance later appeared on the poster advertising Ondekoza's concert at the Espace Pierre Cardin in May of 1975. Despite this apparent precedent, there is disagreement about whether the style of performing taiko in this manner dates from this time.

Although Den decided that the drummers should perform at the Naked Festival wearing only *fundoshi*, he has said that the idea to perform in this style, which contributed in his opinion to the legitimation of taiko as an art form, came from Pierre Cardin during Ondekoza's first performance in Paris: "The establishment of taiko as a performing art was to a large extent attributable to the 'shock' of seeing [Hayashi] Eitetsu's 'Ōdaiko,' especially the image of him playing in a *fundoshi*. As I always say, this was Pierre Cardin's idea" (1994, 4).

The custom appears to have begun a few days after Ondekoza began performing at Cardin's theater, and in a manner that seems greatly understated for the impact it would later have. According to Den, Cardin approached him to ask whether he would be willing to extend Ondekoza's concert appearances. After consulting with the group, Den told Cardin that they could perform for another three days. In a small gesture that ultimately had quite profound implications, Cardin responded with a "thank you" and a request that Hayashi Eitetsu, the featured taiko player in "Ōdaiko," perform the piece in a loincloth for the upcoming concerts. Den promptly refused. In an interview, Den later recalled that his refusal stemmed from a belief, or perhaps some insecurity, that the "Japanese body" was not something to put on public display, "even if it was Hayashi's impressive physique" (1994, 4). Some who knew Den attributed this hesitation to his early experiences with his German shipmates. Whatever the reason, the hesitation was short lived. Knowing how much the extra money would help the group, Hayashi quickly agreed to do it.[21]

Audience approval of the change was not immediate, but emerged gradually, with a distinctly homoerotic twist. Den recalled the change, probably with some exaggeration, as follows:

> On the fourth day, we skipped "Yatai-bayashi" and went immediately into "Ōdaiko," with Hayashi wearing the loincloth. When we finished, the concert hall was completely quiet. No applause at all. People slowly filed into the lobby in a daze. They spoke to each other in hushed tones. . . . A strange kind of gloominess filled the air. I thought to myself, "Oh no, we must have offended them."
>
> The next night, the same thing happened. No applause, some conversation,

and then everyone leaving. I said to [Hayashi] Eitetsu, "Maybe we shouldn't do it like this anymore?" "Well, we already got the money, so there's not much we can do," he responded unflinchingly.

The next day or so, the theater was full but this time there were surprisingly few women. And there was something odd about the air that night. It was mostly men, but the scent of perfume kept wafting up.... For the first time, "Ōdaiko" received a huge applause. Around this time, we also noticed the long line of gay men waiting outside the theater to see us. It was quite a scene! I still remember the looks on the faces of the security guards at the U.S. Embassy across the street.... It was from this time on that we started receiving standing ovations. (1994, 5)

It is not entirely certain why Cardin suggested that Hayashi wear a *fundoshi* while playing the big taiko. Some former members of Ondekoza suggested that he had seen film footage of Ondekoza's performance at the Naked Festival and that the concert poster made him recall the scene. Other informants told me that the suggestion derived from Cardin's long-standing interest in sumo wrestling.[22] Whatever its source, Cardin apparently imagined this to be the way that "Ōdaiko" was commonly played in Japan. Ultimately, this image of "Ōdaiko" performance became reality; the group continued to perform the piece in this manner and wore loincloths in another piece in their repertoire. More important, adopting the *fundoshi* transformed Ondekoza's performance of "Ōdaiko." It became a kind of stage "costume" that emphasized the impressive bodies of the male drummers, not just the movements and sounds these bodies produced (figure 13). Ondekoza had always been concerned with artistic presentation: the placement of instruments, choreography, and the progression of pieces. But with this change in costume, suddenly the drummers themselves—or more precisely, their toned, muscular bodies—became a central, if not *the* central, means of expressing their guiding ideology and artistic vision. Forged as they were in an attempt to re-create the folkways of premodern Japan, these bodies came to represent the ideals that their cinematic predecessor, Muhōmatsu, had embodied. In fact, concert programs dating from the period between their performance in Paris and Den's departure from the group in 1981 state explicitly that Ondekoza's goal was not merely to preserve Japanese folk entertainments, but "to *embody [taigen]* in the present the very life force at the roots of Japan's folk performing arts" (emphasis added). Through "Ōdaiko," and perhaps through the gaze of an influential European observer as well, Ondekoza now revealed these bodies for all to see.

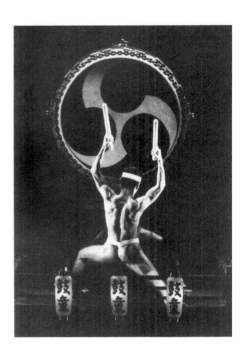

FIGURE 13. Kodo's "Odaiko" in 1997. Conserving Hayashi's innovation, the drummer's back faces the audience. The lanterns circling the raised platform recall Muhōmatsu's original cinematic presence. Photo by Mark Coutts-Smith.

"MONOCHROME" AND THE BIRTH OF KODO

A month before their visit to Paris, Ondekoza had performed "Yatai-bayashi" and "Ōdaiko" soon *after* finishing the Boston Marathon. The combination of events, orchestrated by Den, made a considerable impression on onlookers. Indeed, the sheer feat of completing the twenty-six-mile race and then executing another strenuous performance of taiko is impressive.[23] Not only did it manifest the group's training regimen of marathon running and musical practice; like "Ōdaiko," it also visibly demonstrated the results of their intense training.

During their time in America, the members of Ondekoza were introduced to the Japanese composer of "modern music" *(gendai ongaku)* Maki Ishii by the Japanese conductor of the Boston Symphony Orchestra, Seiji Ozawa. Ishii would go on to compose a piece for Ondekoza, and the collaboration with Ishii marked the first time that the group enlisted the help of an outsider in the composition of one of their own pieces. It also marked the first time that they learned a piece that was scored, rather than memorized through repetition. Even though nearly six years had passed since the group's inception, the majority of Ondekoza performers still could not read staff notation. Completing the arduous process of learning Ishii's composition "Monochrome," however, gave them confidence that they were musicians who could play contemporary music, not just arrangements of folk performing arts. Furthermore, having a piece which they could call their own, even though they themselves did not compose it, contributed to their feeling more like professional musicians. As Hayashi Eitetsu remarked in an interview, "With folk performance pieces based on local rhythms, I often felt that I was an outsider playing someone else's music and that no matter how hard I tried it was impossible for me to feel the way a local feels" (1999, 37).

That said, the process of creating the piece did not take it entirely out of the realm of their former efforts. The piece itself is arranged for seven *shime-daiko* drums, three *chū-daiko* drums, and one *dora* (gong). It begins with the drummers playing a nearly imperceptible alternating pattern that builds in a long crescendo to an ear-splitting cacophony and then decrescendos into light tapping. The rest of the complex piece is characterized by similar use of contrasts between crescendos and decrescendos, evoking the summertime buzz of Sado's cicadas, interspersed with skillfully arranged percussive effects and dramatic use of silence. The piece climaxes with three of the *shime-daiko* players rising in unison, turning, and then sitting in front of the three *chū-daiko*—in a position akin to that used in "Yatai-bayashi"—with their backs to the audience.[24] Indicative of its "post-Cardin" creation, the drummers then proceed through a series of highly scripted motions to remove their *happi* (kimono-like topcoats) and reveal their bare backs, which are criss-crossed by the two straps holding on their *haragake* (wrap-around carpenter aprons).[25] One after another, the drummers then launch into the *chū-daiko* pattern of "Yatai-bayashi" as the remaining *shime-daiko* players transition one by one from a series of syncopated percussion riffs to the supporting pattern that normally accompanies the *chū-daiko* in "Yatai-bayashi." In a sense then, "Monochrome," as a piece of music in itself, artistically represents the point of contact between the avant-garde and the folk that was embodied, quite literally, in the meeting between Ishii and Ondekoza.

"Monochrome" signals how Ondekoza's new circulation in the emerging global market for world music affected the group's repertoire and sense of mission. At the same time, it highlights an aspect of the group's character that had hitherto been implicit, but that these pieces make explicit—that is, the avoidance of combining recognizably Western (classical/modern) and Eastern (Japanese) music within their own performance. It is significant that, as much as "Monochrome" represented a move to integrate Western forms of compositional structure, arrangement, and staff notation, the performance is restricted to Japanese instruments and its composer was a Japanese man who constructed the piece around the sound qualities of Japanese instruments. Whether this avoidance was conscious or unconscious, it is a common thread that runs through Ondekoza's performances to present-day Kodo and ties both groups to the other two influential taiko ensembles discussed earlier.

In the years following the debut performances of Maki Ishii's "Monochrome" in 1976, Ondekoza's history was marked by increasing devotion to performing, both in Japan and overseas in Europe and America, and continued marathon running. It was not until 1978 that the group had received enough exposure to settle into a stable touring schedule. Starting in July of that year, the group toured continuously for five months, arranging four performances a week. Interviews with informants about this period, however, primarily reference what eventually came after it: Den's departure from the island and the creation of Kodo in his wake.

Most of the informants with whom I spoke attributed the proximate cause of the break with Den to the making of the second documentary film about the group, *Za Ondekoza* (The Ondekoza), a film directed by the Japanese filmmaker Katō Shun that began shooting in February of 1979. By this time, five other documentaries had already been made about the group.[26] Ondekoza's (or, to be more precise, Den's) previous forays into movie production had been meant primarily as an audiovisual means of chronicling the group's development. However, the group had grown increasingly suspicious of Den's fascination with filmmaking. The films cost the group lots of hard-earned money, which they never saw returned to them in the form of box-office receipts or wide distribution. In fact, some members wondered whether the impulse to continue producing films was merely an expression of Den's fascination with the cinematic image of Muhōmatsu.

Eventually, these tensions escalated into a standoff between Den and the young performing members, many of whom were now entering their thirties. This conflict resulted in Den's abrupt decision to leave, but the operations of the group did not cease so quickly. The film remained unfinished and Ondekoza already had concert appearances scheduled for the upcoming year. Out of a sense of responsibility and pressing economic need, the group kept their performance engagements, including a tenth-anniversary concert that they organized by themselves. They continued to perform as Ondekoza until Den demanded that they discontinue the practice. By that time Den had left for Nagasaki—with all the group's instruments in tow—to start a new Ondekoza.[27] For a brief period, the two groups performed contemporaneously, each claiming that it was the "real" Ondekoza. In the fall of 1981, the two groups reached a decision: Den would retain rights to use the name Ondekoza and the former members of that group would reassemble themselves under the new name Kodo.[28] The reasons for this choice of name and the fallout from its adoption yield some insight into the character of the group at this time and the nature of its evolution.

Although the leader and manager throughout this period of transition was a player named Kawauchi Toshio, the featured stage performer remained Hayashi Eitetsu, the drummer primarily responsible for arranging the group's standards "Ōdaiko" and "Yatai-bayashi." In the period following Den's departure, Hayashi advocated that Ondekoza focus on maintaining high-quality performances. For him, this seemed essential to the group's survival, since the economic base of Ondekoza's activities depended on revenues earned at concert performances. In contrast, many others in the group, such as Kawauchi Toshio, were still captivated by Den's original vision of creating an "artisan academy" and were not concerned with the group's financial stability. According to Hayashi, it was at this time that Den's vision of a "university" gradually shifted into a desire to create a "village" that would have the artisan academy at its center.[29] Even so, it was from Hayashi's minority voice and from the long experience of being with Ondekoza that the group's new name, Kodo, emerged. As he explained to me in an interview:

Den always exhorted us to think of ourselves as *oni* [demons] when we performed—unsmiling ferocity, deliberate intensity. While his exhortations had a basis in our group name and compelled us to perform with great passion, there was something in the sound of the taiko that was for me much gentler. Mothers often came up to us after our show to tell us how their children were lulled to sleep by the sound of our taiko. I always thought this was interesting, and it made me recall a story I had heard about the sound of the taiko resembling the way a mother's heartbeat sounds to a fetus in the womb.

It was in this universal human experience of motherhood that I began to see the reason why foreigners listening to our performance could be moved to tears, and why our audiences abroad comprised so many different kinds of people. At our first few performances in Los Angeles, our audiences were overwhelming Asian American. But over time we began to notice people of all ethnic varieties—white people, black people, Latinos—at our performances. What attracted them all, I figured, was that primordial sound that we've all heard but forgotten. I took these two images of "drum children" and "heartbeat" and came up with Kodo.[30]

According to Hayashi, when he suggested this name in a meeting, he noticed that no other player shared this vision or experience but, since there were no other ideas, they agreed to it. When he saw Kawauchi announce to the audience at their debut performance in Japan that they, as a group, had chosen the name out of a desire to play the taiko "with the unspoiled heart of a child," he decided that it was time for him to leave this group of performers. He eventually began a new career as a taiko soloist. Personal conflicts aside, the new group name also exchanged an identification with the folk culture of Sado Island for something approaching a universal humanism. The shift in nomenclature anticipates Kodo's increasingly global perspective and its look outward to world music for musical inspiration.

THREE DECADES OF KODO:
FROM DEMONS TO HUMANS

Established in 1981 and still going strong today, Kodo has already outlasted its antecedent group on Sado by two decades. The interest in the folk performing arts, admiration for the artisan, emphasis on intense physical conditioning, and refinement of such signature pieces from the Ondekoza era as "Yatai-bayashi," "Ōdaiko," and "Monochrome" all remain integral to contemporary Kodo performances. Nevertheless, there have been some significant changes in the size, scope, and artistic direction of the organization following the turbulence that accompanied the change in name and leadership. With the departure of Den and Hayashi Eitetsu, the duties of overall group leadership and management fell to Kawauchi Toshio (affectionately called *hanchō*, or "leader," by group members), and it was he who provided the inspiration and direction for the group over the next several years. Left without any musical instruments, tools, furniture, books, or records, the group spent its first years without Den rebuilding the organization and acquainting Ondekoza's fans and business contacts with the new group name. Gradually, Kodo's name recognition grew and its touring schedule stabilized.

During this time, some important additions were made to the repertoire. Soon after the break with Den, a contingent of drummers from the group journeyed to Miyake Island, one of a group of islands several miles away from Tokyo, to study a drumming pattern played during festival celebrations in the island's Kamitsuki Village. "Miyake," the piece that developed out of this interaction, positions three or five *chū-daiko* horizontally on low stands, arranges them at the points of a triangle, and places a drummer on opposite sides of each drum. Musically, the piece consists of a repeating four-measure, odd-time pattern derived from the Kamitsuki festival drumming pattern, which is interspersed with solo performances by the two drummers at the apex of the triangle. Because the drums lie only inches off the stage, the drummers have to stretch their legs out wide and lower their bodies down to a height of only a few inches from the stage. The drum is struck in a series of coordinated arm and lateral body movements. The combined effect is signature Kodo (Ondekoza): a folk rhythm rearranged for stage performance coupled with impressive choreography and physical display.

In this formative period, the group also refined a piece based on a deer dance *(shishi odori)* from northeastern Japan that had been integrated into the repertoire of Ondekoza shortly before the break with Den. This deer dance, "discovered" by the group when Hayashi Eitetsu went there to study folk *shamisen* playing, involves carrying an *okedō-daiko* that one plays while dancing. In the past, Den had resisted a performance piece in which players carry drums and dance because he associated it with Korean drumming, which he thought did it much better. Ever conscious of the Japaneseness of their performances, however, Hayashi found a style of *okedō-daiko* drumming that locals said was distinctly Japanese, and the group moved swiftly to feature it in their performance.

Along with these changes to the repertoire, several changes occurred on the level of the organization. During the Ondekoza era, romantic relationships and marriages between members had been strictly forbidden. (Some informants told me, however, that toward the end of the Ondekoza period it became clear that some male and female members had become romantically involved.) Upon the change to Kodo and to managing their own affairs, relationships among members came to be permitted. Many in the group who had joined Ondekoza in their late teens and early twenties had by now entered their thirties and increasingly looked forward to marriage and family. The group had been living communally in the former Daisho Elementary School building, and the members who wanted to marry and start families gradually moved out of the building into homes in the neighboring towns of Ogi and Mano, as it was difficult to manage children and family in such a confined setting.

The separation of these members from the group was assisted by the creation of a legal corporation to handle salaries, employment, tour booking, and other management issues. During the Ondekoza years, members did not receive salaries, as Den and his small staff pooled monies earned from concerts and donors to provide the group with room and board. The distribution of salaries thus ensured a new level of financial independence for members of the group. The name the group gave this corporation, Kitamaesen, reflects the enduring vision of the group members as ambassadors of local culture. During Japan's Edo period (1603–1868), the ship *Kitamaebune* traveled from Osaka to Hokkaido, stopping at a number of harbors on the Japan Sea along the way, one of which was Sado Island.[31] Along with trade in goods, the *Kitamaebune* facilitated the transmission of culture from place to place along its route. Much of Sado's distinctive local culture, Kodo members told me, dates from the era of the *Kitamaebune*.

With the creation of Kitamaesen, the group started on a path that would transform it from a small group driven by the pursuit of common goals into a collectivity of individuals with often conflicting desires and artistic objectives. No longer subject to Den's surveillance, members decided that they would now monitor themselves; as a result, bans on popular media were relaxed and morning runs were left up to individual desire and decision. One veteran member of the group, playing on the two names of the group, summed up the change in mood that accompanied the shift from Ondekoza to Kodo: "We changed from demons back to humans."

One thing that did not change entirely with the shift from Ondekoza to Kodo, however, was the individual nature of group management. Although group responsibility was distributed for some of the matters outlined above and a legal corporation was created, the responsibility for the overall direction of the group, its financial management, and its tour booking remained in the hands of Kawauchi Toshio. Those who knew him describe Kawauchi as a talented, contemplative visionary who kept much of the group's accounting and tour information in his prodigious memory. He also had a penchant for taking solitary fishing vacations. On one of these vacations, in 1987, he drowned. The group was thrown into utter disarray, desperately struggling to recover information about their finances and impending tour bookings while coping with the shock of Kawauchi's death. Kawauchi had been the lifeblood of Kodo since Den's departure, and his tragic loss left an indelible mark on the organization. To this day, Kawauchi's former office at the converted Daisho Elementary School remains untouched and Kodo's administrative center, built after his death, has a small room set aside as a miniature shrine to the former leader.

Having suffered from the sudden disappearance of two important leaders, the remaining members of Kodo regained their footing and established a more formal system of accounting and tour management. Their tour schedule and name recognition now established, they continued to move forward on two important initiatives set in motion by Kawauchi before his death. The first of these, Kodo Village, broke ground in the mid-1980s and came to fruition in 1988 with the opening of the administrative center in a newly carved-out section of Ogi Town on the southwestern tip of Sado Island. Kodo Village was the culmination of several years of sometimes tense negotiations with residents of the surrounding community, and it marked the implementation of the desire to establish an "artisan village" at the center of Kodo's activities first articulated by Den Tagayasu and conserved by Kawauchi. Although Den's original plan called for the development of an "artisan academy," Kodo Village began as a central location for the group's management and tour staff. A rehearsal hall, dormitory, and reception house on the property followed and were all completed by 1992. While relations with surrounding villagers were discouraged during the Ondekoza era (drummers were supposed to concentrate exclusively on training), Kodo Village represented the desire of the Kodo organization to establish itself as a permanent presence on Sado Island (not just renters in abandoned schoolhouses) and a new emphasis on integration with, not distance from, its neighbors on Sado. Over the years, members of the group built homes and took up residence outside the boundaries of Kodo Village, further blurring the distinction between Kodo and the surrounding community. The desire to have an "artisan academy" at the center of the group continues to resonate within Kodo, and something akin to such a school is institutionalized in the Apprentice Centre.

In 1988, in addition to founding Kodo Village, the group held its first "Earth Celebration" festival, another proposal envisaged by Kawauchi Toshio. The inaugural Earth Celebration brought together musicians from around the world for a week of concert performances, workshops, and other activities on Sado Island. Kawauchi intended the Earth Celebration festival to be an extension of Kodo Village's function as a place not only for the revitalization of the culture of Sado Island but also for the exchange of culture between Sado and the rest of the world. The Earth Celebration gave Kodo an opportunity to invite the many individuals and groups that it had met in its years of touring back to its home ground of Sado Island and to introduce visitors and local residents to a variety of world musical forms. *Tataku* (the Japanese word used to describe the "beating of a drum") has been the theme of every Earth Celebration, and it signifies Kodo's emphasis both on the global diversity of ethnic music and on a celebration of the group's belief in the universal human desire to "beat." The festival has continued every year virtually uninterrupted since 1988, and it remains one, if not the only, collective event that the entire group—performers, staff, and apprentices—works together to carry out.

Artistically, the period shortly before the founding of Kodo Village until its completion in 1992 was dominated by the artistic director Leonard Eto. At the time of his arrival, most of Kodo's repertoire had been inspired by the folk performing arts or composed for them by outside professionals. Since most drummers had come to Kodo without prior musical experience, it was enough for them just to play these inherited pieces with aplomb. Leonard Eto, by contrast, proved to be a talented composer of original ensemble taiko pieces. In fact, he composed a number of the classic Kodo pieces from this period, including "Irodori," "Zoku," and "Lion." Leonard Eto left in 1992 to pursue his own solo career as a taiko drummer but, as one longtime fan mentioned to me, seeing a Kodo concert during the height of his influence on the group was like "seeing 'Leonard Eto with Kodo,' rather than 'Kodo.'" Eto still retains close ties to the group, and his interest in composing original pieces was taken up by such Kodo members as Naito Testurō, who tended to favor pieces based in odd-time meters, and Kaneko Ryūtarō, who liked to compose works sprinkled with Asian motifs.

Kaneko's integration of Asian musical influences into what was formerly a strictly Japanese repertoire is illustrative of a trend that has marked the group's activities since the early 1990s. Although the base of its stage performance remains rooted in pieces inspired by the folk music of Japan— such as "Miyake," "Monochrome," "Ōdaiko," and "Yatai-bayashi"—several Kodo members have taken up the task of composition and have introduced international motifs, and even foreign (but non-Western) instruments, into the group's performance repertoire. Leonard Eto's "Irodori," which borrows its shoulder-harnessed okedō-daiko playing technique from the Korean group Samul Nori's style of janggo playing, was probably the first of these.[32] Since this time, the group has inserted musical instruments from Korea and Southeast Asia into its performances and incorporated musical motifs from an even wider array of countries.

Several outside observers of Kodo's performances remarked to me that this trend has diminished Kodo to just another "percussion group" without a distinctively Japanese sound. This is probably an unfair criticism, as the group still bases its performances in the pieces mentioned above. However, these critics do point to what I would agree is an increasing interest on Kodo's part in developing not only as a group that plays a distinctive kind of Japanese music but as a group of (mostly) Japanese performers who put on a distinctive performance. When asked about the conflation of Ondekoza-era pieces and new ones, players uniformly told me that they saw no incompatibility; in their view, this was merely the natural outcome of dozens of years of international tours. Kodo's promotional literature, too, reflects this perspective. It states that the group's repertoire derives from three sources: pieces rooted in the folk performing arts that the group has arranged, pieces written for the group by outside composers, and pieces created by individual members based on their experiences with cultures outside of Japan.

It is perhaps this emphasis on a broader array of musical influences and performance styles that most distinguishes contemporary Kodo from its antecedent group on Sado. Yet Kodo still places an important emphasis on maintaining a tie to the performing arts and local culture of Japan, much of which continues the original vision of Ondekoza in institutional form. In 1997, Kodo received permission from the Niigata prefectural government to establish the Kodo Cultural Foundation, a nonprofit foundation on Sado Island that oversees those aspects of Kodo's mission peripheral to the performance management of the Kitamaesen Corporation. The Kodo Cultural Foundation administers Kodo's enhanced apprentice program and supports research into the folk culture of Sado Island.

Although the desire to create an independent "artisan academy" has waned, some of its spirit lives on in the form of Otodaiku (a neologism that means "sound carpenter"). Established in 1988, Otodaiku Ltd. handles the management of Kodo's copyrights and audiovisual recordings.[33] True to its name, in the past it also distributed crafts made by Kodo members and affiliates.

These three divisions of Kodo's contemporary organization thus complete the institutional distribution of responsibility and management expertise within the group following Kawauchi Toshio's death in 1987. Along with the commitment to Sado Island that is evident in Kodo Village, these additional institutions distinguish Kodo from other music groups that have transformed themselves from local folk revivalists into entirely commercial popular-music groups.

. . .

Hayashi Eitetsu, the Ondekoza member who departed shortly after contributing the name Kodo to the group, has gone on to a critically acclaimed career as the first solo taiko performer in Japan. Since beginning his solo career, Hayashi has pushed the artistry of taiko performance to a level of lofty refinement that some say extends beyond that attained by his former group. Settling this issue is, of course, largely a matter of taste. Of more academic significance, however, are the numerous professional taiko groups that have appeared in Japan since the 1980s. Like Hayashi, these groups have artistic intentions without an identity rooted in a particular locality. For these groups, taiko drums are musical instruments and taiko performances are intended to express artistry alone. By contrast, the close ties to festival, community, and the folk performing arts represented in the histories of Osuwa Daiko, Sukeroku Daiko, Ondekoza, and Kodo appear anachronistic.

Nevertheless, while these artistically inspired ensemble taiko groups represent a recent trend, their numbers remain small compared to the number of amateur and semiprofessional ensemble taiko groups in Japan that do have local roots. The following chapter turns to a discussion of these groups and of the remarkable proliferation of ensemble taiko beyond the settings of Osuwa Daiko, Sukeroku Daiko, Ondekoza, and Kodo into the many communities of Japan—in other words, the "taiko boom."

FOUR

Placing Ensemble Taiko in Japan

FESTIVAL CREATION AND THE TAIKO BOOM

OSUWA DAIKO, SUKEROKU DAIKO, ONDEKOZA, AND KODO represent the main stylistic variants of ensemble taiko performance, but they do not encompass the larger cultural phenomenon it has become. Since these groups first cleared out a space for ensemble taiko groups in Japan, the number of taiko groups has risen into the thousands. Social, religious, and demographic factors have all contributed to the proliferation of taiko ensembles, but three related factors are of central importance: first, the increasingly democratic nature of participation in community festivals in Japan; second, the decline in vitality of older shrine-based festivals; and third, the creation of new community festivals by local governments intent on enlivening community life. The popularization of ensemble taiko is thus closely correlated with changes in the character of Japanese festivity. These formative factors continue to be reflected in the membership, instrumentation, repertoire, and performance sites of contemporary taiko groups.

My debut with Miyamoto Daiko, the amateur taiko ensemble I joined during my fieldwork, helps illustrate how the changing nature of Japanese festivity facilitated the popularization of Japanese taiko. A fellow graduate student at the University of Tokyo first introduced me to this group of drummers. He invited me to one of their weekend practices, where I learned that they were scheduled to perform at a local children's festival the following week. I tagged along with him that day, intending to watch the group perform. Prior to the start of the performance, we met the other group members and began chatting. One drummer took a tally and discovered that they were short a member. They began to tease my friend, telling him that he was going to have to play an extended solo to make up for the absent player.

Soon this teasing died down, and they suddenly turned to me and asked if

I wanted to play. This took me by surprise, since I had been to only one practice session and had not yet learned any of their pieces, much less joined the group. Nevertheless, being an eager field-worker, I decided that the opportunity to perform with them was worth the potential embarrassment. Minutes later I was squeezing myself into the group's stage costume of tight-fitting *pacchi* pants, sleeveless *haragake* vest, and wrap-around *happi* topcoat. I climbed onto the stage with them and stood as far to the rear as possible. (If I could have stood behind the stage, I would have.) Once the performance started, I followed along, playing simple rhythm patterns on a high-pitched *shime-daiko* drum. My friend subtly tried to signal to me when to start or stop, but I failed to recognize most of his signals and made a mess of mid-piece breaks and synchronized endings. My debut was far from perfect, but fortunately it was not too horrible. I was able to practice and perform with the group for the rest of my year in Tokyo.

I recall this experience not to boast but rather to draw attention to the openness with which I was received by the group, the ease with which they allowed me to participate, and the site of festival performance. For scholars familiar with Japanese festival entertainments, this degree of openness might appear surprising.

FESTIVALS IN JAPAN

In the prevailing scholarly literature on Japan, festivals—or *matsuri*—are regarded as events that affirm religio-communal ties and boundaries. The boundaries of this festival "community" are usually coterminous with the parish boundaries of the local Shinto shrine, which houses a tutelary deity, or *ujigami*. Those responsible for organizing the festival, carrying out its rituals, and performing the music and dance that accompany it are the "children of the shrine," or *ujiko*. Inclusive as the festivals are for these shrine children, those outside the parish community—for example, residents of a different community in Japan—would normally not be allowed to participate in performances associated with the festival. Moreover, this exclusion extends even to residents who recently moved to neighborhoods within or bordering the boundaries of the parish, often even after several years of residence.

The common English translation of the Japanese *matsuri* as "festival" lacks the nuance of the Japanese term. Although "festival" sometimes marks a religious event, the English term typically signifies a large, accessible gathering and a generalized atmosphere of levity and openness. In contrast, the Japanese term has historically referred to a distinctly religious occasion, albeit one that is usually accompanied by enthusiastic ritual fervor. As urbanization and rural depopulation in Japan have accelerated since the end of World War II, large-scale festivals, such as those held in major urban centers, have become better known as tourist attractions than as communal outpourings of religious sentiment (Ikeda 1999). The meaning of the term *matsuri* has accordingly expanded beyond its formerly strictly religious basis to include the sense that the English term connotes (J. Robertson 1991, 39–40).[1]

Bemoaning this hollowing out or, worse still, withering away of traditional Japanese religio-communal life is a common theme in the literature on Japanese festivals, and it has received much more attention than patterns of exclusion and inclusion.[2] As one scholar wrote decades ago, in contrast to urban festivals that are "fast losing their ritualistic symbolism and are becoming simply festivities of a purely secular nature . . . old traditions are still a living reality [in village Japan]" (Moriarty 1972, 91–92). Yet, this scholar notes, village communities have not gone untouched by modernity. As young people from the community slowly drift away, "they do not understand the meaning of the symbols used in the ritual and, because of urban entertainment, they do not feel the need for the festivity of the *matsuri*. If they do return to the village for the celebration it is out of loyalty to the community and to enjoy the festivity" (136). A more recently published book-length study of a Japanese festival recognizes the difficulty that residents have had continuing the *matsuri* as "movement from the old neighborhoods in the center of town to the outlying areas creates a drain of talented young people necessary for learning and passing on the traditions. As a result, 'time-honored' traditions are in danger of fading away" (Schnell 1999, 278). Taking such sentiments as a given, one anthropologist examined festivity in a provincial urban center to explain why it has even been maintained at all (Ashkenazi 1993, 14).

While festivals have certainly changed in response to new economic and social circumstances, ethnographic analysis of urban, and suburban, festivals suggests that they are characterized not by *loss*—whether of ritualistic symbolism or authenticity—but by *creation*. In the late 1980s and 1990s, the anthropologists Theodore Bestor (1989) and Jennifer Robertson (1991) explored how local governments created entirely new festivals as a means of integrating the increasingly differentiated populations within their jurisdictions. An important corrective to studies that have minimized the salience of the insider-outsider division, the work of these two ethnographers tends to emphasize how the new festivals can be problematic, interfering with the kinds of community making they hope to encourage.[3] Yet these studies consider less thoroughly how new community festivals have also had a range of positive effects, even when they have made only a modest or even negative contribution to local community building. Among other things, they have often created a space for participation in festivals, particularly festival performance, in ways that were not possible before—a space filled in part by members of the amateur taiko ensembles that are the subject of this book. The same holds true for established festivals, where the weakening of hereditary authority has opened up opportunities for participation and involvement.

During my fieldwork, I was struck by the number of people involved in ensemble taiko performance who expressed to me that their interest in participating grew out of exclusion from shrine-centered festivals conducted by "natives" of their hometown. One of my clearest memories of this was a young woman whom I met on Sado Island at Kodo's annual summer concert, "Earth Celebration." She had come to the island from a bedroom community on the outskirts of Osaka for a series of workshops held during the Earth Celebration weekend. I asked her whether there was a taiko group in her area and she replied that there was. If this was the case, I asked, then why had she come all the way out to Sado Island to learn about playing taiko? "Because," she told me, "the drum group plays as part of a local festival. The longtime residents of the community consider the festival to be theirs, and they won't let us participate in it."

It is often a desire to simulate the atmosphere of communal festivity that leads individuals to participate in taiko and, in some cases, to start their own groups. The majority of amateur ensemble taiko groups I encountered recruited members openly without regard for parish affiliation. At the same time, the groups did express a preference for residential affiliation, because they were invariably involved in community-based festivals and were in a sense attempting to create new bonds of community. (Such was the case in the group in which I participated, but, as I have already described, this did not preclude my involvement.) Thus, while these groups recapitulate the emphasis on community in parish-based festival groups, they base membership on residence, regardless of duration and shrine affiliation.

This emphasis on residence rather than shrine affiliation is not just the limited preserve of taiko enthusiasts with whom I came in contact. In fact, it is representative of a larger trend toward increased festival participation more broadly across Japan, even in shrine-based festivals. Although participation in shrine-based festivals was typically reserved only for the men of certain

FIGURE 14. "It's Festival Time": a poster soliciting palanquin holders for a summer shrine-based festival in a Tokyo neighborhood. As in many Japanese festivals in recent years, participation is much more egalitarian and open than in the past. The poster reads: "Adults, Children, Men, and Women. All welcome." It also assures prospective participants that festival garb is available for loan. Photo by author.

families, declining fertility in regional communities has left fewer younger men who are ready to take up these inherited responsibilities. Some regional communities have responded by accepting male participants from outside hereditary lineages, while other localities have extended this privilege beyond men alone.[4] Women and girls are thus finding new roles in festival processions and in folk performances that were traditionally closed to them.[5] The shift is evident even in metropolitan areas that have suffered less from a loss of young people.[6] In fact, in areas like Osaka and Tokyo, it is not uncommon to see posters soliciting individuals of all ages and genders to help carry festival palanquins (figure 14).

FESTIVALS AND TAIKO

As with more and more festivals and folk performing arts groups, openness to nonresidents and women is a characteristic shared by ensemble taiko groups. However, openness in itself does not explain the widespread participation of taiko groups in new festivals or the rapid increase in the number of groups, which began in the 1980s. What accounts for the role of ensemble taiko groups in new festivals and the growth of those groups since the 1980s?

First, when considering the presence of ensemble taiko groups in contemporary Japanese festivals, it is important to remember the long association of taiko with religious activity in Japanese history. Before the first taiko ensembles emerged in postwar Japan, the sounding of taiko drums as accompaniment for religious ritual music and dance was common, from Buddhist chanting and Bon dancing to Shinto rituals and festival processions. This was particularly the case in shrine-based Shinto festivals. When I asked informants about the presence of taiko groups in these festivals, they would typically respond with some variation of *"taiko naki matsuri nante nai yo!"* (a festival without taiko is not a festival).

Second, with respect to the spread of ensemble taiko groups in the 1980s and 1990s, it is helpful to get some sense of scale. Given the historical tie of taiko to Buddhist and Shinto ritual, it would not be surprising if the close relationship between taiko groups and festivals that I observed in and around the Tokyo area was representative of Japan as a whole. Although a truly comprehensive census of all taiko groups in Japan was beyond the scope of my own research, in 1999 another organization, the Nippon Taiko Foundation, surveyed 3,389 local government bodies in Japan about their knowledge of taiko groups in their administrative districts. The survey indeed found evidence of a close relationship between taiko groups and festivals. Of the 97 percent of local communities that stated that they had some involvement with taiko groups, nearly 60 percent reported that this involvement came in the support of community festivals and events (Nippon Taiko Foundation 1999, 6). Furthermore, 83 percent reported that their communities hosted a festival or similar event that involved the use of taiko (14). The survey also found that the vast majority of contemporary taiko groups had originated in the period since World War II, with nearly half of all groups (46 percent) originating in the ten-year period between 1988 and 1998. While more comprehensive and recent data would strengthen these initial findings, the connection between taiko performance and community festivals that I observed in selected field sites appears to be reflected in these empirical data.

Additional evidence of this connection in western Japan—an area that I was not able to visit for an extended period during my fieldwork—is provided by a 1991 survey of taiko groups in Hiroshima Prefecture (Yagi 1994). The survey found a total of 73 taiko groups distributed over the area of 86 local administrative divisions. Of these, 64 groups (88 percent) were new taiko ensembles not associated with inherited folk performing arts. A similar survey in 1989 in Nagasaki Prefecture found 75 taiko groups spread over an area of 79 administrative divisions, of which 61 groups (81 percent) were taiko ensembles. Extrapolating from this baseline yields an approximate estimate of 3,000 taiko ensembles in Japan.

Along with these estimates, these surveys also found a close relationship between community revitalization efforts (or, alternatively, efforts directed toward enhancing community ties) and the establishment of taiko groups in these two prefectures. Analysis of these surveys by historical period reveals a trend similar to the one found in the Nippon Taiko Foundation survey— that is, one showing that most taiko ensembles have originated in the period since 1988 (Yagi 1994, 26). Furthermore, at events featuring presentations of "local culture" in both Hiroshima Prefecture and Nagasaki Prefecture, ensemble taiko groups made up the overwhelming majority of performers on stage (29), thus expressing their identification with local culture (and, perhaps as well, the diminished prominence of the folk performing arts that formerly signified localism).[7]

Most of my informants anecdotally attributed this growth in the number of taiko groups to the "Grants for the Creation of Native-Places" program implemented by Prime Minister Takeshita's government in 1988. This program distributed grants of one hundred million yen to 3,269 local government bodies over the course of several years. These individuals told me that many communities used the seed money received from this program to "revitalize" festivals for community development or to encourage tourism. Though they are inconclusive in themselves, the Nippon Taiko Foundation's survey and the data from surveys in western Japan provide some statistical credibility for the claim that most ensemble taiko groups emerged in conjunction with increased funding for community revitalization and festival creation.[8]

CHARACTERISTICS OF TAIKO ENSEMBLES

The changing nature of festivity and the effects of government investment in community building help explain the growth in the number of Japanese taiko ensembles. They help illuminate as well what distinguishes these groups from inherited folk performance groups and contemporary pop groups. These distinctions in particular lead to my conceptualization of taiko ensembles as new folk performance.

First, much like their progenitors Osuwa Daiko, Sukeroku Daiko, and Ondekoza, amateur taiko ensembles have a repertoire that is characterized by innovation and emphasizes artistic expression, not inherited custom (where ritual meaning, in many cases, has been lost over time). In this way, these ensembles differ from folk performing arts groups, whose activities are defined by a strong adherence to an inherited repertoire. Furthermore, in contrast to folk performance troupes and classical Japanese music, taiko ensembles display a distinct lack of self-conscious traditionalism. Most young people become involved in these groups as a creative outlet rather than as a means of expressing an attachment to a specific tradition. To my surprise, interviews with taiko players consistently revealed that they saw performance on Japanese taiko to be no more Japanese than performance on Western drums or any other genre of Western music. In fact, for many young Japanese, playing taiko is actually more exotic than playing Western instruments, since Western instruments have much more thoroughly permeated Japanese society than Japanese instruments (Mathews 2000, 37–48). There are individuals in Japan who resist this failure to distinguish Japanese and Western drumming, however, as I discuss in more detail in chapters 5 and 7.

This does not mean that taiko ensembles have no interest in the folk performing arts. Although ensemble taiko groups place near-exclusive emphasis on drums and differ markedly from folk arts in this respect, they nevertheless often adapt folk rhythms and motifs in a manner similar to professional ensembles like Ondekoza and Kodo. While widespread borrowing may seem to threaten the integrity of the folk performing arts, where authentic performance is identified with the residents of a particular locale, it has also led to a market for instruction in these folk rhythms of which local "experts" can take advantage. This is particularly the case when groups that arrange local styles do so successfully, thereby increasing their popularity and market value. In addition, as performance venues for ensemble taiko groups apart from community festivals increase (that is, in locally or nationally sponsored taiko "festivals," contests, or concerts), venues also grow for the original folk performing arts that inspired them. As taiko ensembles adapt folk performances for stage performance, this process of exchange, in a kind of feedback loop, also engenders shifts in the character of local folk performances themselves. Making new taiko ensembles "local" thus sets in motion a cycle of exchange that affects both new ensembles and the regional groups from which they take inspiration.

The experiences of drummers on Hachijō Island and Miyake Island, both located approximately one hundred miles south of Tokyo, illustrate this process at work. In response to increased interest from tourists and audiences on the mainland in the 1970s and 1980s, one of the many versions of *Hachijō daiko*, the two-person improvisational drumming indigenous to the island, became standardized and ultimately transcribed as "Hachijō Daiko." Taken to different parts of Japan, this rhythmic pattern and its characteristic arm movements and mallet twirls have become well known (and widely copied). As the demand for performances grew, groups of young drummers from the island began touring across Japan to perform this "new" standardized form of *Hachijō daiko*. In fact, one member of the amateur group I joined proudly showed me the notated score of "Hachijō Daiko" that he obtained on a short trip to the island. Soon after his visit, he and the other members of the group moved to integrate elements of its rhythms into the group's repertoire. Standardization and notation of *Hachijō daiko* thus facilitated the movement of the rhythmic pattern to areas outside of Hachijō. Of course, the distinctive body movements of the Hachijō drummers did not travel so easily, reserving a place for their authentic performance and direct instruction.

Similarly, *Kamitsuki kiyari daiko*, a kind of taiko performance specific to the Kamitsuki Village of Miyake Island, underwent several changes in response to tourism and the demand for stage performance. Although it is probably best known for providing the inspiration behind Kodo's piece "Miyake," even before the drummers from Kodo encountered it in the early 1980s, performances for tourists visiting the island and at events on the mainland had led to changes to the inherited form. Coordinated arm and leg movements were standardized, and the drum, which had formerly been placed horizontally at shoulder height, was instead placed on a lower platform that raised it only inches from the floor. The new placement not only positioned the drum closer to the level at which it is hit during the annual festival (the drum actually rests on the ground when it is played during the festival) but also allowed the drummers to show off their strength and power better. To overcome the limitations of one repeating phrase, the drummers modified the festival pattern slightly so that they build up to a dramatic climax by gradually accelerating the tempo of the pattern. Ironically, then, the folk performing art Kodo came to learn and adapt for stage performance had by that point already been modified for stage performance.

Third, taiko ensembles commonly integrate motifs and rhythms taken from folk performing arts groups located quite far away (for example, Chichibu *[Chichibu yatai-bayashi]*, Hachijō Island *[Hachijō daiko]*, and Kokura *[Kokura gion daiko]*). As a result, since key elements of new taiko ensembles often do not originate in the locality where they are performed, there is no greater right for longtime residents to have control over them. The disembedding and delocalizing of taiko pieces and motifs, through travel and technology, instead erects a different structure of performance authority that operates between localities rather than within them. To be sure, in some cases certain styles are incorporated in local communities because they are part of greater prefectural identity (as when groups in Saitama Prefecture take up Chichibu's *yatai-bayashi*). In other cases, though, groups maintain informal rights to artistic control over significant distances. These new spatial relations undercut claims to authority by longtime residents of a locality, while making those of nonresidents more salient and persuasive. The rhythmic "roots" of new folk taiko ensembles, in striking contrast to inherited folk performing arts, thus often stretch well beyond local boundaries.

Fourth, while some taiko ensembles have the financial wherewithal to bring instructors from regional areas to teach them directly, taiko ensembles more typically invite current or former members of professional ensemble taiko organizations to teach them. Consequently, professional taiko groups like those reviewed in the last chapter, as well as theatrical groups such as Warabiza, serve as intermediaries in the flow of taiko culture among regions in Japan. Among professional groups, Osuwa Daiko has been most active in providing instruction in its playing technique and repertoire to fledgling taiko groups. It has done so not just to teach a generic approach to taiko performance but, rather, with the intent of teaching its unique Osuwa Daiko style of taiko performance (in other words, it intends to create a hierarchical link between its own lineage and the new branch group). For this reason, the number of groups in Japan that trace their initial instruction and much of their repertoire to Osuwa Daiko reaches well into the hundreds. Kodo also instructed a number of amateur groups in its approach to taiko performance in the years after its formation, but it did not share Osuwa Daiko's interest in cultivating a number of subordinate groups. In fact, in response to the tendency of some taiko ensembles to play only what Kodo taught them, the group no longer teaches its own performance pieces. Instead, it has opted to teach only simple techniques or to offer suggestions, in the manner of a business consultant, to taiko groups in need of inspiration. In contrast to inherited performing arts, therefore, structures of taiko instruction, even by professional groups, do not further claims to performance authority by community elders. Instead, much like the flow of performance patterns and motifs, taiko ensembles that organize to express new kinds of communal affiliation often perform a repertoire that connects (and often subordinates) them to a musical lineage extending beyond the borders of their communities.

Fifth, although these groups are distinct from inherited folk performing arts organizations, methods of transmitting taiko techniques to neophytes typically replicate those found in other folk performing arts. In ensemble taiko groups, instruction is usually limited to oral and visual means; experienced players literally "show" novices how to play. As the example of Ondekoza demonstrated, in some cases this is merely an adaptive mechanism, since most taiko performers do not know how to read music. In other cases, however, the restriction of instruction to oral and visual means turns out to be motivated by a frustration with Western staff notation. This is not for nationalistic reasons, although they may be at work, but derives from the belief that Western notation is incapable of capturing the dependence of taiko performance on tightly choreographed movement and sound.[9]

Sixth, taiko ensembles tend to be much more open than inherited performing arts to participation by a wide range of individuals within localities. Because many of the festivals in which taiko ensembles play are civic and secular, newcomers to a community have as much right to play as natives. In addition, because these secularized festivals lack an association with ideas of female pollution based in Shinto, taiko groups are typically as open to women as they are to men. Women have begun to participate in taiko in quite large numbers. In fact, an annual taiko performance at the National Theater in Tokyo that I attended during my fieldwork in 1999 drew on this popularity and featured amateur and professional taiko groups in which women play central roles. A high level of participation by women in taiko groups, however, does not mean that gender inequality is absent. There remains a strong masculine ethos in contemporary taiko, which affects the range of expression available to women. The gendered dimensions of Japanese taiko, particularly its effects on women, are treated in more detail in chapter 6.

Finally, the number of ensemble taiko groups is increasing, in contrast to the folk performing arts groups from which many take inspiration. In 1950 and again in 1975, the Japanese government passed legislation in an effort to save what remained of inherited folk performing arts in locations where "long traditions" of transmission and performance were jeopardized by rural depopulation. By classifying certain important folk performing arts as "cultural properties," public funds were made available to help preserve and maintain local traditions in danger of extinction (Thompson 2006). In one study of the folk performing arts, Barbara Thornbury credits the efficacy of this legislation when she remarks that "to no small degree, the folk performing arts survive today because they are cultural properties" (1997, 66). Ensemble taiko groups are currently not categorized as examples of traditional folk performance, because their origins lie outside of religious ritual. But their integration into festivals and community life seems to justify their consideration as elements of a *new* kind of folk culture, one that expresses the cosmopolitanism of the contemporary more than the sentimentality of "vanishing" tradition (Ivy 1995).[10] In fact, the Festival Law, passed in 1992 to promote domestic tourism, encourages the promotion of local festivals and "regional traditional performing arts" *(chiiki dentō geinō)*, a category that includes both "traditional performing arts" *(dentōteki na geinō)*—that is, folk traditions established before World War II—and "regional traditions . . . transmitted as part of regional-communal life," for which date of origin is not important (Thornbury 1997, 68). This law, therefore, clears the way for more extensive state support of new forms of local culture exemplified by contemporary taiko ensembles.

In sum, taiko groups, while using drums derived from parish-level religious ritual and folk entertainments typically closed to outside participation, have been a response to the call and felt need for new, more open, geographically broader, largely secular, but still distinctly vernacular community festivity. In this sense, reports of the death of communality and festivity in the ethnographic literature on Japan have been exaggerated. Instead, what has in fact occurred is the very reemergence of communality and festivity, sustained in part by the stimulus of a government program. The widespread creation of festivals has provided support for taiko ensembles, which in turn have been embraced enthusiastically by large segments of the population. This has led to the development of a new folk culture, one characterized by innovation, a broad range of popular participation, robust cultural exchange among regions, and claims to authority over performance that stretch beyond the local.

PART TWO

Discourses of Contemporary Taiko

(Dis)Locating Drumming

TAIKO TRAINING, EMBODIMENT,
AND THE AESTHETICS OF RACE AND PLACE

> See, look at them clapping their hands, gazing up at the sky, smiling and singing. Now look at us doing *kyōgen,* our shoulders rigid and our legs tucked underneath us in *seiza* [formal sitting position]; our hands clenched, resting on our laps; our eyes fixed on the earth beneath us; our voices low and guttural. We drive our words into the dirt; we don't lift our hands up and smile at heaven. Your god is in the sky, right? Our spirits are in the ground, you see. That's cultural difference ... that's cultural difference.
>
> INSTRUCTOR, *Kodo Apprentice Program,*
> *contrasting two groups of apprentices*

ON SEPTEMBER 27, 1945, the Japanese emperor Hirohito and the American general Douglas MacArthur posed for a picture before meeting for the first time to discuss the American occupation of Japan. The photograph, which was splashed on the front page of newspapers throughout Japan the following day, has since achieved fame as a representation of the political relationship between the two countries following the defeat of Japan. General MacArthur, who appears relaxed, resting his hands on hips that rise to the height of his former enemy's chest, towers over the diminutive Hirohito, who is dressed formally and stands rigidly beside the new commander, as if at attention. For Japanese readers, the meaning of the photograph was clear enough: "In contrast to the tall general full of pride, the figure of the emperor's worn-out body wrapped in morning dress was nothing but the evidence of defeat" (Ide Magoroku, quoted in Igarashi 2000, 33). Japan had been conquered by an enemy not only materially richer and militarily stronger but also taller, more physically imposing, and more powerful. For many Japanese, the prolonged postwar military and economic dependence of Japan on the United States was first understood in starkly racial terms.

Here my intention is not to recall the racial contours of World War II or to trace the development of postwar Japan-U.S. relations. Instead, I reference the encounter between Hirohito and MacArthur to frame more broadly the importance of the Japanese body in discursive constructions of national and regional distinctiveness among Japanese taiko drummers. As I observed and participated in the instruction of taiko technique in a number of sites across Japan, I was repeatedly struck by the attention paid to refining the presentation of movement in a performance that one might expect to focus on the sound of drums. Whether it was the exaggerated gestures of Osuwa Daiko, the acrobatics of Sukeroku Daiko, or the controlled ferocity of Ondekoza and Kodo, visual presentation of drumming bodies was as much a part of taiko performance as the rhythms these bodies produced. In a sense, this should not have been surprising; all ritual drumming in Japan either accompanies dance or features choreographed physical movement. For both newer and older forms, movement and sound are inseparable.[1] Distinctions of style between Oedo Sukeroku Taiko and Sukeroku Daiko, for example, depend solely on the way drummers hit their drums.

The concern with tightly choreographed movement is also central to the way taiko is invested with meaning as a distinctly Japanese activity. In the discourse of taiko pedagogy, the size and shape of the stereotypically Japanese body is considered to be not only ideally suited to the performance of taiko but also the very foundation of performance aesthetics.[2] Rather than being the source of a perceived sense of "inferiority," as the emblematic comparison between MacArthur and Hirohito suggests, the Japanese body is imagined as the wellspring of Japanese taiko. But, it turns out, not all bodies are alike. This articulation of Japanese bodies with Japanese culture in effect constructs yet another hierarchy by which bodies are differentiated. Taiko drummers insist that "authentic" performance of local styles depends not just on one's "race" but also on one's "roots"—an association from birth with the locality in which the performance style originated, not merely mechanics or techniques. Locals embody and express this connection to place in a way that is impossible for nonlocals to replicate. Just as a racially non-Japanese person will never be able to play Japanese taiko as naturally as a Japanese person, a nonnative will never be able to replicate local drumming techniques as well as a native. In both cases, authentic performance is expressed by and through bodies associated racially and culturally with particular places.[3] The following account of learning taiko in Tokyo helps illustrate how these processes play out in practice.

BLISTERS, BODIES, AND PLACE:
LEARNING TAIKO IN TOKYO

In the initial stages of my fieldwork among taiko groups in Tokyo, I measured progress by the presence of blisters on my hands. In the first few weeks, blisters served as tangible markers of the advancement of my field study. Later on, I discovered that their placement also indicated the degree to which I had acquired proper playing technique. At first, blisters emerged at the base of my forefinger and the crook of my thumb. Teachers and fellow students quickly recognized this as evidence of flawed playing technique. In the Sukeroku style of drumming that is popular in Tokyo, drummers who play medium-size taiko drums use thick drum "mallets," measuring 1 to 2 inches in diameter. These mallets are much bigger than the drumsticks used in orchestral or jazz percussion.[4] My blisters indicated that I had been applying techniques borrowed from my prior experience as an orchestral and jazz drummer, where the drumstick is held between thumb and forefinger and snapped with the wrist and fingers to maximize speed and accuracy. The size of the mallet reflects the amount of force needed to compress the thick head of the drum and produce the proper sound. In an inversion of my understanding of drumming up to that point, my teachers stressed that I grasp the mallet at the bottom of my hand between my palm and little finger, as if it were a club. Speed and dexterity mattered little; what mattered was volume and power. If I struck the drum using the correct technique, they told me, blisters would develop at the base of my little finger. Incredulous, I asked them to show me their hands, and, indeed, there at the base of their smallest finger were calluses (not blisters, since they had developed their hands past this point). An entry from my field notes some months later cites jubilation at finding a small red spot at the base of my right pinkie.

As trivial as they may seem, these blisters and calluses encoded in microcosm cultural conceptions that extended beyond mere differences in playing technique. The difference between upper and lower—a fulcrum at the top of the hand versus a fulcrum at the bottom of the hand—replicated distinctions implicit in informants' descriptions of aesthetically appropriate taiko technique and the relationship of bodies to culture. Blisters at the top of the hand indicated overuse of fingers and hands—essentially wasted effort, since using the top of the hand vibrated only the top of the drum, muffling subtleties and creating an indistinct sound. Producing a good sound meant driving the compression through to the bottom of the drum by using the bottom of the hand. But using hands, arms, and shoulders only—the "top" of the body—failed to generate enough power. Building momentum in the hands, arms, and shoulders meant twisting the hips and torso for power. And, ultimately, power in the hips and torso depended on strong legs and feet—the "bottom" of the body. In this conception, power generation begins in the feet, firmly planted on the ground, moves up through the legs and torso, rushes through the arms and hands, and surges through the drum stroke to penetrate into a drum angled down toward the ground.

Proper form and proper movement, then, were of critical importance. The wall of floor-to-ceiling mirrors, found in every practice room I observed, symbolized this emphasis on bodily form. During practice, we were advised to surveil our bodies to make sure that we were maintaining proper posture, keeping our hips low, and summoning the strength of our legs to put power into our stroke. After learning how to strike the drum, we immediately moved into learning how to play the five basic pieces that constituted the repertoire for the group. There were no basic exercises, no series of steps through which one proceeded in a rationalized manner before attempting an entire piece. Each piece required different playing positions, different movements, and different rhythmic patterns. They were studied in isolation and combined during practice only sequentially, in the order in which they were played during stage performance. No general philosophy of performance applied to these pieces; deviations from the appropriate form were corrected in a diffuse, hands-on manner ("more like this," "less like that," and so forth) and the ideal form was never articulated, only demonstrated. It was left to us, the students, to discern what merited correction and emulation, with the fear that we might be the subject of our teacher's extended (and often heated) admonition as incentive. The process of learning to play taiko at Sukeroku Daiko, therefore, was essentially the process of learning to play a particular kind of taiko in a particular place. Experimentation was openly discouraged. "Basics" did not exist. "Getting it right" meant embodying the inherited form.

Observation of more advanced players at the school confirmed that the pattern of strict observation continued even after mastery of elementary playing technique. When practicing alone or with others, advanced players constantly monitored their own movements. What's more, since drumming patterns were predetermined, players did not look to expand their technical competence but continually strove to refine their form and movements to greater levels of aesthetic presentation. This is not to say that maintaining rhythm was unimportant. Rather, performers tended to assume that one could stay on beat as long as one's form was correct.

This concern with the movement of the body in performance also related to a particularly local aesthetic distinction. The Sukeroku Daiko Hozonkai in which I studied was a "preservation society" devoted to the maintenance of the repertoire of the group of the same name, which was established thirty years earlier in the *shitamachi* area of "downtown" Tokyo. Informants told me that the distinctive aesthetic of this group is expressed by the term *iki,* which describes a particular way of moving with flash and flair that evokes the sophistication of "old Edo" (old Tokyo). In this sense, the drumming choreography of Sukeroku Daiko expresses a distinctly local aesthetic.[5] Movement not only contributes to artistry but also demonstrates one's rootedness in place. Working through the feet and body, these "roots" not only give power to performance but ground one's identity as well.

For me, a person who lacked any ready endowment of *iki,* moving the body in the prescribed manner proved difficult. While my previous experience with drumming enabled me to pick up rhythmic patterns faster than most beginners, it was of little use in learning to maintain proper form when playing. I was criticized to the point of exasperation for not putting enough power into my strokes—for using too much upper-body "top" and too little lower-body "bottom." Yet the substance of these criticisms commonly fed into another distinction between "top" and "bottom," one that reflected a racialized discourse about the intimate relationship between specific types of bodies and the specific kinds of culture they produce over time.

Two examples from my fieldwork will help make this discourse clear. The first concerns the particularities of my own body and that of another white American man, Richard, who attended practices with me. Richard and I had been taking lessons together for several weeks at the Sukeroku Daiko Preservation Society. On a day when Richard had not come to class, my teacher commented that both Richard and I had a tendency to strike the drum too much with our upper bodies at the expense of using our lower bodies. Part of this, he said, was due to the fact that we were approaching the drum as "foreigners" *(gaijin)* would.[6] In this regard, Richard was more typical than I. We were both pale in complexion, but he was tall (about six feet) with long legs and lean musculature, whereas I am of a shorter and stouter physique. The teacher compared our difficulty in playing the drum to the way in which foreigners wear their Japanese summer kimonos during the July through August Bon festivals. He explained: "It's obvious that they are trying to blend in, but they wear their *obi* [belts] too high up on their torso, around their waist, instead of lower down around the hips where we Japanese wear them. This probably feels better, because it's where one would wear a leather belt, but it just looks funny." The implication, especially for Richard, was that our foreignness led us to approach the drum from the same "high" position.

Across town at the Nihon Taiko Dōjō, a taiko group founded by a former member of the original Sukeroku Daiko, my difference was handled in much the same way. After I had finally become able to hit the drum with some skill and power, my teacher admonished me for overusing my upper body in striking the drum and advised that I use my whole body instead. Without missing a beat, he then added that my relative upper-body strength differentiated me from Japanese students in the class and came from "eating meat." In this way, I was like other "meat-eating animals" *(nikushoku dōbutsu)* he had observed in America, who had similarly strong (upper) bodies but who overused them without realizing that "real" power comes from the legs and torso. Later, when it came time for me to return to the United States, he exhorted me to take what skills I had learned back with me to teach Americans how to play taiko better, meaning with their entire bodies. Of additional concern, he stressed, were those risqué female players in the United States who shake their rear ends too provocatively when playing the large *ōdaiko* drum, a problem compounded by their longer legs and fuller figures.

I do not know how seriously my teachers took the comments they made to me. Probably out of deference, Japanese students in these classes never spoke out against these cultural-racial comparisons, which were often made with a smile to soften their effect. Some students, though, asked me later in private whether I had taken offense, which indicated to me that even to native speakers the comments were not entirely innocuous. The comments also seemed to draw from a broader cultural discourse in Japan called *nihonjinron* (discourses of Japaneseness), in which intellectuals and pseudo-intellectuals commonly attribute cultural differences between Japanese and non-Japanese to differences in race and biology (Befu 2001; Dale 1986; Yoshino 1992, 1998).

Indeed, this tendency to interpret difference in performance capacity between Japanese and non-Japanese on the basis of anatomical distinctions is not limited to taiko. A similar comparison of foreign with Japanese appears within discussions of modern Japanese theater. In a translated collection of influential essays (Suzuki 1996), the distinguished Japanese theater director Suzuki Tadashi responds to a colleague's suggestion that Japanese actors should perform only in plays written by Japanese playwrights. Attempting to replicate foreign theater in translation, the colleague argues, is futile because Japanese people are physiologically limited: "Our appearance is wrong; our arms and legs are too short" (quoted in Suzuki 1996, 3). Suzuki agrees, but only to a degree. Attempts at imitation are ultimately pointless, since movement is related to gesture, which for him is merely another form of language: "However long our arms and legs may grow, however our physical appearance may improve, no Japanese actor can imitate the Chekhovian manner as well as his Russian counterpart—as long as he is speaking in Japanese" (5). Linguistic handicaps aside, in Suzuki's view the goal of true performance is not successful *imitation,* even performance in a foreign tongue, but *transcendence* of one's nationality and physical limitations.

Just as he differs from his Japanese colleague, Suzuki does not countenance the exasperation of American actors who complain that their inability to perform the series of theatrical exercises he designed stems from the physical "handicap" of having legs that are generally longer than those of Japanese actors (Suzuki 1996, 13). Even though some members of Suzuki's organization agree with this interpretation, Suzuki remains unconvinced. The exercises are directed toward "discover[ing] a self-consciousness of the interior of the body" (12). An actor's success at performing these exercises relates directly to the actor's ability to make this discovery: "A Japanese actor has no special claim to success, or to developing those skills in his own body, any more than anyone else" (12).

Suzuki's sentiment is a nice one, a democratic and inclusive one, which resonates well with the contemporary neoliberal zeitgeist because it suggests that through individual effort one can overcome personal obstacles; the body is an empty container and hard work is all that is needed to fill it up. Yet in this apparent universal humanism, Suzuki differs dramatically from the taiko drummers I encountered in my research. Setting aside questions of whether taiko drumming is best conceived as a type of music, a type of dance, or some other hybrid, proper physical movement and the expression of vigorous spirit through these movements are the purpose of performance, not a means of self-discovery. What's more, bodies and movement are meant to locate one firmly within the boundaries of a national-cultural site, not to transcend it. Among taiko players, a native-foreigner dichotomy replaces the promise that difference can be overcome through universal humanism with a locative counterdiscourse founded upon not relativism but radical alterity and race.

When confronted with physical differences among the Japanese people themselves, though, this racialist logic encounters problems. In his book of essays, the taiko soloist Hayashi Eitetsu remarks on his difficulties teaching both foreigners and young Japanese how to play "Ōdaiko," a piece based around a solo performance on the large *ōdaiko* drum.

> I've had the opportunity to teach my "Ōdaiko" to tall white guys. They can move their arms pretty well, but their knees are weak. They start to shake, and their stance falls apart. *The same is true for tall Japanese people.* They either have to spread their legs out really wide or put the drum up really high to make it at least not look painful. I once taught the members of a popular "boy band" how to play "Ōdaiko." Their [tall] foreigner-like bodies made it hard to teach them the piece, and it took a long time to make them look presentable. . . . In my view, my "Ōdaiko" playing style fits best the "old-model" Japanese person, with short legs and a long torso. (1992, 55, emphasis added)

Hayashi's anecdote encapsulates well the thrust of the preceding discussion. "Ōdaiko," although a product of the new performing art of ensemble taiko, is performed best by a player with a specific type of racialized body—namely, that of an "old-model Japanese," like the now middle-aged Hayashi.

As if in a series of concentric circles spiraling out from the hands and enveloping more and more of the body, the binary oppositions between "top" and "bottom" found in the discourse of taiko pedagogy first map a set of aesthetic, racial, and spatial distinctions and, second, apply a similar logic of inversion in each case. Hitting the top of the drum quickly with the top of the hands (fingers) and the top of the body (arms and shoulders) is emblematic of *pākasshon* (percussion), a term used generically to refer to Western-style drumming. The "foreign" bodies of those who play percussion, with their long legs and big upper bodies, are further emblematic of the universalistic aesthetic of "percussion," one that stretches away from the ground to lift up, to transcend. In contrast, hitting through to the bottom of the drum with the bottom of the hands (wrist) and the bottom of the body (legs and torso) reflects the particularistic aesthetic of Japanese taiko and the goal of its performance. The bodies of those who play taiko, with their short legs and long waists, sink close to the ground in a performance that aims to ground performer and listener in space. Short legs, long waist, and small body size, therefore, become the quintessential foundation for aesthetically rich taiko performance, while the often-envied long legs of "foreigners" and younger, "new-style" Japanese are understood as obstacles to overcome.[7]

As Hayashi's anecdote demonstrates, the same forces of modernization and westernization that gave birth to taiko ensembles have also given birth to generations of Japanese youth whose bodies do not "fit" well with them. Perhaps more important, their adaptation to westernized Japan has dislocated them from the local folkways within which both new and old forms of taiko were originally forged. For these young Japanese who are, from this perspective, "other" to themselves *as* Japanese, renewed acquaintance with the rural culture of Japan, where "tradition" purportedly still survives, presents a means through which this "lack" can be recovered.[8]

Within the genre of ensemble taiko, the Kodo Apprentice Program is the location where an attempt to overcome the deficiencies of "new-style" Japanese is given the most sustained attention. As described earlier, since Kodo's establishment on Sado Island in the late 1960s, one of its primary goals has been to express the energy of Japan's locally based folk performing arts through creative stage performance. Yet, the modification of folk arts for presentation on stage by individuals who lack the "roots" of traditional inheritors presents both opportunities and obstacles. Japanese individuals can work to overcome their physical and cultural limitations. The embodied detritus of modern Japan can be replaced with the "new" self of a Kodo performer, one that evokes older, now "vanishing" (Ivy 1995) ways of the past. At the same time, the process of developing this new self alienates participants from this older folk culture as much as it gives them a new one. A professed belief in the connection between local roots and authentic performance discursively renders Kodo members forever inferior to the inheritors of the traditions they cleverly rearrange. In this sense, Kodo members are paradigmatic of "new-style" Japanese who attempt to overcome their physical limitations and lack of roots by taking up ensemble taiko. While the ensuing discussion focuses on the particular context of the Kodo Apprentice Program, it is therefore meant to extend more broadly to the ranks of amateur and professional groups in Japan that model themselves after Kodo.

MIMESIS AND AUTHENTICITY:
TRAINING KODO PERFORMERS

The Kodo Apprentice Program is a two-year training program for individuals who wish to become performing or nonperforming members of Kodo. Roughly twelve apprentices enter the program annually, each paying fifty thousand yen (approximately five hundred dollars) per month for the opportunity to participate.[9] The apprentices live in the Apprentice Centre, a renovated junior high school. Kodo sectioned off former classrooms to create bedrooms for the apprentices and added bath and laundry facilities. However, the group does not own the complex; at the time of my study, it rented it from the municipality of Ryōtsu, which had jurisdiction over the hamlet of Kaki-no-ura in which the Apprentice Centre is located. Accordingly, there is always the possibility that Kodo may have to return it to the city. This fact is stressed on the day that the program begins and compels the apprentices to take even greater care of the place.

Symbolically, the Apprentice Centre is more than just a building; it is a structural metaphor of the very purpose of the Kodo organization. Initially abandoned as a result of the depletion of young people from the area, the building is now filled with idealistic young people interested in recapturing the energy of Sado's disappearing folk culture. Walking around the Apprentice Centre, one sees traces of the building's former life: classroom and office signboards, posters exhorting students to pay attention and study hard, and plaques charting institutional chronology. All are tangible reminders that the presence of the current occupants may be equally transitory.[10] The building as an old-yet-new space and the interior as an assemblage of apprentices from "northernmost Hokkaido to southernmost Okinawa" materially signify the apprentices' task: to embody Kodo's repertoire of pieces, many of which borrow motifs from regional traditions, while working to overcome the encumbrance of their own individual pasts.

The task of self-transformation begins in early April, when the apprentice program commences. On Sado, farmers begin to rework their fields for rice planting in April, and villages hold Shinto festivals celebrating the start of the planting season. The festivals feature dynamic performances of the folk performing art *ondeko* ("demon drumming"), from which Kodo's antecedent group Ondekoza took its name. The significance of this confluence of planting and festival performance is not lost upon the organizers of the apprentice program, nor is the manner in which the self-sufficiency of local farmers is premised on the skillful manipulation of the natural world.

As prospective members of Kodo, first-year apprentices learn how to make items necessary for their livelihood and future performances. On the first day of the program, first- and second-years proceed to a workroom to begin a basic class on woodworking, an activity that has both practical and symbolic value. Their task is to whittle a section of bamboo into the one pair of chopsticks that they will use for the rest of the year. (Second-years have the chance to correct the mistakes of the previous year.) Those who are not used to working with bamboo have to learn quickly, a process complicated by the fact that there is very little in the way of detailed instruction. After a few perfunctory remarks about how to avoid cutting oneself when whittling, the apprentices—even those without any experience using hand tools—are left to figure things out on their own. Of course, chopsticks are available for purchase all over the island. But the symbolic value of the activity is found in the stress on providing for oneself by embodying the mechanical skills one needs. The emphasis is on learning by doing, watching closely, and "stealing" what one needs to complete the task.[11] Later in the week, apprentices return to the workroom to fashion their own drum mallets out of small blocks of wood using only a hand lathe and sandpaper. Like chopstick making, the activity stresses self-sufficiency, working with one's hands, and the conversion through manual labor of natural materials into tools for human use. The value of "making things by hand" is encoded in activities throughout the program and reflects the legacy of the "artisanal ethic" that developed in Ondekoza, as well as respect for the agricultural patterns of regional Japan.

In the days after they arrive, the apprentices engage in two activities that seem unrelated but are in fact closely connected in the logic of the program. In the daytime, the apprentices begin preparing a small rice field and two vegetable gardens for planting. Second-year apprentices pass on their knowledge of farming techniques to first-year neophytes, mimicking the process of transmitting rural culture among their neighboring villagers. In the evenings, the apprentices visit a small Shinto shrine in Kaki-no-ura where (male) locals practice *ondeko* for the upcoming festival. The first-years watch as the second-years, who have practiced the movements and simple drum patterns of *ondeko* over the past year, join in.

Participation in farming and dancing reflects these beliefs in the intimate connection between practical labor and folk culture. The movements of "demon drumming" and other folk performing arts are believed to both mime the movements of agricultural activity and rely heavily upon the lower-body strength developed in them. The belief in this connection underlies much of the apprentice program and supplies the logic for integrating agriculture into a program ostensibly meant to train stage performers. Importantly, though, it is rarely articulated. Instead, a connection between these two different activities—daily labor and festival performance—is wrought through rigorous physical training.[12] Through participation in these activities, apprentices come to *feel* the linkage between the two in an intuitive way. Farming and *ondeko* practice are thus two important means by which the program disciplines apprentices and inscribes in them an (unconsciously) embodied attachment to Sado Island.

The preparation of food further reinforces this process. Apprentices are taught not only how to cook, but how to cook *well*. The task comes with considerable pressure, since cooking duties are rotated and one usually prepares dishes for fifteen to twenty other people. (The same holds true at Kodo Village.) It also has considerable meaning: communal preparation of food coupled with the communal growing of food not only affirms the ties of apprentices with each other (and, at Kodo Village, of the members with each other), it also emphasizes the value of physical labor, of using one's body to grow food for oneself and then using one's hands, and embodied "knack," to prepare it with flair.

Apprentices learn cooking, much like they do woodworking and farming, mostly "by feel," since directions regarding proportions of water, sake, salt, and other ingredients come primarily in the form of vague "a little," "some," "a lot" kinds of commands. The man in charge of instructing the apprentices in farming, woodworking, and cooking, himself quite a gourmet, often admonishes apprentices for their collectively low level of cooking acumen. They had, he pointed out, become too reliant on eating out and quick-and-easy instant foods before coming to the program. To rectify this, the apprentice program (and Kodo more broadly) prohibits the use of packaged foods, stocks, sauces, and chemical additives, stressing the use of naturally grown ingredients and the value of spending labor on cooking rather than saving it.

Foodstuffs at Kodo are always fresh and in season, reflecting the changes in the growing season and sensitizing the bodies of apprentices to the rhythms of their local environs. Vegetables are bought whole and chopped with knives (not by a food processor); fish are bought whole and filleted by hand; rice is bought unrefined from local vendors, run through a machine to remove the husks, rinsed repeatedly by hand in water, and then cooked fresh for each meal. In making the miso soup that furnishes the basis of each meal, apprentices begin not with the concentrated soup stock Japanese households use as a time-saver, but with the constituent ingredients of dried kelp and dried bonito flakes. Food is usually simmered and sometimes fried, the former not only allowing for the most flexibility in terms of quantity and preparation but also drawing on the wonderful-tasting water of Sado. Later in the year, apprentices proudly announce dishes made from vegetables grown in their own fields.[13]

The value placed on building bodies from local food and local knowledge was made readily apparent to me a couple of weeks after the apprentices arrived at the Apprentice Centre. By this time, the chill of the long cold winter had yielded to the gentle warmth of springtime. On the hills and shallow marshes surrounding the Apprentice Centre, wild vegetables *(sansai)* sprouted up ripe for the picking. I accompanied the apprentices one day as one of their instructors led us on a journey to pick these vegetables, a task more difficult than it may seem. The vegetables are usually found in soggy, hard-to-reach locations and it is difficult to get at them. On a personal level, it was also hard for me to remember the names of all the obscure vegetables that our instructor told us to pick. "That's okay, Shawn," several apprentices told me, "Japanese people don't even know these words." Indeed, it was true that the apprentices, most of whom had grown up in urban areas, had never heard of or tasted these vegetables either. After we finished picking the vegetables, we brought them back to the Apprentice Centre, cleaned them, dipped them in batter, and had a feast of *sansai tempura.*

Later in the week, a similar event took place at Kodo Village for Kodo staff and players. "Enjoying Sansai" was led by a resident expert on wild vegetables in the area and emphasized the same connection to the local landscape as the informal one at the Apprentice Centre. As I watched staff members and players quiz each other on the names of different vegetables, comparing the subtleties and sharp contrasts in taste among them, it became clear that the enjoyment of a tie to their local surroundings resonated even with older members of Kodo who had lived on Sado longer. In fact, longer residence meant even greater familiarity with the local environment and a more finely cultivated ability to discern the peculiarities within it. The "Enjoying Sansai" events emphasized the connection between local "nature" and local "culture," between the bounty of the forest and the transformation through human labor of these materials into food—food that constituted the bodies of not only Kodo apprentices but Kodo members as well. Bodies joined with place once again.

At the Apprentice Centre, the process of food consumption has an additional purpose beyond mere sustenance: training apprentices in proper sitting technique. During meals, apprentices assume a formal sitting position called *seiza,* which literally means "the correct way to sit." To sit in *seiza,* one sits on one's heels, back straight with hands resting lightly on one's lap. It is an uncomfortable position. Blood slowly recedes from the lower extremities until toes and feet are completely numb. (This anthropologist has about a fifteen-minute limit.) Nevertheless, *seiza* is recognized as the proper way to sit on formal social occasions in Japan and in classical Japanese performance. At the Apprentice Centre, it is rumored that one can become "better at *seiza*," and observation seemed to confirm that this was, in fact, the case. At first, new apprentices routinely switched from *seiza* to a more relaxed sitting position after about twenty minutes. Nevertheless, second-year apprentices exhorted first-years to continue doing *seiza* despite the intense pain with promises that they would eventually "get used to it." However, even second-years had trouble enduring *seiza* for the several hours that *kyōgen* (classical comic theater) practice required. While sitting in *seiza* during meals, right-handed apprentices also disciplined their hands by holding their chopsticks in their left hand, a practice that is atypical in Japan.[14]

Much like their level of cooking skill, the inability of incoming apprentices to sit in *seiza* for extended periods concerned some in the organization, since it indicated how far Japanese society had detached itself from its "roots." According to this view, with the introduction and eventual predominance of Western styles of interior design, more and more Japanese had become accustomed to sitting on chairs and eating at high tables. In the process, they had lost the ability to sit in *seiza*—a distinctly Japanese way of sitting—for prolonged periods.[15] The insistence that apprentices sit in *seiza,* therefore, was integral in helping them replace the modern "habits" *(kuse)* they had incorporated before entering the program with new ones. (The case of sitting accords quite well with the aforementioned binaries of low/high, bottom/top, and Japanese/Western.) While ultimately it intends to prepare apprentices for stage performance, the Kodo apprentice system extends bodily discipline in a totalizing manner to activities such as sitting, eating, cooking, and farming that relate only tangentially to performance. Tangential as they seem, these activities work by accretion to cultivate an attachment to Sado and shape the kinds of bodies suitable for Kodo's stage performance.

Training in the classical Japanese arts—tea ceremony *(sadō),* theater (Noh), and comic theater *(kyōgen)*—functions similarly to discipline apprentices' bodies for performance but bears a more direct relationship to actual stage performance than tool making, farming, or cooking. Although professional practitioners of the classical arts routinely train for ten or more years, Kodo believes that apprentices benefit from practicing these venerable activities even for a short time. The apprentices hope that some measure of these traditions might "stick to their bodies" and be expressed during stage performance. What's more, training in the classical arts recapitulates the emphasis on cultivating a distinctly Japanese sensibility in two important ways. First, these activities stress "economy of movement." In tea ceremony, for example, apprentices pay close attention to the proper way of sitting (in *seiza,* of course), opening doors, moving across a room, serving and drinking a cup of tea, and so on, all while moving in a smooth, prescribed manner. Every action is stylized and formalized, with all but essential movement eliminated. *Kyōgen* practice applies a similar principle to entering, exiting, and moving around the stage.

Second, all of these activities emphasize mastery of a specific set of movements, not a generic set of skills applicable to any kind of tea ceremony, Noh, or *kyōgen.* Each teacher (they were all from outside Kodo) hails from a particular artistic "school" and teaches apprentices only the techniques of this school. Practice, therefore, consists of repetition and perfection of movements specific to the school. Much like training in Sukeroku-style taiko in Tokyo, training in the classical performing arts contributes to a localization of performance. The techniques apprentices learn are tied to specific schools of performance, just as the performance pieces they will soon master are associated with a particular group (Kodo) that is rooted in a particular place (Sado Island). Like their training as amateur woodworkers, farmers, and cooks, training in the classical performing arts eliminates vestiges of nonlocal habits and replaces them with a new set of embodied dispositions, which are both created by and expressive of a distinctly local culture.

HIERARCHIES OF PERFORMANCE: KODO AND ITS "FOLK"

Although apprentices spent a great deal of time in the aforementioned activities, the bulk of program time is understandably reserved for training in Kodo's performance repertoire. That said, apprentices do not practice the complete repertoire—only a subset of older pieces derived from the folk performing arts.[16] This is not because these pieces are easier than newer ones. Rather, by practicing pieces derived from the folk performing arts, apprentices affirm the logic of localization upon which the apprentice program functions: the movements of farming and rural labor find expression in the folk performing arts; the folk performing arts provide an artistic foundation for much of Kodo's repertoire. At the same time, the nature of these pieces as essentially part folk–part Kodo creates an opposition between Kodo's cosmopolitanism and the parochialism of folk performance. Kodo's desire to venerate the folk arts as authentic expressions of local culture implies that modifications of folk performances must necessarily remain inferior to the original. In contrast to the racial distinction outlined earlier between Japanese and foreigners, where the stereotypical Japanese body is believed to be the foundation of taiko performance, this discourse of localism distinguishes between local and nonlocal Japanese bodies based on the belief that authentic performance accrues from birth in a particular place.

Kodo strives to remain engaged with inheritors of the folk performing arts that originally provided artistic inspiration for many of its pieces. Apprentices and other members of the group often travel to the local areas where selected varieties of folk drumming are maintained by preservation societies and performed in festivals. During my time with Kodo, members of the group visited two locations, Miyake Island and Chichibu City, to observe performances of folk drumming. While contact with local folk performers proves edifying for most members, these interactions also seem to confirm the pervasiveness of a belief in the connection between local bodies and local places, a belief that ultimately alienates Kodo members from folk performance even as it attempts to bring them closer to it.

After Kodo members returned from observing festival drumming on Miyake Island, for example, Kodo held a meeting where returning members demonstrated differences in technique between Kodo's version of this drumming (in a piece called "Miyake") and the "original" version performed on the island.[17] The presenters also played a video of local people performing the rhythmic pattern during the festival. As the group watched their original teacher, Mr. Kimura, on screen, a young presenter remarked in awe at how powerfully and smoothly he hit the drum and commented, to the general agreement of those watching, on how robust he looked for a middle-aged man. Mr. Kimura's seemingly effortless display of drumming prowess not only affirmed a belief in the vigor of rural individuals but also illustrated how local people embody folk performance to a degree that Kodo can approximate but never quite equal. What's more, the enthusiasm of other individuals featured in the video affirmed the challenge of communicating the energy of Japanese festivity in a stage performance divorced from a festival context. Whereas locals can put energy pent up over a year (or even longer in the case of Miyake Island) into a festival, Kodo has to muster this level of energy on consecutive nights of stage performance, a task many players believed to be near impossible.

Similar sentiments regarding the difficulty of matching the ability of native performers were expressed several months later when a group of probationary members and apprentices returned from a trip to Chichibu City to observe the city's annual night festival. The drumming pattern of this festival procession provides the rhythmic foundation for one of Kodo's featured pieces, "Yatai-bayashi," and the returnees told me how thrilling it was to hear Chichibu drumming in its original festival context. The drumming at the festival had a unique "spirit," they told me, which they believed was nearly impossible to express fully on stage, but which they hoped to re-create nonetheless. The visit also marked the first time that many of these individuals had heard the difference between the original Chichibu festival rhythm and the one arranged for performance by Kodo, which substitutes a steady underlying drum pattern for a slightly unsteady original. In creating their version, Kodo's arrangers believed that they would never truly be able to capture the distinctly local nuance of the Chichibu original and changed it to suit their own limitations and artistic preferences.

A similar concern with local "feel" became apparent later in my fieldwork when a group of dancers from northern Japan came to instruct apprentices in the techniques of their native *Kurokawa sansa odori* dance. Just as Kodo members take trips to observe folk performances, these performers occasionally visit the Apprentice Centre to conduct short workshops. On this occasion, apprentices had been learning the dance since the start of their program, and the practice session focused on acquiring a "feel" for the dance that better approximated the original. Although the Kurokawa dancers modeled movements that apprentices then tried to replicate, the whole exercise appeared to be predicated on the assumption that apprentices would never really be able to master the dance. This was not because the apprentices were poor dancers or students, however. From the start of their nearly twenty-year relationship with Kodo, the Kurokawa dancers have instructed Kodo performers and apprentices on the condition that the group not perform the dance on stage until given permission. It is unclear how long this will take, but it is expected to be at least several more years. Only after this amount of time will the level of "naturalness" that the local dancers consider necessary to distinguish real performance from mere imitation reach a level that satisfies both parties.

This agreement, of course, has no legal force. But if Kodo were to violate it, the group would not only lose the opportunity to continue nurturing their relationship with the Kurokawa dancers but also sacrifice the moral sanction at the heart of their activities—that is, the acknowledgment that they borrow from local areas with longer ties to the performing traditions that they happily rearrange.[18] In addition to this moral sanction, the group recognizes that local people retain a proprietary claim to those pieces in Kodo's repertoire that derive from the local performing arts no matter how well Kodo performs them.[19] As one probationary member commented to me about the Kurokawa dancers: "It's so beautiful to watch [the local people] dance. It's such a part of them. The way they move—it's so natural." The reason for this, he and other Kodo members repeatedly told me, is that local people like Mr. Kimura of Miyake Island, the Chichibu drummers, and the Kurokawa dancers are believed to be quite literally "grounded" in their performances. By virtue of being born and raised in a particular place, locals have embodied to an almost mythical extent their native folk arts. This makes them able to perform this local performing art better than any newcomer or imitator, no matter how long his or her engagement.

Like the discourse of race and taiko discussed earlier, the discourse of localism at the Apprentice Centre dissolves performance culture into physical nature. This is not a nature that is reducible to biology alone, however, but rather one that is embodied organically over time by accident of birth. In the same way that drumming bodies articulate racial distinctions between Japanese and non-Japanese in the context of taiko practice in Tokyo, the Kodo Apprentice Program thus discursively constructs an unbridgeable gap between local inheritors and nonlocal borrowers.

SOUNDING LOCAL: LEARNING TAIKO AT KODO

Of all the forms of training discussed so far, this gap is manifest perhaps most clearly when apprentices learn Kodo's repertoire of drum pieces. At first, the practice of drumming in the apprentice program proceeds in a manner very similar to the practice of drumming in Sukeroku Daiko and Nihon Taiko Dōjō. Apprentices start on small *shime-daiko* drums. They learn the proper playing position—legs akimbo, back straight, chest out, arms in—and the proper drum stroke, with the latter being the hardest to master. Apprentices are critiqued at every step to ensure that the motion of their arm is consistent throughout the arc of the stroke. They are taught to "remove power" from their arms when playing so that the motion looks smooth, in the same way that efficiency of movement is stressed in the classical arts they study. Apprentices practice this movement repeatedly to replace any habits they acquired before coming to Kodo with a standard way of playing *shime-daiko* at Kodo. As in Tokyo, there are no exercises, no basic techniques, no set of drills, and no articulated theory of performance for apprentices to learn as they strive to refine their drum stroke. Instead, they practice alternating patterns of right-left drum strokes over and over while their teacher looks on, offers criticism, and models the appropriate way to hit the drum.

As apprentices shift from the smaller *shime-daiko* to the mid-size *chū-daiko* drum, they begin learning the aforementioned piece "Yatai-bayashi," which uses three mid-size *chū-daiko* drums. The process of learning here stresses proper movements of the body to produce proper sounds as much as the training at Sukeroku Daiko in Tokyo detailed earlier. The horizontal position of the mid-size *chū-daiko* drums in this piece makes it such that the drummers must lie with their legs straddling the underside of the drum. This obviously neutralizes the use of the legs in the piece, but in contrast to the *shime-daiko*, the size of the drum and mallet and thickness of the drumhead shift the axis of motion from the arm and wrist to the arms, shoulders, and back (with the muscles of the abdomen providing support). As with the *shime-daiko*, apprentices play the pattern over and over, receive criticism on the movement of their arms, and play again. Three *chū-daiko* players play at the same time, leaving the remaining apprentices to provide accompaniment on *shime-daiko*, collectively producing a sound that is near deafening (figure 15).

After gaining some proficiency playing "Yatai-bayashi," apprentices move on to the even more physically demanding "Miyake." "Miyake" is Kodo's signature piece, marking the group's first creative effort after the departure of Den Tagayasu, and it taxes the bodies of apprentices and players like no other piece in their repertoire. In "Miyake," five *chū-daiko* drums are placed horizontally on small drum stands that lift them only a few inches off the ground. Drummers position themselves at the front and back of these drums, spreading their legs out wide in an effort to get their hips as low to the ground as possible. They move back and forth only laterally, closer to and then farther away from the drum, as they strike it. Each foot remains planted, so that at each extreme one leg is extended at an angle and the other is bent ninety degrees at most. The movement requires considerable strength and flexibility in the legs, hips, and lower back, and, when accompanied with arm movements, considerable coordination as well. The size and length of the drum mallets (they are longer than, for example, the ones used in "Yatai-bayashi," but not quite the length of those used in "Ōdaiko") make it such that all power and movement in the stroke comes from the torso, shoulders, and

FIGURE 15. An instructor watches closely as Kodo apprentices practice "Yatai-bayashi." Posture, movement, and power all receive extensive comment and criticism. Photo by author.

arms. Each stroke is accompanied by a movement of the body either toward the drum (right arm) or away from it (left arm). The rhythmic pattern of the piece is rather simple. Its artistry derives from the skillful arrangement of the drum pattern, the choreographed movement of the five drummers, and the sheer physical spectacle of watching drummers perform in this position for the length of the piece. Apprentices are evaluated on their ability to play powerfully without ruining the smooth flow of the piece. They are critiqued on the extension of their legs and arms and the proper placement of their mallet strikes on the drum. The sound that comes out of the drum is important, but as at Sukeroku Daiko and Nihon Taiko Dōjō, it is imagined as the end result of a set of bodily movements that are emphasized as being equally, if not more, important. In addition, the emphasis in both of these pieces on staying low to the ground, generating power in the lower extremities, and then propelling this power into the drum recapitulates the distinction between "bottom" and "top," "low" and "high" discussed in the first section of this chapter.

In contrast to Sukeroku Daiko and Nihon Taiko Dōjō, however, the language of pattern memorization used by Kodo reintroduces an opposition between local and nonlocal into the apprentices' training regimen. Before apprentices actually touch the drums in either piece, they must first memorize its *kuchi-shōga,* onomatopoeic vocalizations that correspond to a particular kind of drumbeat, stroke, or pattern. For example, the *kuchi-shōga Do-Ko* refers to the sound of two right-left (R-L) drumbeats. Similarly, *Do-Ko-Do-Ko* stands for two R-L drumbeats in quick succession. *Do-Ko-Don* stands for two R-L drumbeats followed by a strike of the drum with the right hand to produce the sound *don,* which has the length of two R-L drumbeats. (*N* is considered its own syllable in Japanese, and hence has the same duration as *do.*) Combining these syllables with the syllable for rest (*tsu*), drummers can vocalize sophisticated rhythmic patterns in a manner that is relatively easy for individuals who lack formal musical training to remember. As a result, *kuchi-shōga* is the predominant form of communicating rhythmic patterns at Kodo (and in most other taiko groups as well). Moreover, in contrast to Western systems of notation that specify pitch and duration but not timbre, *kuchi-shōga* represents all three. Accordingly, by memorizing *kuchi-shōga* first, drummers have an idea of how a piece should sound before they even play it. For example, the rhythmic pattern utilized in "Yatai-bayashi" is not particularly difficult, but it is not easily notated on a consistent three- or four-beat measure like that in popular or classical music. Despite the difficulty of representing this rhythmic pattern with standard musical notation, apprentices had the *kuchi-shōga* memorized by the end of the day—an impressive feat.

Nevertheless, as I alluded to earlier, there is a limit on how closely apprentices can approximate the original. As with dialects, *kuchi-shōga* vary regionally in Japan. Attempting to mimic folk dances or drum performance is believed to be tantamount to learning a regional dialect—a task that is difficult if one has not lived in a particular area since birth and unconsciously acquired its accent or dialect. As a result, Kodo's arrangements of traditional folk drumming, while lauded for polish, power, and sophistication, are often believed to lack the *namari,* or "local nuance," of the original. One example referenced earlier is the loss of local nuance in the transformation of Chichibu festival drumming into Kodo's "Yatai-bayashi." The fact that Kodo usually replaces the *kuchi-shōga* of folk drumming with its own in itself signifies the impossibility of replicating the nuances of local performance in an alien context. Local flavor, in a sense, is lost in translation.

Training in the other performance pieces featuring taiko at the apprentice program follows the same pattern of memorization and repeated practice of specific physical movements I have discussed here. Taiko instruction, arguably the most important part of the Kodo apprentice program, recapitulates the intense physical discipline that manifests in all aspects of the program. Although its approach to performance and its repertoire distinguish it from Japanese taiko groups like Sukeroku Daiko and Nihon Taiko Dōjō, Kodo is similar to these groups both in its attention to the training of the body for performance and in the way that performers' bodies come to express conceptions of local identity. In contrast to these groups, however, Kodo's apprentice program illustrates how physical movement in taiko combines with an aesthetic of "rootedness" that differentiates local and nonlocal Japanese. Just like foreigners, whose bodies hamper their ability to incorporate the techniques of taiko drumming, Kodo apprentices represent those "new-style" Japanese, whose lack of local "roots" prevents them from ever fully embodying the folk motifs at the foundation of ensemble taiko performance.

. . .

On the final day of Kodo's apprentice program, the second-year apprentices appeared before an audience of Kodo staff, teachers, and first-year apprentices for a small graduation ceremony. By this point, the apprentices knew who would become probationary members (and thus have a chance to join the group full time) and who would be going home. With the pressure off, the new graduates had an opportunity to reflect and share their thoughts with those assembled. The occasion was formal: male apprentices arrived in suits and ties, female apprentices in kimonos and elaborately manicured hair. At this particular ceremony, one male apprentice stood out. Unlike his fellow apprentices, Daisuke dressed formally except for a black leather jacket with a studded collar and lapel, chains, and bright silver buttons. A few of those assembled chuckled when Daisuke walked in, but the snickers quickly changed to rapt attention when he began to speak.

Daisuke explained his choice of dress. This was the same jacket that he wore on the day he arrived at the Apprentice Centre. And he had worn it for a purpose. The jacket expressed who he was—a drummer for a punk band, with an attitude and record of delinquency to match. He arrived at Kodo to play taiko, to show how good he was, and to become the best taiko drummer he could. It was hard at first. There were lots of new things to learn, lots of annoying authority figures telling him where to go, what to do, and how to behave. But now sitting here (in *seiza*) in this place in this jacket, he had come to realize just how poorly it "fit" the new him. Two years after wearing the jacket to his first day at the Apprentice Centre, he announced that this would be the last time he would put it on.

Daisuke's words spoke to a transformation of self—one that occurs subtly, nearly imperceptibly, over time as one engages in the rigorous physical discipline to which Kodo apprentices are subjected. The emotion on the faces of the younger apprentices, several weeping openly, impressed on me just how widely felt his sentiments were. Daisuke's words are recalled here so as not to diminish the potential for self-transformation in the Kodo apprentice program. Indeed, this is its central point—not just to train the next generation of Kodo performers but also to create new selves grounded in the local style of Kodo performance and the local environment of Sado Island.

This chapter has tried to contextualize such self-transformation by placing it in the discursive context in which it is interpreted and assigned meaning. As an intensively physical practice, ensemble taiko encodes and articulates notions of identity and difference in Japanese bodies through repeated bodily practice. The chapter began with a reference to the famous photograph of MacArthur and Hirohito standing side by side. The comparison between the two served as shorthand for expressing a sense of "inferiority" many Japanese feel toward the comparatively tall bodies of stereotypically white, male foreigners. Among ensemble groups in Tokyo, however, Japanese bodies are hardly inferior. Instead, taiko is conceived as an activity that developed from and suits best the stereotypical Japanese body.

At the same time, the emphasis on roots and localism that extends out of this aesthetic discourse creates a hierarchy by which the bodies of some Japanese are believed to be better suited to the performance of certain kinds of taiko than others. Those who have lived since birth in a particular region have embodied folk performance in a way that enables them to perform it better than a nonlocal practitioner ever will. This sense of local entitlement is so powerful that even the most accomplished professional practitioners of taiko drumming in Japan, those in Kodo, routinely defer to the prowess of the local inheritors of the folk arts from which they take artistic inspiration. Although it operates in one instance to subvert a hierarchy based in race, the aesthetic discourse of taiko ultimately erects another rooted in the ineffable particularities of place.

SIX

Woman Unbound?

BODY AND GENDER IN JAPANESE TAIKO

ON SEPTEMBER 22, 1999, the National Theatre of Japan hosted the first night of an annual taiko concert series called "Taiko of Japan" (Nihon no Taiko). Since it began in 1977, the "Taiko of Japan" series has showcased professional taiko ensembles and a wide variety of local festival groups from various regions in Japan. The length of its run, along with its base at the National Theatre, the home of Japan's classical performing arts establishment, has helped "Taiko of Japan" legitimate ensemble taiko as a new genre within Japanese performing arts. On this particular day, the series drew attention to an emergent trend within the Japanese taiko community: the dramatic rise in the number of female taiko drummers. Over the past twenty years, it has become increasingly common to see women performing alongside men in taiko ensembles. Even so, male performers have tended to receive the greater share of the limelight. By naming the series "Women Play Taiko," concert organizers sought to shine the spotlight on taiko ensembles that feature women drummers.

Even without being able to read Japanese, a concertgoer might infer from its poster advertisement that the event had something to do with women (figure 16). At the center of the poster is an image of a seminude woman floating among the clouds, hair wafting out behind her, playing a taiko drum fastened around her waist. While the poster plays on depictions of the thunder god Raijin (traditionally represented as a male dressed similarly but without the taiko drum), the composition of this image conjures up a different mythology, one that is closer to taiko folklore than the god of thunder. Pale white except for bright splashes of red on her cheeks and chest, the goddess's body and the adjacent vertical text evoke the colors of the Japanese flag and their origins in the legend of the Japanese sun goddess Amaterasu.

FIGURE 16. "Women Play Taiko": a poster for the annual "Taiko of Japan" concert implies continuity in women's drumming from the goddess drummers of the mythic past to the female drummers of the present.

As the ancient creation myths tell it, Amaterasu was so offended by the actions of her brother Susanō, the god of the sea, that she shut herself inside a cave, plunging the world into darkness. Her fellow deities begged Amaterasu to come out of the cave, but to no avail. It was not until the goddess Ama-no-uzume organized a celebration, rousing the attendees by banging on an over-turned tub and then jumping on top to dance around nude, that Amaterasu peeked outside the cave to see what was causing the commotion. Once she revealed herself, the god of strength, Tajikarao-no-kami, pulled her out of the cave and blocked her reentry, bringing light to the world once again. For many of the drummers I encountered, the overturned tub upon which Ama-no-uzume danced is believed to have been one of the first taiko drums. Hence, Ama-no-uzume, a female goddess, can be considered the first taiko drummer.[1] Deftly mixing religious and secular symbolism, the poster implies a continuous arc of association from the goddesses of the past to the female drummers of the present.

As noted in the preceding chapter, however, it has historically been quite rare for women to play taiko drums. In fact, with few exceptions, women's performance on traditional Japanese instruments has been tightly restricted, at least since the early seventeenth century. Starting in the 1980s and 1990s, however, women began taking up taiko drumming in significant numbers, eventually reaching contemporary levels equal to and possibly even greater than men.[2] There are many all-female amateur taiko groups and several successful professional groups that feature women prominently. In 2005, a Japanese American woman even won the solo competition at the Tokyo International Taiko Contest. Taiko drumming is thus a new and conspicuously public site where women perform professionally on Japanese musical instruments in numbers comparable to men.

Evidence of the enthusiastic entry of women into its ranks brings into fuller relief gendered aspects of taiko that have been implicit in the preceding chapters. As much as taiko drumming is a new practice that allows for the participation of new groups of people, its development has had a distinctly masculine orientation. All of the progenitors of ensemble taiko on the Japanese mainland were men, and the influence of their view of the ideal taiko player continues to resonate in contemporary taiko aesthetics. Ondekoza's valorization of the peasant class and celebration of folk performing arts was premised on sentimental images of the artisan, the farmer, and, of course, the rickshaw driver Muhōmatsu—all distinctly masculine in orientation. Tokyo's Sukeroku Daiko grew out of a competition among young men to stand out at summer Bon festivals. Perched on the taiko platform way above the dancers, the young drummers devised acrobatic choreography to win the adoration of the crowd below, especially young women. Oguchi Daihachi's reimagination of Shinto ritual drumming in his Osuwa Daiko departed significantly from ritual performance but conserved the taboo on female drum performance derived from Shinto notions of ritual pollution. Women did not join his ensemble group until the trend had been established elsewhere.

Given its postwar origins and the significant number of female participants, taiko drumming appears to hold potential as an artistic site for the reworking of prevailing gender ideologies in Japanese music. On the basis of interviews with professional taiko players, however, it appears that this revision has yet to take place. Instead, as women have taken up taiko drumming, they have had to contend with a set of aesthetic standards and gender norms that derive from the original (and still prevailing) male dominance of taiko performance. Moreover, as a kind of musical performance that places particular emphasis on the stylized presentation of the body, these aesthetic standards have been discursively constructed around male bodies. Women taiko players have therefore had to grapple with a "hegemonic masculinity" (Connell 1995, 77–78) within the sphere of taiko performance. This hegemonic masculinity discursively elevates male taiko players over female taiko players, who are believed to lack the natural physical endowment necessary to play taiko like men. Men's bodies are the standard; women's bodies are the exception.

The effects of this hegemonic discourse have been twofold. First, those women who have been successful within contemporary taiko performance have felt the need either to match men through powerful playing or, conversely, to accentuate their femininity in line with dominant gender norms. Second, the entry of female bodies into the highly masculinized site of taiko performance has provoked complementary reactions of titillation and abhorrence. This has been managed particularly by the use of clothing, either to reveal the eroticism of powerfully built "masculinized" female bodies or to shroud them within the boundaries of convention.

In this respect, the image of the goddess on the poster proves instructive once again. Soaring high in the heavens, naked from the waist up, the female (goddess) drummer is literally "unbound" from both the pull of gravity and the sartorial strictures of custom. Yet, at once unbound, she is presented anew with breasts and torso exposed as an eroticized object of the male gaze. This tension between liberation and titillation finds expression in not only the artistry of the image but also the narratives of men and women in the taiko community. The locus of these narratives on the body—its limits and potentialities, its exposure and obfuscation—recalls the emphasis on bodies and embodiment discussed in the preceding chapter. Whereas in that case distinctions of race and place were believed to limit the potential embodiment of taiko technique, in this case distinctions of sex and gender are given similar weight.

Before analyzing the narratives of taiko drummers, it is useful to contextualize the taiko drumming of today within the history of female stage performance in Japan. Reviewing this history does not merely help clarify why taiko drumming has proven so popular with women. Many of the concerns in the contemporary taiko community with women's stage costumes, the exposure of women's bodies on stage, and the capability of women to perform alongside men have antecedents in the evaluation of women's performance in the past. Thus, while discontinuity has characterized women's drumming over the last several hundred years, there has been significant continuity in the interpretation of women's stage performance. Examining key moments in the history of women's performance in Japan not only illuminates the nature of these continuities but also underscores the contemporary significance of "*women* playing taiko."

BOUND THROUGH HISTORY

The transgression of everyday gender norms characterized by contemporary female taiko players has a long history in Japan. Kabuki, one of Japan's best-known classical performing arts, began as a form of gender-bending street theater led by a woman. In the early seventeenth century, a Shinto shrine maiden named Izumo no Okuni began leading theatrical performances on the banks of the Kamo River in the former capital, Kyoto. Wearing the clothes of a man, a Christian cross around her neck, and a samurai sword on her side, Izumo gave avant-garde performances that attracted a considerable following (Foreman 2005, 38). While today *kabuki* is typically translated as the "art of singing and dancing," the word in fact derives from the verb *kabuku*, which means "to lean" or "to behave bizarrely." The so-called *kabuki-mono*, literally "bizarre people," referred to nonconformists who flaunted authority through unconventional dress, hairstyles, and accessories (41). At a time when roles for men and women followed a strictly prescribed Confucian social order, Christianity was being vigorously suppressed, and laws prohibited the carrying of swords by anyone other than samurai, Izumo's kabuki surely seemed nonconformist and threatening to the ruling Tokugawa authorities. Of course, the female actresses were often available as prostitutes, which surely added to the allure of the emergent theater. It also led to additional problems, as fights over women commonly broke out among patrons.

In response to these brawls, in 1629 the Tokugawa shogunate took the aggressive step of banning women not only from the kabuki stage but from all manner of public performance (Shively 1978, 7). Female performers were moved from the public sphere of the open stage to private entertainment houses located in the licensed pleasure quarters of Japan's larger cities. Spatial and sartorial confinement in turn came to define women's performance in Japan for the next two hundred years. While female entertainers were freed from the pressures of marriage and motherhood that constrained other women in feudal Japan, they remained territorially bound and literally (and symbolically) "wrapped" in the multiple layers of kimonos worn while performing for their patrons. With women marginalized, public stage performance developed in a distinctly masculine direction. Even the men who played female roles in the flourishing kabuki theater were believed to embody the essence of true femininity better than ordinary women (J. Robertson 1992b, 424).

The reentry of women into the masculinized space of the stage was thus bound to be transgressive and fraught with gendered and sexualized overtones. After the modernizers of the Meiji government (1868–1912) rescinded the ban on female public performance in 1877, female *gidayū,* musician-singers who provide musical and narrative accompaniment in Japanese puppet theater, were some of the first women to retake the stage (Coaldrake 1997). Resplendent in their kimonos, the young female *gidayū* tended to receive more adulation for their looks than for their virtuosity. Perhaps out of frustration, in 1882 a female *gidayū* broke out of the confines of her kimono and donned the trousers and broad-shouldered top of male performers, establishing a custom that continues to this day.

A step forward for equality, this early cross-dressing came with unintended consequences: the new performing costume proved just as stimulating for young male audience members as kimonos. Male students from elite universities in Tokyo soon formed fan clubs around popular female *gidayū* performers. In response, and in keeping with older concerns over the dangers of female theater performance, the Ministry of Education in 1900 prohibited male students from attending *gidayū* performances. Later, the Department of Public Morals and the Tokyo Metropolitan Police Department began to censor scripts. Evoking Edo-era policies, authorities also restricted puppet theater performance to areas beyond municipal borders (Coaldrake 1997, 21). On stage, as women achieved greater equality with men, they also began to be held to the (male) performance standards established in their absence from mainstream performance. Female *gidayū* were criticized for their inability to duplicate the articulation and vocal power of leading male performers (215n33). Eventually, governmental regulation, the incompatibility of long-term apprenticeship with the demands of motherhood, and competition from new mass media led to a decline in women's *gidayū*. Having reached its zenith in the Meiji period, *gidayū* remains a performance genre dominated by men.

This early experience of female *gidayū*, particularly the focus on dress and performance ability, has parallels in other classical performing arts as well as contemporary taiko drumming. Since the late nineteenth century, women have slowly made inroads into genres of classical stage performance formerly restricted to men. Women now play *shamisen* and perform in theaters without fear of stigma, but the custom of professional all-male kabuki continues, limiting opportunities for female performers even if there is interest. Professional Noh theater and *bunraku* (puppet theater) also remain overwhelmingly male. In fact, the professional involvement of women in all varieties of classical Japanese theater and music pales in comparison to that of their contemporaries in orchestral and popular music. Because these types of music were popularized in the modern period and are clearly identified with the West, there has been no significant difference in women's participation in them. Women have embraced new instruments of social distinction, such as piano and violin, and female pop singers have performed on stage since the beginning of the twentieth century.

Nevertheless, recent studies of musical (Yano 2002) and theatrical (J. Robertson 1998b) genres that emerged in the first decades of the twentieth century suggest that female performance even in "modern" genres has been fraught with gendered associations similar to those of earlier eras. One example is the popular musical genre of *enka*. Derived from urban protest songs of the late nineteenth century, *enka* mixes Western instruments, melancholic chords, and languid melodies with Japanese vocal stylizations. Women have faced no significant barriers in *enka* singing, in contrast to the classical performing arts. However, male and female *enka* singers differ significantly in their performance costumes. The different clothing customs reflect early twentieth-century associations of the male with the modern, Western public sphere and the female with the traditional, Japanese private sphere. Male performers typically wear suits on stage, while women customarily perform in kimonos (Yano 2002, 172). The persistence of these conventions can be frustrating for younger entrants into the world of *enka*. A singer in her early twenties told one scholar:

The image of *enka* singers is very fixed. In the beginning, I thought I would break the rules. In other words, I would not wear a kimono, I would sing wearing a short dress, etc. I thought I would try that but it was all wrong. In the end, wearing a ribbon in my hair and a dress just didn't work. I was scolded [and told] that an *enka* singer has to be graceful and adult-like in a kimono, and if I tried to buck the system, I wouldn't sell any recordings. That's how it was. (Quoted in Yano 2002, 64)

As her frustration indicates, even in the "modern" genre of *enka,* women still cope with constraints on performance. Not only are women who sing *enka* bound by tightly drawn hair and snug kimonos, their songs, drenched in nostalgia and odes to maternal sacrifice, keep them well within the Meiji ideological framework of "good wife, wise mother" and sanitized of the ribaldry associated with the pleasure quarters.[3]

As much as women's clothing is fixed in *enka,* it floats much more freely on the Takarazuka Revue stage, but not to entirely different effect. The all-female Takarazuka Revue theater, founded in 1913, is the foremost example of "modern" female theatrical performance that emerged after the end of the ban. As a type of theater in which women play both male and female parts, Takarazuka theater corresponds most obviously to all-male kabuki. But, the intent of such cross-dressing differs between the two genres (J. Robertson 1992a, 1992b, 1998b). While the male playing a female role in the kabuki theater modeled femininity for ordinary women, the female playing a male role in the Takarazuka Revue was not meant to be a model for men to follow. The education of the actor, not the audience, was of more concern.

> The *otokoyaku* ["male"-gender specialists] ... were to glorify masculinity and ultimately to enhance the "good wife, wise mother" gender role for women. Kobayashi [the male founder of the Takarazuka Revue] theorized that by studying males and performing men, the *otokoyaku* would learn to understand and appreciate the masculine psyche. Consequently, when they eventually retired from the stage and married—which he urged them to do—they would be better able to perform as "good wives, wise mothers," knowing exactly what their husbands expected of them. (J. Robertson 1992a, 49)

The Takarazuka Revue thus demonstrates gender play within specific boundaries: the identification of sex and gender can be transgressed on stage, as long as the ultimate purpose of this transgression is the maintenance of accepted gender roles offstage.[4] Although they can adopt the manners and dress of men in performance, the women of the Takarazuka Revue are kept within the boundaries of Meiji-era gender ideologies as much as kimono-laden *enka* singers.

In sum, over the last several hundred years in Japan, the evaluation of women's stage performance has been guided less by concerns about quality than by anxiety over its social effects. From at least the days of early kabuki, authorities have been sensitive to the effects of women's performance on male audiences. Feudal and modern governments ultimately monitored these effects by strictly regulating the availability of women's performance. For male stage managers in the modern era, the tendency has been to rein in the eroticism of women's performance through the use of kimonos (such as in classical performance and *enka*) and through adherence to prevailing gender ideologies (such as in Takarazuka).[5]

It is thus not surprising that interpretations of women's taiko performance bear the traces of earlier debates. Concern over the appearance and behavior of women on stage figures importantly in evaluations of taiko drumming, particularly the degrees to which women's bodies are exposed. This concern is striking in a performance genre in which exposure of the male body is commonplace, even encouraged, and in which the reaction of male or female audience members to the eroticism of male bodies is considered unproblematic. Yet the tremendous physical demand of taiko drumming on performers makes the body a highly charged site for the articulation of gender difference, just as it marks differences of race and place. In a manner reminiscent of early Meiji debates about the ability of women *gidayū* to match the power of male performers, female taiko players largely comprehend performance ability in physical terms.

GENERIC MOTIVATIONS, GENDERED LIMITATIONS

During the period of my fieldwork, roughly half of Kodo's twenty apprentices were women, a ratio the group tries to maintain. For these new female apprentices, in their late teens and early twenties, the unique opportunity that taiko presents for Japanese women factored little in their interest in playing taiko professionally. Rather, a consciousness of their gender most often emerged as they progressed through the program. Overwhelmingly, female apprentices were drawn to the idea of playing taiko professionally for many of the same reasons as their male counterparts: they found it enjoyable and looked forward to expressing that delight on stage with Kodo.

In contrast to more senior female performers, who had joined the group a decade or so earlier, most first- and second-year apprentices had previously played taiko in local groups. Kimiko, a nineteen-year-old first-year female apprentice from a small town in Shizuoka Prefecture, had played taiko for several years in a group started by local officials for community revitalization purposes and had found the experience empowering.

> In my experience, I've found that playing taiko on stage, really enjoying it, communicates that joy to the audience. The audience starts to feel as good as the performers. The first time I felt that way as an audience member was at a Kodo performance. I felt like I received a kind of courage, strength, and joy from them. I thought that it would be great to be able to give that kind of feeling to people in the audience. That's when I decided I wanted to apply to the Kodo apprentice program.

Tomihisa, a twenty-two-year-old first-year male apprentice from Okinawa, similarly emphasized the power of taiko to elicit emotions in audience members:

> In my second year of university, I joined a taiko club. We mostly played at local festivals and events, but in my final year we rented out a space and held a solo concert. Some of my male university friends who attended that night were moved to the point of tears. After only two years of practice! [He laughs.] This made me think about the power of taiko performance. I thought about making a life playing taiko. When I researched professional groups to join, Kodo looked to be the best run and best organized. So I decided to apply to the apprentice program.

These narratives of joy and exhilaration when playing taiko were not only representative of Kodo's apprentices but also similar to narratives I heard in other groups, at short-term workshops, and at taiko classes. More than any other factor, taiko held appeal as a fun and enjoyable activity.

For some apprentices, the desire to communicate joy was coupled with a near-existential desire to make taiko a part of one's life. Again, both male and female apprentices shared this feeling. Yuriko, a twenty-three-year-old first-year female apprentice from Hokkaido, stressed the joy of performing and the construction of identity through taiko performance:

> Right around the time I was preparing to take my teaching certification exams, my mother told me that I should stop playing taiko and concentrate on my studies, but I couldn't stomach the thought. If I stopped playing taiko,

I thought, my "self" would disappear. People always told me that I looked happiest when I was playing taiko and I always got excited when the conversation turned to taiko. Around that time I saw Kodo perform. Compared to other professional groups I had seen, Kodo seemed to be playing freely and with lots of enjoyment. I thought, "that's the kind of taiko I want to play," and I applied to the apprentice program.

Daisuke, a nineteen-year-old second-year male apprentice from Osaka whom we met at the end of the last chapter, felt that he had been "saved" by taiko. Daisuke had a troubled personal history that distinguished him from his fellow apprentices but resonated with the experiences of many of the male performing members. Like these men, Daisuke came from a working-class background and was an unenthusiastic student. Fighting and improper behavior at school led to his being sent to an educational institution for troubled youth.

> My high school was not very good. A lot of bad students with bad grades, bad recommendations, and bad attitudes, like me, went there. I hated studying and got caught up in drugs, alcohol, girls, and gang activity. But that school had a taiko drum club and I joined. I found I loved it. Taiko became my life. I realized that if I got arrested, I wouldn't be able to continue playing. It would be like my life had ended. So I stopped all my illegal activities.
>
> I saw Kodo play in Osaka and it had a huge impact on me. It gave me a huge energy boost, like a nicotine or caffeine high. I wanted to continue playing taiko and I decided that these were the people I wanted to play with. I soon applied to the apprentice program.

In each of these stories, themes of personal development and emotional communication dominate much more than a concern with gender or an interest in preserving Japanese tradition. In fact, gender was conspicuously absent in apprentices' discussions of initial interest in the group. Only one female performing member among my informants mentioned noticing a gender distinction before joining the group. Asako, a twenty-seven-year-old female member from a small town in Saitama Prefecture, was initially surprised that women could actually play taiko in the group.

> I first saw Kodo in ninth grade. I went with my mother and we sat right in front. At that time, there were no women playing taiko in the group, but the performance, especially the solo drummer playing on the huge taiko ["Ōdaiko"], moved me. I got goose bumps and tears welled up in my eyes.
>
> When I was deciding on my future in my final year of high school, I

recalled that performance. At first I thought that Kodo was just for men, since I hadn't seen any women playing on stage. But later I found an advertisement soliciting apprentices in the group's monthly newsletter to which I had subscribed. I called to see if women could play, too. The head of the apprentice program at that time told me, "As long as you play taiko 'as a woman,' you can play." Wow, I thought. I want to play!

Like other apprentices, Asako was clearly emotionally moved by seeing Kodo's performance. However, she also perceived taiko as a male endeavor, and the absence of female taiko players on stage was a source of some concern. Having received assurance from the director of the apprentice program that women could indeed play, albeit "as women," Asako felt comfortable enough to enter the program.

A concern over whether women could play taiko emerges in Asako's discussion about her decision to join the group, as it did for a number of more senior players in their thirties and older. Yet I found that even if gender rarely figured into the initial decisions of younger female apprentices to play, these apprentices, and other female performing members, became more conscious of gender differences as they continued through the program. After having practiced standard Kodo pieces alongside male apprentices for months, these women spoke of what they perceived to be the physical difficulties they faced in trying to meet an established male standard.

Yoshiko, a twenty-two-year-old second-year female apprentice, realized these difficulties over the course of her apprenticeship.

> Most women arrive at the Apprentice Centre with the attitude that they will "not be beaten" by the guys. I was the same way. I had noticed that women don't appear on stage as much as men in Kodo concerts. At first I thought that women weren't allowed to play drums, which isn't the case. I was determined to play as well as men and earn my place on stage. But over time I've realized that physically I just can't keep up. I've had to admit that there is a real gap in terms of stamina and strength. At the same time, I don't think that women should receive a "handicap," as in golf, during practice. In fact, although it was tough, being pushed to play as hard as the guys has actually been a source of self-confidence for me.

Yoshiko recognizes a gender disparity and uses it as motivation to work harder. Significantly, Yoshiko feels this disparity in her body, as a lack of physical strength that men have. Kana, a twenty-one-year-old first-year female apprentice, also recognizes gender difference in physical terms and, like Yoshiko, uses it as motivation.

> I've come to see that I can't match the guys in terms of power. When I'm playing the *chū-daiko*, I have a tendency to hold back a little. I know that that's a bad thing to do. But in my head I'm thinking, "I don't have enough strength . . ." Second-years say, "even if you lack power, you still have something you can communicate to the audience." So, even though I'm not as strong as the guys, I can't hold back. I want to keep trying to play just as the men do.

While Yoshiko and Kana use their frustration to motivate themselves, Yumi, a twenty-three-year-old second-year apprentice, is less sanguine about the ultimate effects of such efforts: "Here we play a kind of taiko that has historically been played by men. No matter how hard we try, I think it's impossible for women to match the volume, strength, and power of the guys, especially in such pieces as 'Yatai-bayashi' or 'Miyake.' In any case, it's fruitless to even try, since women aren't able to play these pieces on stage. If we were able to play these pieces on stage, I think we could bring something special to them other than power and strength."[6] Ultimately, Yumi appeals to a "special something" besides strength and power that women can bring to Kodo performances. In doing so, she affirms a conception of gender difference between men and women that inheres in their "natural" physical endowments. Instead of celebrating gender egalitarianism in training and performance, Yumi gestures toward a recognition of gender *difference,* one that is not unique to Kodo but is found in many taiko groups throughout Japan. Unfortunately, the lack, in her opinion, of a suitable place for women in the Kodo organization led Yumi to give up on the goal of becoming a performing member of the group. Even if she were accepted, she told me, she planned to decline and join a different group where women had more performing opportunities.

Frustration at being held to a male standard emerged as well in discussions with women who had been longer-term members of the group. Earlier I referenced Asako's excitement at finding out that women could play taiko in Kodo. Since becoming a performing member, she has distinguished herself as an impressive dancer. In an interview, she explained to me that her interest in dancing in fact arose directly from her frustrations playing taiko (as well as commentary on her playing by male supervisors).

All along I knew that I wanted to play taiko. In my first year of the apprentice program, I tried to play hard, just like the men. One of the male supervisors noticed how much I was straining to keep up. He said, "Just having the appearance of a woman, you start out with a strike against you if you play like that." But I still didn't listen. I didn't want to try dancing; I wanted to focus on taiko. Intense pieces like "Miyake" and "Yatai-bayashi"—I put my all my energy into them.

In my second year I recalled what I had been told on the phone about playing taiko "as a woman." I decided to use it to my advantage. The gentleness and refinement of a woman—to develop it and use it to my advantage was my only option. That's when I developed an interest in dancing and singing. Even now, after trying for many years, I still can't quite get rid of that face I make when I play—my "trying-too-hard face." I'd say that playing taiko with the "gentleness and refinement" of a woman is still a work in progress for me.

The perceived physical inability of women to match the strength of men as they play intense pieces like "Yatai-bayashi," "Miyake," and "Ōdaiko" very likely derives from the actual experience these women have when practicing alongside their male counterparts. Nevertheless, the comments of Yoshiko and Asako indicate that this embodied disparity in strength and stamina also reflects a structural difference in the performance roles of men and women with the organization. Since the Ondekoza era and until recently, opportunities for women in the organization to play taiko have been rather limited. In the Ondekoza era and in the early days of Kodo, women's roles were largely restricted to dances performed between taiko pieces or alongside them.[7] As if symbolizing their tightly constrained roles, the women of the group appeared on stage only in formal kimonos or summer kimonos *(yukata)*. In the late 1980s, as women who had an express interest in playing taiko joined the group in increasing numbers, wardrobe became a source of contention. Later, arguments over wardrobe would serve as a proxy for the issue of women's position within the group.

Hana, a female staff member of Kodo who has been a member of the group for over ten years, recalled for me the process through which the wardrobe of the women shifted:

When I arrived at Kodo, there was a general attitude that women ought to just dance. Indeed, most women in the past were dancers and singers. When I tried to practice taiko, two of the male lead players chided me, "Why don't you just practice dancing?" All the while they knew that I wanted to do more than just dance. I wanted to play taiko.

As it happened, a senior male player went to Africa. That opened up a space for someone to play instead of him. When I tried it, some audience members reacted, "Oh, there's a woman playing taiko." After that, I was able to play taiko more but still not as much as I had hoped. I remember one day I was really frustrated and I broke down in my dressing room. A female member of the tour staff came in to check on me and I told her of my frustration. This staff member had a husband who was a performing member of the group. Not long after our conversation, she wore his stage costume to a meeting of the entire group. "I don't look bad, do I?" she announced. "Even on women, it looks good, doesn't it?"

Soon after, things started to change. We had begun performing a new piece ("Zoku"), which featured men and women playing medium-size *chū-daiko* together. We put on the same costumes as men and we also started helping out between numbers. Before that time, even if you were new, women just sat and waited between performance numbers.

Interestingly, the resolution of the conflict over dress—the wearing of formerly male costumes by women—parallels the example of Meiji practitioners of *gidayū,* who wore masculine wardrobe in order to demonstrate their liberation from feudal mores and newfound equality with men. Having broken free of their previously stereotyped and limited roles, female taiko players soon came to be judged according to new standards. Much like Meiji *gidayū,* the women of Kodo began to encounter similar positive and negative evaluations of their taiko-playing ability by audiences. Some audience members reacted to the "violation" represented by women playing taiko. On postconcert surveys in the past, Hana told me, it was not uncommon to encounter comments like "women are dirty," an idea that harks back to Shinto notions of women as polluting beings. (The half-naked men who play alongside them incur no such invective.) I was struck by how, on more recent surveys, audience members remarked that these female taiko players appeared "sexy," evoking the response of audiences to the female *gidayū* of an earlier era.

A continuum between transgression and titillation thus continues to mark the evaluation of women's performance, even among the taiko players of today. On the one hand, women remain within stereotypical and, some would say, antiquated notions of femininity, wearing kimonos and accepting a separate status from men; on the other hand, they are "liberated" to compete equally with men. In the latter case, they tend to be either judged negatively—by themselves or others—for failing to match the playing power of men or evaluated positively for the sensuality they bring to performances.

Kodo's gendered division of labor on stage is reflected in the feelings of female apprentices and performing members. However, a concern with the presentation and limitations of the female body emerges even in groups that feature female players more centrally. The first mainland taiko group to highlight a female performer was actually the "new" Ondekoza that Den Tagayasu formed in Nagasaki after breaking with the original Ondekoza on Sado Island. At the center of this new Ondekoza was Takakubo Yasuko, whom Den chose for the group not because of her taiko-playing acumen (she had never played taiko before joining the group) but because she was "petite" and had "big eyes." Frequently praised by audiences and (male) critics for her "cuteness" and combination of feminine "delicateness" and "toughness" (Kuwahara 2005, 6–7), Den required her to perform in a *yukata*. This set her off from the male players of the group, emphasized her femininity, and constrained her movements. Evidently, just like some members of Kodo, Den wanted a female taiko player who would stay within the limits of a particular conception of femininity. Takakubo did play "Ōdaiko," a traditionally male performance piece, but she performed it wearing the aforementioned *yukata,* which prevented her from spreading her legs wide and raising her arms over her head to put power into her drum strokes. In hopes of performing with more volume and power, Takakubo initially resisted the request to perform in this manner, but she eventually relented to Den's demands, and the performing style stuck (11).

Other than Ondekoza, the two most prominent professional ensembles that feature female taiko drummers are Honō Daiko and Amanojaku. Both groups were formed in 1986 and have multiple women playing taiko. While women take lead performing roles, men played central roles in founding both groups. Honō Daiko, which is composed of three female taiko drummers, was organized by Asano Akitoshi, a senior manager at the Asano Taiko drum company. Amanojaku, a three-person unit that features one man and two women, was founded by Watanabe Shōichi, formerly a drummer with Sukeroku Daiko. What is striking about the performance styles of these groups is the way in which they each highlight the muscularity of women playing taiko, a stark contrast to the presentation of women in groups like Ondekoza and Kodo.

Women playing taiko vigorously was a theme that emerged clearly in an interview with Yuka. Formerly one of the lead drummers from Honō Daiko,

Yuka is in her late twenties and worked for a number of years in offices and at other odd jobs. When I asked about her reasons for joining the group, she told me that she happened to see an actress playing taiko on television one day during her shift as a waitress in a coffee shop. According to her recollections, she didn't give it much thought other than thinking, "Hey, that looks kinda cool," but she did recall that one of her customers mentioned to her that playing taiko would "suit her." (This was likely a reference to her hard-edged personality.) She didn't know much about taiko or other taiko groups, but it was attractive to her because, she thought, "it'd be nice to sweat some and get in better shape." In the end, she knocked on the door of a school affiliated with the taiko manufacturer Asano Taiko in Ishikawa Prefecture. The woman who answered suggested that Yuka come to one of her upcoming performances at a summer festival to get a better sense of the kind of taiko she teaches. Yuka attended, and the event proved transformational. The following is a selection of her comments to me about how moving she found the event:

> At the festival, there was a special stage set up for taiko performance. A number of taiko troupes representing localities across Japan appeared on stage one after another and I wasn't so impressed. Finally, the group I had come to see took the stage. As if on cue, the skies opened and rain started coming down so hard I could barely see. Knowing that I was going to attend a festival, I had dressed up in a *yukata* and I had taken extra time to style my hair in the customary way. Once the rain started to come down, my clothes and hair got soaked. People around me started to file out. But I was transfixed. I couldn't leave. I knew I wanted something, and I couldn't leave.
>
> Suddenly, the lights went out and they began covering up the big taiko drum to protect it from the rain. Right at that moment, I heard a woman on stage announce—no, better yet, scream—that she was going to start playing. I thought to myself, "Wow, there really are exceptional women in the world." At that moment, she started to play—huge taiko mallets pounding against the drum, her hair flying up around her. It still was raining so hard, I could barely see, but the image I saw before me moved me profoundly. I was looking at something that blew away the world of the typical office lady, the very road that I had been following up to that point. I realized that women *can* put themselves out there, forcefully and wildly. I thought of myself, coming there in makeup with my hair done up nicely. I realized that I had spent too much time worrying about the small, irrelevant things in life. All I had been told about being a woman—that you shouldn't speak too loudly, that you shouldn't lose yourself in laughter, that you shouldn't speak your mind too openly—suddenly seemed silly. After she finished playing, I went backstage and asked her to be my teacher.

Yuka's account of joining a taiko group was unusual both for its vividness and for her explicit emphasis that it was a woman playing taiko that had inspired her to join. Her immediate realization of a contrast between the freedom represented by this woman's performance and the limitations of the preordained path she had followed up to that point figured importantly in her decision to join a taiko group.

This emphasis on "freedom" is emblematic of the approach to performance in her group and in Amanojaku. Female members of the Honō Daiko and Amanojaku groups were concerned less with maintaining ties to the Japanese past than with exploring new directions for the Japanese drum. Amanojaku's website states, for example, that the group seeks to create "a new form of music by adding the elements of modern and western music to its base of taiko, an ancient Japanese art."[8] Honō Daiko emphasizes gender explicitly as a group that "aspires to express the delicate beauty and passion of women through the medium of taiko drumming."[9] I asked Yuka about the connection that she felt with other taiko groups. She told me that she felt that she had little in common with other taiko groups in Japan, and that she had little interest in maintaining a connection with Japanese "tradition." This is not surprising, given women's alienation from folk and classical drumming.[10]

This emphasis on freedom is also reflected in the ways in which these groups display women's bodies. Much like the taiko-playing bodies of the men of Kodo and Ondekoza, the muscular bodies of these taiko-playing women are showcased. From inception, Honō Daiko's manager at Asano Daiko took this into account.

> I wanted to see what would happen if I had women train to play taiko on stage just as men would. One thing is the musculature, of course. Up to this point, men have played taiko and proudly displayed their bodies. It wasn't good enough to have women just imitate men. I wanted to express the kind of eroticism that develops in women through intense training [kitae-ageta erosu wo dashitakatta]. So, I hired a designer to create costumes that would highlight this. With those costumes, the beauty of those well-trained bodies shines through. There's nothing at all obscene about it. (Asano Akitoshi, quoted in Kuwahara 2005, 8)

The revealing snug-fitting tops and straps permit the female drummers to display their muscular shoulders and arms (figure 17). Along with the loose-fitting skirts they wear, these outfits permit a freedom of movement not possible with kimonos or *yukata*. In fact, one of the first pieces the newly

FIGURE 17. Honō Daiko's costumes highlight their muscular physiques. Photo courtesy of Asano Taiko Company.

founded Honō Daiko performed was a version of Ondekoza's "Ōdaiko," in which one female drummer performs with exposed back toward the audience. The attention to muscularity in this version stands in sharp contrast to Takakubo's *yukata* version. The women of Amanojaku use a similar wardrobe, which permits greater freedom of movement and draws attention to their muscular upper bodies (figure 18).

These groups thus make greater attempts to put women on a level of equality with men than groups like Ondekoza and Kodo. At the same time, and as might be expected, the women's performances were held to masculine standards, and gendered differences among bodies again became the focus of

FIGURE 18. A female drummer for Amanojaku poses before an *ōdaiko* with her muscular shoulders and back exposed.

attention. Members of these groups told me that they believed men's bodies naturally develop the musculature needed to play taiko through regular practice and performance alone.[11] Women who want to play taiko, however, need to supplement the "natural" weakness of their bodies with extra training, like weight lifting. As one male member of Amanojaku put it to me, "Playing taiko requires a lot of physical strength. Women who want to play alongside men need to develop extra strength in order to produce the same amount of power as men. That's why the [two] featured women of Amanojaku lift weights and bodybuild in addition to practicing taiko."

The female members of Honō Daiko expressed similar sentiments to me in interviews; in fact, one television documentary on the group features scenes of the group training intensely and lifting weights before a practice session. The two groups share the belief that women need to train beyond normal taiko practice in order to produce the same amount of power that men naturally generate through the course of typical playing. In the prominent display of these "unbound" female bodies, there is evidence of the same kinds of hegemonic masculinity that keep women's bodies contained in groups like Ondekoza and Kodo—namely, the belief that women's bodies are naturally weaker than men's bodies. Whereas this is covered up through wardrobe and restrictions on the kinds of pieces women can play in Kodo and Ondekoza, Honō Daiko and Amanojaku compensate for this perceived weakness through training and bodybuilding. The masculine standard remains, and women have to strive to reach it.

One factor that contributes to the different presentation of female bodies in these groups is the attitude toward the attractiveness of female performers on stage. Honō Daiko and Amanojaku attempt to use the eroticism of "masculinized," muscular female bodies as a selling point in a way that Ondekoza and Kodo do not. At the root of this difference lie two competing notions of what makes female performers attractive: a demure "traditional" femininity or a more "progressive," sexually assertive femininity. But it is not just the different philosophies of male artistic directions that are at work here. The featured female players also have a higher degree of control over their stage presentation in each of these groups. The emphasis placed by women in these groups on freedom from traditional music and gender roles thus manifests materially in their self-presentation. Liberation from traditional methods of playing and notions of gender roles means freedom from the constraints of traditional costume.

An understanding of why greater artistic control by women leads to greater display of female bodies in contemporary taiko benefits from comparison to strikingly similar tendencies among female pop "idol" singers in Japan. Whereas in the 1970s and early 1980s female pop idols embodied a diminutive, "cute" femininity, the "post-idol" idols of the last fifteen years are characterized by a much more aggressive, sexually suggestive kind of femininity (Aoyagi 2005, 104–107). Contemporary young women find the latter to be more liberating and the former, "cuter" sensibility to be more constraining. Accordingly, a tendency toward greater exposure of the body and sexually aggressive gestures, like crotch grabbing and the touching of breasts, emerges when young pop idols are granted more freedom over their self-presentation (118–119). Much like the pop idols of a previous era, the women of Kodo and Ondekoza have had to adapt themselves to a particular kind of tightly bound femininity, which they find to be confining and frustrating, both literally and figuratively. The more aggressive sexuality that emerges when male control recedes in the training of idols is analogous to the kind of gender and sexual expression that emerges when women have increased control over their performance in taiko groups such as Honō Daiko and Amanojaku. Of course, the women of Honō Daiko and Amanojaku do not touch their breasts or grab their crotches during performances, but the exposure of skin and musculature parallels the physicality of "post-idol" idols. It is true that men still have key roles in the presentation of women's bodies in both of these taiko groups. As much as these are masculine projections of female sexuality, however, they are quite different in form than Meiji notions of "good wife, wise mother," and are consonant with newer interpretations of feminism that view exposure of the body as liberation from patriarchal control over women's self-presentation.

Nevertheless, the parity with men in performances of Honō Daiko and Amanojaku ironically makes them less interesting to many taiko enthusiasts. Inasmuch as women in these groups play drums with the power and enthusiasm of men, they are uninteresting, even uncomfortably transgressive. But if they do so while maintaining a modicum of femininity, they remain intriguing. This attitude, which I encountered frequently during my fieldwork, was summarized in an exchange I had with a male member of the amateur taiko group I joined during my fieldwork:

"I'm going to interview members of Honō Daiko. Have you ever seen them?"

"Um, are those the ones from Ishikawa Prefecture? Yeah, I've seen them. Kinda boring. The ones from Tokyo are better."

"You mean Amanojaku?"

"Yeah," he responded, with one eyebrow raised, "they're good."

"You mean you like the way they play better?"

"No, they're *cuter*."

This sentiment regarding sex appeal and "cuteness" was echoed in a magazine interview with Nishitsunoi Masahiro, a highly respected scholar of taiko in Japan. Nishitsunoi remarks, "It's now okay for women to play alongside men, to establish their own groups, or to play solo pieces like 'Ōdaiko.' But if the performance features a woman who is not beautiful or does not naturally exude sex appeal or cuteness, then I doubt anyone will have an interest in going to see it" (2001, 7). Women's bodies that cross too far over into the realm of "female masculinity" thus risk disapproval by some. In short, "naturally" weak bodies need to be strengthened to meet masculine performing standards, but if these bodies in turn become too masculinized, "natural" femininity and attractiveness suffer.

What's more, female taiko players who go too far beyond performance conventions also risk audience disapproval. The performance at the National Theatre I mentioned at the beginning of this chapter featured two additional groups led by women (not including Amanojaku and Honō Daiko) who played taiko with what could only be described as wild abandon. They pounded the drums furiously, jumped up and down, and screamed and shouted throughout their performance. Sitting in the audience, I personally found the performance exhilarating. So I was surprised when I asked one informant, a middle-aged woman who curates a popular taiko museum, what she thought of the drummers. "That's not taiko. It's nothing more than [Western] percussion. I think it's horrible." "Western" percussion for her functioned in a derogatory way to mean that the performance lurched into excess, beyond the limits not just of gender roles but also of national-cultural borders. This reaction was not atypical for senior members of the taiko community. A senior male manager at Kodo, who has been a member since the group was founded, reacted to the same performance in a way that reflected a concern both over female bodies and appropriate movement on stage.

> Women are just not endowed with the same kind of natural muscular beauty that some men have. Sometimes, in fact, too much musculature on a woman can be unattractive. So, when women scream and yell and show off their muscles when playing, I don't think it's very attractive. When women play like that, I think it looks more hysterical than beautiful. That's probably my own prejudice, but as long as I am here at Kodo I don't want to see or hear that kind of female performance.

These two comments reflect a belief that a woman who is too "unbound" steps into excess, beyond the confines of properly gendered behavior (into unattractiveness) or, yet further, outside the genre of Japanese drumming itself (into "Western" percussion). The gender expression of female taiko players, much like that of contemporary female pop idols, typically oscillates between confinement within norms of classical femininity and transgression of those norms through assertive expressions of physicality. Though the latter may seem to represent liberation, it can also transform women into objects of erotic desire or derogate them as inferior imitations of men.

AMATEUR DRUMMERS, COCON,
AND THE FUTURE OF WOMEN IN TAIKO

Women in professional taiko groups thus appear to work within rather strictly defined gender boundaries. My experience observing amateur taiko groups, however, suggests that rigid distinctions between the sexes are less pronounced, although there are gendered differences in performance that parallel those of professional groups (for example, women typically do not play strenuous taiko pieces like "Yatai-bayashi" or "Ōdaiko" as often as men).[12] In addition, gender difference is frequently marked in uniforms (that is, in pink versus blue headbands). This relative lack of distinction in performance is likely the reason that many new Kodo apprentices do not perceive gender as a constraining factor prior to participating in the apprentice program. Nevertheless, women in amateur groups also bow to societal pressures that routinely face women in Japan. Married women with children do not participate as actively in amateur groups as nonmarried women or married women without children, and even professional female taiko players commonly suspend their performance activities to take care of children and family (Kuwahara 2005, 10).

In the amateur group that I joined, for example, there were two couples that had met through their participation in the group. One couple with a three-year-old boy had married before I arrived. Prior to the birth of their child, husband and wife were both active performers in the group. While they both continued to attend practice sessions after the birth of their son, the wife sat on the stage away from the group watching over the little boy while her husband practiced with us. During breaks, the little boy would grab a pair of drum mallets and start banging on the drums as his mother watched over him. She would occasionally play as well, but typically just to demonstrate simple techniques to her son as he pounded away. Her role had shifted from performer to watchful mother and gentle teacher. The other couple became pregnant toward the end of my initial fieldwork in 2001. When I returned in 2004 for a follow-up visit, the couple had had a child and followed a similar pattern to the first: the wife brought her child to practice but had stopped performing actively with the group.

It is possible that these women will return to playing as their children age. This was the case for one father in the group, whose two children (a boy and a girl, ages seven and nine, respectively) regularly attended practice with him while his wife stayed home. During my initial fieldwork, the children learned basic playing patterns and positions along with another child from the local community. When I returned in 2004, the boy and the girl had both begun performing on stage together with the adults. The one woman in the group who had children and *did* participate, albeit peripherally, was in her fifties. Given occupational trends in Japanese society, these avocational patterns are not surprising. Women's occupational participation in Japanese society tends to follow an "*m*-shaped" curve: women work until they get married, leave work once they get married or have children, and then return to the workforce in their forties or fifties, once their children have grown (Ogasawara 1998; see especially chapter 1).

Still, it struck me that, more than any other aspect of my study, gender dynamics within the taiko community were changing significantly even while I was studying them. In the spring of 2008, a number of years after the conclusion of my initial fieldwork, I attended a concert at a "children's festival of the traditional arts" in the suburb of Osaka in which I was living. Out of the thirteen groups that appeared on stage, five were taiko groups. The children in these groups ranged in age from kindergartners to high school students. Most striking to me, however, was the overwhelming representation of girls relative to boys in these groups. Girls outnumbered boys in every group that appeared. Admittedly, this is an unrepresentative sample, but it does reflect anecdotal evidence of a trend toward greater numbers of girls and women participating in amateur taiko more generally.

At the same time, like the significant disparity between the small number of female senior managers and the large number of working women in Japan's largest corporations (Ogasawara 1998), there is a great disparity between the large number of players who are women and the very small number of women who are senior leaders within the taiko community. The Nippon Taiko Foundation, which I discuss in more detail in the following chapter, is the largest national organization of taiko groups in Japan. In 2008, the foundation comprised forty-two divisions, slightly fewer than the number of prefectures in Japan. Out of forty-two divisional presidents, only two were female. It appears then that the gap between the number of girls and women who play taiko and the number who rise to the level of leadership within the community remains quite wide. But, given the relatively brief history of women in taiko, it is reasonable to expect that this will change over time. As women begin to assume leadership positions not only within individual taiko groups but also within taiko associations like the Nippon Taiko Foundation, it is possible that the masculine aesthetics of taiko performance might change as well.

Even in the formerly masculine world of Kodo, there are indications of a shift in gender consciousness. During the time of my initial fieldwork, one young woman had recently advanced to become a performing member of the group and eventually became the first woman to play taiko alongside men in a piece called "Chonlima."[13] "Chonlima" positions each of four drummers side by side behind a small, high-pitched *shime-daiko* and a lower-pitched *okedō-daiko* drum. Behind these four stands one drummer who plays a *chū-daiko* drum positioned vertically on the floor. The piece involves extremely fast movements and considerable coordination among the drummers, much like the drum line of a marching band. Until this woman, Tomomi, the group had held the belief that there was no woman who could play with the speed and dexterity necessary to perform the piece. In this respect, her performance represented a hallmark.

Having talked with so many female apprentices and members, I was curious about how easy it seemed for Tomomi to play taiko within the group, instead of being confined to dance. In contrast to other female performers in Kodo's history, Tomomi had been a semiprofessional drummer in a punk band before joining the group, and she still had the tough attitude and brusque manner one might expect of a punk musician. When I asked her whether she felt that group members steered her away from drumming toward dancing, as other female members had indicated to me, she responded flatly, "Well, when I joined, I told them straight up that I wanted to play taiko. No one has ever told me to dance."

Given how confident Tomomi was that she could play alongside the men, I was surprised to learn that she took the initiative to form a decidedly female small group with three other female members in 2007. (Kodo has several such small groups, but this was the first ever all-female group.) According to Tomomi, the smaller group was formed in order to experiment with a kind of "feminine" taiko, free from the artistic control of men. The group cocon was conceived in distinctly feminine, even maternal, terms. An article in the English-language newsletter of the group explained that the origin of this name comes from the French

> for "cocoon" or "chrysalis." A chrysalis is similar to the uterus, the sacred chamber in which life is created and nurtured. [Tomomi] aspires to get in closer with their [sic] own humanity and gender, which can be covered up on stage by the masculine costumes and roles normally associated with taiko. *cocon* is envisioned as a platform for the women of Kodo to share and freely express themselves with the drums, song, dance, and other instruments they usually travel the world with. (Taylor 2008, 2)

In contrast to the typical Kodo performance, women in this group had complete control over their instruments, pieces, and costumes. Yet this control led

FIGURE 19. Members of cocon in their loose-fitting stage costumes. The white tones of the costumes evoke the innocent and unthreatening femininity at the core of the group's identity. Photo by kawashima kotori.

them not to present themselves on stage in the manner of other female-centric groups in which women dominate. Instead, cocon remained within the boundaries of the conservative femininity that has marked Kodo throughout its history. The description of their activities is replete with generative metaphors of maternal femininity—"cocoon," "chrysalis," "uterus," "sacred chamber." Their white stage costumes hang as loosely as kimonos hug the body snugly, masking their taut physiques and shrouding their sensuality (figure 19).[14] One publicity photo even shows them resting, perhaps gestating, inside a cocoon.

•   •   •

The white costumes of cocon evoke the adolescent purity of Japan's ancient and modern Shinto shrine maidens, the "original" female taiko drummers, with which this chapter began. The virginal innocence projected by these costumes contrasts starkly with the more aggressive sexuality of Honō Daiko and Amanojaku, among other female groups, just as the patches of red stand out from the white on the body of the goddess in the "Women Play Taiko" poster. The juxtaposition of red and white, of passion and purity, so close to the national symbolism of Japan, expresses as well the boundaries within which women perform contemporary taiko. For the last several hundred years, women's performance in Japan has been marked by the perception of sexualized excess and by the attempts of authorities to rein it in. While taiko clearly marks a new site for women's performance in Japan, the discursive construction of women's taiko performance continues to reflect the debates of the past.

At the same time, the physical demands of taiko newly direct attention not merely to the superficial differences between the sexes but to corporeal distinctions as well. While the gendered boundaries of an earlier era were marked primarily on the surface through clothing and observed behavior, in the contemporary period gender difference is experienced through a sexed body, which clothing either reveals or obscures. Dominant masculinity is defined by the capability to perform taiko with one's inherent physicality alone; subordinate femininity is defined by its lack. Aesthetic display of muscular male bodies is unproblematic, even encouraged; display of female bodies is fraught with social sanction. Women respond to this inequity either by accepting it (and risking frustration) or by challenging it (and risking objectification). While to some they may seem to be goddesses floating high above a world of convention, female taiko drummers remain tightly bound by the social strictures of their brethren down below.

SEVEN

The Sound of Militarism?

NEW TEXTS, OLD NATIONALISM,
AND THE DISEMBODIMENT OF TAIKO TECHNIQUE

DURING ENSEMBLE TAIKO'S relatively short history in Japan, few taiko drummers have seen much in common between their activities and those of other taiko groups. Many of the drummers with whom I spoke even questioned the degree to which ensemble taiko could be considered a cohesive "genre." The identification of local groups with local communities, and the discourse of localism that both constitutes and reflects it, has yielded an assortment of taiko groups organized vertically along lines of descent from an original progenitor (or set of progenitors) rather than horizontally through feelings of solidarity with other drum groups.

While the concern with lineage continues to contribute to weak ties of solidarity, some influential members of the taiko community have tried to organize distinctive regional forms into a centralized procrustean bed. Buttressed by intellectual and institutional support of national scope, the push toward centralization emerged in response to the popularity of taiko and has advanced through years of negotiation. The end result has been the creation of a new cultural category of "Japan Taiko" (Nihon no taiko).[1] Although this may seem to be just another way to refer to the groups discussed throughout this book, it should not be taken as such. Rather, this term intends to assimilate the loose association of Japanese taiko groups, at least conceptually, into the genre of performance to which it refers. It is therefore a political move as much as an organizational one. Indeed, the push toward centralization has been driven primarily by those with ideological attitudes toward Japanese culture, who see elements of Japan's martial past in contemporary taiko.

Given the importance of embodied movement to the expression of locality in taiko, the discursive articulation of "Japan Taiko" has implications beyond differing interpretations of Japanese heritage. Devising a standard, national approach to taiko instruction and performance necessarily entailed the "disembodiment" of local movement and technique into texts for analysis, classification, and rearrangement.[2] This is not to suggest that the process proceeded with malice. On the contrary, each of the central actors involved believed that they had laudable reasons for carving out a niche for "Japan Taiko": the desire to present performances of taiko alongside performances of other folk performing arts; the wish to preserve styles of folk drumming in danger of extinction; the hope to improve the quality of taiko drumming both in Japan and beyond. Nevertheless, the creation of "Japan Taiko" remains one of the most overtly political moves to reframe ensemble taiko as a national performing art at the very moment of its accelerating globalization. The subtle (and not-so-subtle) relations of power and knowledge enacted by this process once again took styles of taiko drumming out of particular places and set them in motion, transforming local distinction into variation and distilling idiosyncratic styles into generic patterns.[3]

MEMORIES OF WAR

My introduction to this national project of organization began with an experience I had early in my study of taiko. On a beautiful April day in 1999, I drove to one of Tokyo's western suburbs with my research adviser at the University of Tokyo. My adviser had lived for several years in the suburban community before he and his family moved to smaller quarters in Tokyo. He knew of my interest in taiko and told me that he had contacts in his former community who had been active in efforts to invigorate community life through the creation of festival music and dance groups, one of which was a taiko group. This taiko group was planning to perform at the annual O-Bon festival later that summer, and its leaders agreed to have the two of us stop by their practice session to observe and later to chat.

Once we arrived in the city, we wound our way through quiet residential streets to the local community cultural center, where a Bon dance workshop was in session. The workshop wrapped up about forty-five minutes later, and the two leaders of the group, Mayumi and her husband, Makoto, led us back to their home. We sat down at a low table and began to discuss their backgrounds and activities in the community. Both of them had extensive musical training. Mayumi was a graduate of the Tokyo College of the Arts and was proficient in *koto* (thirteen-string zither). Makoto had grown up in culturally rich Kyoto and had studied *shamisen* and *shakuhachi*. They moved out to the suburb in the 1960s, not long after it had been established and when there was little around. Other than the festival traditions of the neighboring farming hamlet in which they could not participate, there was no local "culture," and they soon set about trying to rectify this. They wanted to create for their children and their neighbors' children the same kind of culturally vibrant environment they had had in the cities in which they were raised.

They asked about my research interests, and I told them that I was interested in taiko, its origins and popularization. Mayumi told me that she liked the way that taiko groups helped generate interest in Japanese folk culture. But, while she welcomed the interest of young people in Japanese culture, she also expressed concern at how, in her view, taiko performance evoked the militarism of wartime Japan. The tendency of these groups to "create sound only with power" reminded her of the martial spirit that dominated Japanese society during that historical period. Makoto nodded agreement.

Mayumi's comment about the "sound of militarism" piqued my interest, and I wondered if there was a basis for it in fact. It was not surprising that an observer of ensemble taiko, with its loud booms and fiercely determined youth, might interpret the performance as an expression of martial sentiment. Before coming to Japan, I had seen an example of such an interpretation in the American film *Rising Sun* (Kaufman 1993), which was based on a book by Michael Crichton. The film, which depicts a resurgent Japan using its newfound power to influence American politics and industry, uses taiko as a metaphorical representation of Japanese strength and aggression.[4] In one scene, a group of taiko drummers is playing at a party at a large Japanese company in Los Angeles. The film cuts back and forth between the powerful drumming and a Japanese man having sex with a white woman on a conference table upstairs. The drumming builds to a climax just as the couple does, and the scene ends with the man choking the woman to heighten her pleasure. (Later we find that the woman has died from asphyxiation, at the hands not of the Japanese man but of a white American senator.) The symbolic overlay of national-economic intervention with sexual penetration evokes clear historical precedents. As the historian Yoshikuni Igarashi has written, in *Rising Sun* "the chastity of white womanhood is juxtaposed to American security, both of which have to be protected from aggressive Japanese (male) behavior. Crichton's writing appears to be a simple extension of wartime propaganda, which often invoked white womanhood in need of defense" (2000, 44; see also Wong 2000).

Several months after my visit with Mayumi and Makoto, a Japanese informant told me about a controversy that had erupted in Australia. Japan Australia Professional Exchange Programs (JAPEP) Wadaiko Drummers, an Australian taiko group made up of thirty native Australians and ten Japanese exchange students, was scheduled to play at the opening ceremonies of a festival in Melbourne. The ceremonies were to be held at Melbourne's Shrine of Remembrance—a war memorial—until a veterans' group called the Returned Soldiers' League launched a protest. The group argued that they did not want any form of entertainment to be played on this sacred ground, especially Japanese "war drums." Yet the article's headline, "Veterans Win Fight to Silence Drums of War," leaves little doubt as to the primary reason the event was first cancelled and then later moved to a different venue. The article describes taiko drums as instruments "which were once used to welcome home Samurai warriors."[5] Later in the article, however, a manager of the JAPEP group is quoted as saying that "traditionally [taiko] have been used for festivals and ceremonies. . . . These drummers aren't from the armed forces, they're musicians." My informant, who knew a member of the group, told me that a man in the audience approached one of the Japanese drummers at the conclusion of the performance, looked her in the eye, and said, menacingly, "I've seen *those* shoes before," a reference to the similarity between the drummers' Japanese footwear, which are distinguished by a separation between the big toe and the other toes, and those worn by troops during World War II.

At a number of points in my fieldwork, other foreign visitors to Japan asked me about the connection between taiko drums and war. Yet in my own research I had found little evidence of a connection between ensemble taiko and war drumming or a desire to express the warrior spirit through drumming. None of the amateur or professional taiko players with whom I initially spoke located the goals or the origins of their performance in military activities or interpreted them as martial. In fact, most expressed surprise at the suggestion of such a connection. I passed off Mayumi's comments as personal interpretation, the comments of foreign visitors as cultural misunderstanding, and the American film and Australian reports as misleading.[6]

As I continued to investigate this purported association between taiko and war, however, I found that a particular subset of the taiko community did consider the origin of at least one influential form of Japanese drumming to lie in military use. These individuals were also involved in establishing taiko as a national performing art, a project that depended on the combined efforts of corporate finance and scholarly research. The basis of this project lies in an organization called the Nippon Taiko Foundation (Nippon Taiko Renmei), and the remainder of this chapter takes up a discussion of its organizational aims and interest in creating a standard textbook for use in taiko instruction.

OSUWA DAIKO, REDUX

Tracing the connection between taiko and war drumming also entails retracing the steps of this study back to the progenitor of ensemble taiko, Oguchi Daihachi. As I explained in chapter 2, Oguchi ascribed his inspiration for arranging taiko into ensembles to the models of the jazz drum set and orchestral percussion section. He also has said that the series of innovations leading to the first ensemble group followed the discovery of a drum score in a neighbor's miso cellar. Exactly how that drum score came to be a part of festival drumming in the area in which Oguchi lived had important implications for Oguchi's understanding of ensemble taiko.

In 2001, when I spoke with Oguchi about the development of his drumming style, he mentioned its connection to jazz and orchestral percussion only after telling me how his style of drumming grew out of a custom of military drumming native to the area. Between 1561 and 1568 in the region near where Oguchi lives, a series of battles was fought by armies headed by two legendary generals, Takeda Shingen and Uesugi Kenshin. One of the generals, Takeda, believed in the power of the "spirits" of the local Suwa Grand Shrine, a shrine dedicated to the gods of war and agriculture. Takeda observed how every year villagers came to the shrine from surrounding areas to make offerings for a good harvest. At the time of these offerings, a kind of "drumming competition" took place at the shrine, with the villagers competing among themselves to earn the favor of the shrine deities. Takeda, being— as Oguchi described him—a "smart warrior," recognized immediately the popular association between the taiko drum and the spirits of the shrine. In preparation for battle with Uesugi, he arranged for a legion of drummers to accompany his forces. He called for three groups of seven musicians, the "Osuwa Daiko Group of Twenty-One" (O-suwa daiko ni-jū-isshū).[7] Takeda hoped that the drummers would help raise the morale of his troops by showing them that they had the favor of the shrine gods. Even though the battles ended in a draw, an annual "Seafarer's Festival" (O-funa matsuri) began at the Suwa Grand Shrine in commemoration of General Takeda, and it appears to have continued annually until the end of the nineteenth century.

Oguchi handed me a copy of an English translation of Osuwa Daiko's literature. Entitled "The Japanese Drums of Suwa Shrine," the pamphlet explained the connection of Oguchi's ensemble taiko to General Takeda's war drums as he described it to me. A portion of it reads, with minor grammatical corrections made for clarity, as follows (emphasis added):

> Musicians and dancers belonging to the "Osuwa Drum Group" are not only professionals whose ancestors have, for generations, transmitted from father to son the artistic and religious traditions in the region, but also a number of ordinary people living in this area. . . .
>
> The "Osuwa Drum Group" . . . differs from other [types of festival-based drumming] in that one of its origins can be traced to Takeda's war drum. In other words, this drum art of the Suwa Shrine, performed in a group beating a number of different types of drums, inherits not only the *techniques* but the *basic concept of the Takeda war drum.* Also it *retains in its rhythm* and idea the soul of the peasants of old time who were at time[s] called up for service as soldiers. . . .
>
> During the battles waged against Uesugi, his great rival military commander, between 1561 and 1568, Shingen Takeda ordered that a music band composed of 21 enlisted farmer musicians be organized to boost the morale of his troops. . . . This functional music was called "Taiko" and it in turn had an influence on the performing arts of ordinary people. The musicians switched, with ease, from battlefield to shrine.
>
> During this age, the instruments of drummers be[came] more diversified, and as a result other percussion instruments like "Hyoshigi" [wooden clappers] . . . as well as other wind instruments such as flutes, conch shells, etc., found their way into the group. Thus, more than 18 types of percussion instruments and . . . many kinds of musical instruments are now employed. (Osuwa Daiko Preservation Society, n.d.)

The pamphlet explicitly connects "one of the sources" of the drumming of Osuwa Daiko to Takeda's "war drum" and suggests that it has been transmitted uninterrupted "for generations," albeit in festival form. The latter claim is difficult to take seriously, since, as Oguchi attests, the custom of drumming had already died out years before his childhood; he learned about it only when the score was discovered.[8] Equally troubling is what seems to be an exaggeration of the influence of the original war drum pattern on the form and substance of Oguchi's ensemble taiko. As might be expected, there is no mention of the influence of contemporaneous rhythms or orchestral arrangement on the group, but perhaps more intriguingly, there is no mention of Oguchi's contribution either. Foreign readers unacquainted with the vagaries of Japanese history would likely get the sense that the drumming has emerged organically over time. More knowledgeable Japanese observers, however, have not been so easily convinced.

The folklore scholar Nishitsunoi Masahiro has cast doubt on the relationship between Osuwa Daiko and the war drums of Takeda Shingen. Nishitsunoi confirms that a description of the "Osuwa Daiko Group of Twenty-One" appears in the *Kōetsushin-sen* scroll on which Oguchi bases his claim. However, he argues that the drummers performed not to egg on soldiers in war but to commemorate those who died in combat. While Takeda's incorporation of taiko into musical legions is well known, Nishitsunoi concludes that its connection to Osuwa Daiko has been "manufactured," without a basis in historical fact (1985, 283). Nishitsunoi further disputes Oguchi's claim that his drumming style originated in connection with the Shinto festival music of the Suwa Grand Shrine. Instead, he argues that the basis of Osuwa Daiko's signature piece, "Suwa Ikazuchi" (Thunder at Suwa) lies in the adaptation of the rhythms of a local *mushi-okuri* ritual (a ritual performed for the expulsion of harmful insects from the community) by an area musician in the early post–World War II period, long after the sixteenth-century battle. (Oguchi, though, claims not just to have "arranged" the piece but also to have written it.)[9] Although there is presently a relationship between Oguchi's group and the shrine, it dates from only the post–World War II period. Nishitsunoi remarks that this postwar relationship is an important reason why Osuwa Daiko has not been deemed an "intangible cultural property" by Nagano Prefecture (283).

TAIKO TYPOLOGY

Ironically, even though he has excoriated Oguchi's suggestion of a connection between Osuwa Daiko and Takeda's war drumming, Nishitsunoi created the intellectual framework that Oguchi and others have appropriated to legitimate ensemble taiko as a national performing art. The creation of this framework began when Nishitsunoi set about trying to convince officials at the National Theatre of Japan to allow ensemble taiko to be performed in the theater. For a number of years, the theater, with which Nishitsunoi had recently become affiliated, had sponsored festivals of the folk performing arts. Having been captivated by a performance of Oguchi Daihachi's Osuwa Daiko at the 1964 Tokyo Olympics, Nishitsunoi wanted the National Theatre to dedicate a portion of the concert series to it. Convincing the relevant officials that taiko should be made a part of the concert series, though, proved a challenge.

The National Theatre of Japan is administered by an executive committee at the theater and by the Agency for Cultural Affairs. Nishitsunoi expressed his interest in holding a concert featuring taiko to both agencies and both resisted. They argued that the taiko groups Nishitsunoi wanted to put on stage were "new"—by which they meant "postwar"—and therefore could not be presented on the National Theatre's stage as part of a "folk culture" series. Moreover, according to these officials, performances of "new" performing arts at the National Theatre were taxable. Presenting new performing groups at the National Theatre would not only complicate accounting, it would make ticket prices higher. Mixing traditional and nontraditional motifs, not to mention groups, threatened to complicate financial as well as cultural conventions.

Nishitsunoi's initial proposal was rejected, but he did not give up. Instead, he committed himself to a year of research on Japanese drumming. The result was the creation of a typology of Japanese taiko groups (Nishitsunoi 1985, 302). At first glance, Nishitsunoi's typology of "Japan Taiko" seems to do little to buttress his case. Regional varieties of folk drumming are divided not on the basis of history, repertoire, or region, but along a two-dimensional matrix of group size and instrumentation. Along one axis, styles of drumming are arranged according to whether they feature one drummer or multiple drummers. Along the other, styles of drumming are arranged according to instrumentation (that is, the number and kind of drums). The matrix produces a set of four major combinations: (1) one drummer playing one drum; (2) one drummer playing multiple drums of varying pitch; (3) multiple players playing one drum; or (4) multiple players playing multiple drums of varying pitch. There are additional, finer distinctions for the placement of drums (high or low, or set on a festival cart) and for the position of the drum on its stand (vertical or horizontal), generating even more combinations. By basing a typology on the number of drums and players, it could assimilate a broad array of Japanese drumming. Perhaps, though, it is too broad—one person playing a drum set (combination 2) or several people playing in an orchestral percussion section (combination 4) could theoretically be included. Since the typology does not classify Japanese drumming based on any distinctive qualities of the genre, it would seem to be of limited scholarly utility.

In terms of Nishitsunoi's very practical desire to convince the Agency for Cultural Affairs and the National Theatre of Japan that taiko performance ought to be permitted at the theater, however, his typology is quite ingenious. By not categorizing taiko in terms of history, repertoire, or region, Nishitsunoi reduces the diversity of Japanese drumming to the number of instruments and the number of players alone. Questions of recency and repertoire are left to the side. "New" taiko ensembles like Osuwa Daiko and Sukeroku Daiko are not separated off from "older" festival styles but are integrated into the typology as just another branch of the Japanese folk taiko tree.[10] In fact, they are integrated into the typology more centrally than classical stage drumming, which Nishitsunoi's formulation marginalizes, both literally and figuratively: it is attached to the central branches of the diagram by a dotted line. In fact, by separating out these forms from "Japan Taiko," Nishitsunoi centers his classification of Japanese taiko on folk forms of taiko drumming.[11] Newer groups represent just one structural possibility among many within a matrix of variation that includes older forms of Japanese folk taiko. Historicity is disregarded. What matters is the composition of the particular group in question.

Having completed this typology, Nishitsunoi returned to the Agency for Cultural Affairs and made his proposal once again. While some remained reluctant, agency officials proposed a compromise, telling him that it would be permissible to have performances of taiko at the theater as long as the performances were balanced evenly between "new" taiko groups and "older" festival-based groups. The executive committee of the National Theatre took more convincing, however. After approving performances on a provisional basis, the committee decided to allow them to continue only after seeing how popular the series was with audiences. The "Japan Taiko" concert series launched in 1977 and has continued every year since. A reprint of Nishitsunoi's typology appeared in the program for an inaugural concert that featured both Osuwa Daiko and Sukeroku Daiko.

It is unclear whether Nishitsunoi's research alone persuaded theater officials to sponsor the concert series. As the suggestion of a division in performances between traditional and nontraditional implies, the Agency for Cultural Affairs still takes distinctions between "new" and "old" quite seriously. Beyond its very practical purposes, though, Nishitsunoi's typology also constituted the first scholarly support for considering the many regional styles of drumming in Japan as related yet distinct varieties of a nationally unified core. By presenting the diversity of Japanese drumming on an official, national stage, the concert series is a tangible manifestation of this idea. Nishitsunoi told me that at the time he created his typology, taiko had not yet earned its "citizenship rights"; in other words, it had yet to be taken seriously as a Japanese performing art. Since that time, many taiko players have taken up his typology as an explanation for their particular drumming style, and informants regularly made reference to it when I asked them about the distinctiveness of their style. As such, it represents a major conceptual step in transforming the diversity of Japanese taiko into a more unified genre. With the authority of a respected scholar, Nishitsunoi inscribed into cultural discourse a conceptual map through which taiko drummers newly understood their diverse practices.

THE NIPPON TAIKO FOUNDATION
AND SASAKAWA RYŌICHI

This intellectual apparatus has been taken up by the largest organization of taiko groups in Japan in its drive to inscribe in text a standard approach to taiko instruction. Comprising over eight hundred taiko groups, twenty thousand individuals, and thirty-four prefectural leagues, the Nippon Taiko Foundation (Nippon Taiko Renmei) is the largest organization of taiko groups in Japan. Although it represents only a fraction of the estimated thousands of ensemble taiko groups in Japan, the association has by far the most influence of any organization of taiko groups in Japan; at present, there is no alternative equal to its scale or breadth of activity.

The foundation is the brainchild of Oguchi Daihachi. Its initial membership consisted mostly of groups Oguchi had instructed or assisted. Nevertheless, it appears that he did not establish the organization as a means of consolidating his substantial influence. Instead, as one of Oguchi's colleagues told me, it originated in 1979 with two objectives in mind: first, to promote "good relations" with actively performing taiko groups other than those members of Oguchi's vast instructional and artistic lineage, and second, "to 'make public' and to teach taiko playing techniques."

This second objective makes little sense unless one considers the extent to which prewar folk drumming was confined to village festivals and religious ceremonies. Instruction in playing techniques was limited to small, community- or family-based organizations that had little incentive to "make public" these techniques; in fact, such openness was routinely discouraged. However, in the 1970s, decreasing birthrates and rural depopulation led to fears that some important local festival traditions might disappear. Like government legislation to preserve folk performing arts, the Nippon Taiko Foundation was conceived by Oguchi as a forum in which basic techniques associated with these styles could be taught, practiced, and preserved.

The foundation started in 1979 with approximately one hundred groups and has since grown eightfold. The majority of member groups continue to come from the ranks of Oguchi's disciples or regularly perform in his Osuwa style. But by the 1990s, the foundation had incorporated many ensemble taiko groups from outside Oguchi's artistic lineage and had created an advisory committee consisting of representatives from older, festival-based performing traditions, the academy, and commerce.

Such large-scale organization requires substantial financial support, which the Nippon Taiko Foundation secured through the Japan Shipbuilding Industry Association (Nippon Senpaku Shinkōkai), now known as the Nippon Foundation (Nippon Zaidan), an organization that was endowed by the wealthy entrepreneur and philanthropist Sasakawa Ryōichi. Sasakawa, who died in 1995 at the age of ninety-six, was one of the most notorious figures in modern Japanese history. He was an avowed nationalist and a member of Japan's *kuromaku,* a term derived from the theater to refer to the influential figures manipulating Japanese business and politics from behind the scenes. Many Japanese I encountered viewed Sasakawa suspiciously, and his connection to the Nippon Taiko Foundation gave a number of drum groups pause. Concerns about its source of funding even made some reluctant to join the organization.

A brief review of Sasakawa's background helps make clear why. Before World War II, Sasakawa was already a successful businessman who had made a fortune by speculating on rice futures. He was also very active in supporting right-wing causes. At one point, he was asked to become the leader of the Ultranationalist People's Party. Under his leadership, the party, which was known for wearing black shirts modeled on the uniforms of Mussolini's fascists, grew from one thousand members to fifteen thousand. In fact, Sasakawa was so enamored with the Italian dictator that he flew one of his own warplanes to Italy in 1939 to meet the leader whom he later described as the "perfect fascist" (Katayama 1994, 35). Later in the war, Sasakawa made a fortune mining both in Japan and in the occupied territories of China and Manchuria.

Not long after the war ended, U.S. occupation officials arrested Sasakawa on suspicion of war crimes and placed him in Tokyo's Sugamo Prison. He escaped indictment and was released with other high-profile prisoners three years later. The reason for the release of these prisoners remains somewhat obscure. Most historians believe that the occupation authorities feared the spread of communism in Japan and released the men in a so-called reverse course in order to use their resources and rightist connections as a bulwark against leftist political movements (McCargo 2004, 30–31). Whether or not that was actually the motivation for their release, Sasakawa and his fellow inmates Kodama Yoshio and Kishi Nobusuke eventually became significant players in postwar Japanese politics. Kodama helped provide initial funding to start the Liberal Party, a forerunner of the Liberal-Democratic Party (LDP), which would dominate postwar Japanese politics; Kishi became LDP prime minister in 1957.

Sasakawa maintained ties to political parties through his associations, but he also set about establishing a new basis of financial power. In 1951 the Japanese parliament passed a bill that organized all prefectural motorboat races under one national organization. Sasakawa viewed legalized betting on motorboat racing as a promising economic opportunity and worked toward achieving monopoly control over all races. In 1955, he became president of the Federation of Prefectural Associations of Motorboat Racing. By 1962, the amount of money that organization earned from bets placed on motorboat races had reached such impressive sums that Sasakawa formed a philanthropic organization, the Japan Shipbuilding Industry Foundation (JSIF), to distribute a portion of these earnings (Daventry 1981, 57).

Although the two other state-sanctioned forms of gambling in Japan, horse racing and bicycle racing, are controlled directly by government agencies, Sasakawa's organization is supervised by officials at the Ministry of Transport (Katayama 1994, 37).[12] In exchange for mere supervision, the government requires that 75 percent of the gross total of gambling earnings be returned to bettors in the form of winnings and that approximately 3 percent be used to support the interests of Japanese shipbuilding. The remainder covers operating expenses and is split between the sponsoring city and regional motorboat racing association. Although 3 percent may not seem like a large figure, it is considerable given the amount spent on motorboat racing in Japan. During the economic "bubble" years of the 1980s, this amount of money was subtracted from a grand total of over two trillion yen, which left about seven hundred billion yen ($6.5 billion in 2008 dollars) for the JSIF to divide among the organizations it supported. Since the collapse of the economic bubble, that number has sunk to less than half that amount but remains a substantial sum.

Initially, Sasakawa used the JSIF to support Japanese maritime activities, but later he turned his attention to other philanthropic ventures. One of these was the promotion of Japanese traditional music, which he organized under a division of the JSIF called the Foundation for the Promotion of Japanese Music (Nippon Kokumin Ongaku Shinkō Zaidan). After being approached by Oguchi Daihachi in the late 1970s, Sasakawa agreed to support efforts to create a national organization of taiko groups, and in 1979, he included the Nippon Taiko Foundation among the dozens of organizations supervised by the Foundation for the Promotion of Japanese Music (now the Nippon Music Foundation). The name of the JSIF changed after Sasakawa's death in 1995 to the Nippon Foundation (Nippon Zaidan). At the time of my discussions with a Nippon Taiko Foundation representative around the year 2000, membership and certification fees covered only one-tenth of the cost of maintaining the foundation. The remaining 90 percent was covered by the Nippon Foundation.

Sasakawa's substantial gesture of support for Oguchi's taiko organization did not derive merely out of good will. As one member of Osuwa Daiko who knew him well explained to me, Sasakawa had a particular fondness for the way in which the Japanese drum expressed the "spirit" of Japan.

> Sasakawa was the kind of person who represented the spirit of old Japan. He believed strongly in respect for one's ancestors and in piety toward the gods of Shinto and Buddhism—the kind of person who represented the spirit of the old-time soldier, one who accepted the Imperial Rescript on Education without question.[13] He was the embodiment of *kokusui* [ultranationalism].[14] Some people call this "ultra right-wing"; if so then I, too, would consider myself to share this sentiment. Sasakawa knew that in every temple and every shrine in Japan, there is a taiko drum, that in this taiko lives the heart and soul of Japan and the spirits of departed ancestors. By encouraging people to learn about taiko, Sasakawa believed that more individuals would come into contact with and learn about the Japanese spirit.[15]

Sasakawa's sentiments are expressed in the photograph that adorns the cover of the Nippon Taiko Foundation's Japanese brochure (figure 20). The photograph is of a large *ōdaiko* with the Chinese characters for "Yamato" painted in gold letters on its side.[16] The photograph's caption explains that the characters were drawn by Sasakawa Ryōichi himself.

NIPPON TAIKO FOUNDATION

FIGURE 20. A taiko with the word "Yamato" written on it appears on the cover of a brochure for the Nippon Taiko Foundation. Photo courtesy of the Nippon Taiko Foundation.

TEXTUALIZING TAIKO

The identification of the veterans Sasakawa and Oguchi with the martial spirit of wartime Japan, and the colorful past of the former, made some informants wary of associating their groups with the Nippon Taiko Foundation. Besides politics, many were concerned about how the goals of the organization had changed over time, not to mention the way in which Oguchi seemed to be exerting more control over its artistic direction. As a member of one taiko group expressed to me incredulously, "Oguchi is trying to create something like an *iemoto* system for taiko!"[17]

Despite the reluctance of some, the number of member groups in the foundation rose significantly in the 1980s. Leaders in the organization anticipated that the number of new members would quickly begin to strain the customary oral transmission of playing technique, as relatively few experienced teachers were available to teach new members. As one member of the Nippon Taiko Foundation Skills Committee put it to me: "If the teacher has bad habits, then the students will have bad habits. If those students then become teachers, those bad habits will be replicated, and so on and so on. Proper playing style will degrade. In short, we'll have a mess." Elites in the organization called for the development of an instructional text and appealed to Oguchi and the other members of the advisory committee to produce one.

The "Japan Taiko" textbook published in 1994 was meant to address these concerns. It is not the first taiko textbook ever written, but it has achieved a prominence given the organization's national scope. Oguchi Daihachi took primary responsibility for the text, and it clearly reflects his vision of taiko. Very prominently displayed on the top of its cover page are the words "Instructional Book for Ensemble Taiko—Multiple Players on Drums of Different Pitch," terminology borrowed from Nishitsunoi's typology, which Oguchi has enthusiastically adopted. The use of such a lengthy and technical term on the cover of the book is purposeful and lends it official sanction. The imprimatur of scholarly authority is buttressed by a preface in which Nishitsunoi professes his love of taiko, especially Oguchi Daihachi's style of taiko, and reviews his efforts to arrange the concert series at the National Theatre. The bulk of the book is devoted to descriptions of the various drums used in ensemble taiko performances, the proper method of holding taiko mallets, appropriate playing position, variations on standard instrumentation, and transcriptions of Osuwa Daiko pieces for practice. At the end of the book, there are a few practice exercises and short descriptions of popular drumming groups and styles of Japanese drumming, such as Sukeroku Daiko, *Chichibu yatai-bayashi,* and *Hachijō daiko.* Most important for the argument developed here, though, is the particular vision of taiko laid out in its first few pages.

The first inside page reproduces a painting of the god of thunder lowering a hook out of the sky to pick up a taiko drum floating on the water below. The next two pages contain photographs of mass performances of Oguchi's Osuwa Daiko, one from an event in which 416 drummers play together and another featuring 300 drummers. (Given the backgrounds of Oguchi and his sponsor, it is hard not to see in the inclusion of these photographs a celebration of mass spectacle.) On the following two pages, there are reproductions of screens depicting scenes of taiko being used in war. On one, lines of vertical Japanese script are overlaid with the reproduction of another screen depicting the battle led by samurai generals Takeda and Uesugi. The script tells the story of the Osuwa Daiko Group of Twenty-One, the type of drumming that the screen purportedly depicts. The second photo is taken from a screen that depicts a battle in the late sixteenth century between two rival factions in Japan. At the very bottom of this photo, three men are shown playing a taiko drum fastened to the back of another man. The progression of these images is clearly meant to imply that the use of drums in war was central to taiko history and that Oguchi's ensemble is involved with its continuation. Nowhere is there a mention of the significant influence of Western musical models on the invention of Oguchi's ensemble taiko.

Despite the title *Japan Taiko,* the text looks more like a textbook for the instruction of Oguchi's ensemble taiko. Not surprisingly, several other senior members of the foundation began to disapprove of using a beginner text so obviously weighted in favor of Oguchi's particular method. Along with a desire to produce a more comprehensive instructional text, some felt the need to produce a generic system of "taiko basics" by which student progress could be judged. The organization had been in the process of creating a system of certification (from beginning to advanced), through which taiko students could progress within the organization. They hoped that this system would help legitimate taiko performance and certify appropriate taiko instructors outside the organization.

The difficulty they faced, of course, was that "taiko basics" did not exist. As the previous chapters have shown, taiko performance differs significantly across Japan, from stance, mallets, and subtleties of movement to the placement of drums and timing of rhythmic patterns. Learning to play a particular style is a lifelong process, at the end of which one becomes not a *generically* competent taiko player but, rather, a *specifically* trained local performer. The related concepts of "basics," "standards," "step-by-step," and "progressive" instruction are anathema to this. Therefore, to teach the basics of "Japanese taiko," which would hold for all variations across Japan, the organization essentially had to define, and thus create, a new pan-Japanese taiko in the process.

STANDARDIZATION OF TAIKO PEDAGOGY

The result of these efforts was the release in 2001 of the *Nihon Taiko Kyōhon* (Japan taiko textbook). This book represents a significant departure from Oguchi's first text. While some mention is made of the connection between taiko and war drums and of the distribution of taiko in Nishitsunoi's typology, the bulk of the text is devoted to drumming patterns, after which two transcriptions of Osuwa Daiko pieces again appear. There are drawings of the proper way to hold a mallet to play the taiko and even suggested stretching exercises. The most significant change, however, is the inclusion of marginal caveats mentioning "regional variations" from the techniques depicted pictorially.

For example, on the bottom of one page illustrating how to grip a taiko mallet, there is a short sentence that reads, "This is the basic way to hold the mallets. However, the size and shape of the mallets, the placement of taiko, and the content of performance do *differ slightly by region*" (Nippon Taiko Foundation 2001, 34, my emphasis). Four pages later, in a description of stances appropriate for drums positioned vertically, horizontally, or diagonally, there are two caveats. One notes that "taiko placement and proper playing position *differ slightly depending on region*"; the other states that the "proper playing position *differs slightly depending on region*" (38–39, my emphasis). Another section describes how the organization has standardized the onomatopoeic *kuchi-shōga* used to translate taiko patterns into easily understandable sounds. Yet the very same section cautions that these vocalizations differ importantly among "preservation societies" *(hozonkai)* and concludes with an exhortation to "please exercise care in using/passing down the traditional oral culture preserved in these societies" (53).

The aforementioned caveats express the tensions inherent in creating a textbook and basic approach to taiko performance. Representatives of regional taiko groups only approved the depictions of taiko basics as long as there were caveats that expressed what they took to be significant differences. The chief contributors to the textbook, who came from the ranks of Osuwa Daiko, agreed with this sentiment. They felt that local styles of performance should be preserved. As one of Oguchi's longtime associates put it to me: "we have no reason for denigrating the way they play taiko." However, when instructing novices in basic taiko patterns, they stressed the importance of following what was written in the textbook.

Despite all the caveats about positioning and technique, there are none that comment on the selection of these "basic" taiko patterns. The creators of the textbook argued that mastering a set of basic rhythmic patterns would not affect the actual performances of individual groups. "We told them: Do what you like when performing on stage. That's where difference and local color matter," a contributor to the text explained to me. "But let's all start with the same exercises. Performance is performance; teaching is teaching." This attitude is reflected in the organization's process of certification. After progressing through the basic exercises, students set upon a "specialized course" where they receive direct instruction from a "certified" master (usually the chief representative of a folk performing art).

Even with these caveats, a set of basic exercises still threatens the maintenance of these kinds of local performance. While a text-based approach may make sense for the purposes of applying one's skills to a diverse set of patterns and instantiations, the very nature of progressive instruction—from "basic" taiko to "advanced" taiko—makes the identification of a student with any particular style of performance all the more difficult. What emerges is not an individual who can play a particular regional style in an authentic manner, but a generalist who can play any number of styles without the distinct "local flavor" that defines local authenticity for natives. If the intention of forming a national taiko organization was truly to preserve "vanishing" folk traditions (Ivy 1995), the system of rationalized, progressive instruction inscribed in the text signifies the very disembodiment of these folk patterns, in effect imperiling the integrity of folk styles the foundation wants to help preserve. Much like the placement of classical forms in Nishitsunoi's typology, the text relegates regional traditions, quite literally, to the margins.

The importance of local flavor and the difficulties of maintaining it in textual form exemplify the double bind in which regional groups that join the foundation find themselves. While participating in such an organization may help generate interest in performing arts that are in danger of extinction, these same performing arts are subjected to marginalization from the evolving standard (which minimizes the importance of local identity) and to incorporation into it through the emphasis on cross-regional similarities (which again minimizes the importance of local identity). Moreover, the particular kinds of playing that express local performance identity, especially body positioning and movement, are edited out of the progressive approach to taiko instruction while elements of them are disembodied, reorganized, and reintegrated into a set of basic patterns. The textbook introduction to taiko constructs inherited styles of drumming as deviant at the same time that it gives them a new identity as parts of a greater national whole; much like the many regional dialects of standard Japanese, they are transformed from established "folk performing arts" to incidental local variations of a now-generic "Japan Taiko." Of course, it is possible that the establishment of a standard may lead neophytes to disavow the standard and seek out local forms of taiko culture. The success of such a chain of events, though, depends of course on the survival of present folk performing arts traditions into the future.

TAIKO UNDER A RED SUN

During my fieldwork, I had the opportunity to attend a teaching workshop sponsored by the Nippon Taiko Foundation. Two things in particular struck me about the workshop. First, at the conclusion of the perfunctory opening speeches welcoming participants and with a large Japanese national flag as backdrop, Oguchi led the group in singing the Japanese national anthem. On the surface, this may not seem so surprising. In the United States, for example, it is common to begin professional and amateur sporting events with the singing of the American national anthem. In Japan, however, the singing of the national anthem has been far more controversial. Along with the national flag of Japan (the Hinomaru), the lyrics of the national anthem are thought by many to evoke nationalistic reverence for the emperor of wartime Japan. Advocating the singing of the national anthem (as well as the display of the Japanese flag) at public events has been a distinctive mark of right-leaning individuals in recent Japanese history. The Japanese national anthem was not sung at any of the other dozens of taiko events that I attended, although the Japanese flag was displayed when an event had received funding from public sources.

In addition to the backdrop of Japanese national symbolism, use of the *Japan Taiko Textbook* was pervasive. Buying the textbook was compulsory for all workshop participants. In the morning session of the daylong workshop, Oguchi and others led participants through the pages of the textbook systematically. As the taiko "expert" demonstrated rhythm patterns on stage, junior instructors went around the room fixing technique, adjusting body position, and correcting flawed timing, while participants struggled to follow the patterns in the textbooks splayed out beside them. The lesson illustrated vividly how much the textbook had interceded into the intimate relationship between teacher and student so fundamental to instruction in other spheres of Japanese taiko performance. The expert on stage appeared derivative, his presence in effect a second-order representation of a text already standing in for once-embodied authority.

It is difficult to tell how much impact the Nippon Taiko Foundation's textbook will have on the development of ensemble taiko in Japan, nor is it easy to predict how long Nishitsunoi's typology will continue to be utilized by those inside and outside the ranks of taiko practitioners. While the Nippon Taiko Foundation constitutes the largest organization of ensemble taiko players in Japan, the ensembles that do not belong still outnumber the ones that do. What's more, its claim of having created an authoritative "Japan Taiko" textbook has not gone unchallenged. In 2005, the originality of the *Japan Taiko Textbook* was called into question by members of the Japanese performing arts collective Dengakuza. Members of this group, which is based in the same prefecture as Oguchi's group and is as politically left leaning as Oguchi was right leaning, claimed that portions of the *Japan Taiko Textbook* were copied without attribution from a textbook they published a year prior to the release of Oguchi's first text. (Oguchi admitted that the similarities exist, and the suspect passages have been struck from the text. None of these passages is referenced in the preceding discussion.)[18] Ultimately, in the wake of national curricular reforms implemented shortly after the *Japan Taiko Textbook* was completed, these debates appear less meaningful.

A look at the scale, scope, and impetus behind the activities of the Nippon Taiko Foundation suggests that the answer to the question of taiko's connection with war must in the end remain mixed. While the wartime legacy of ensemble taiko is largely the product of myth creation and selective readings of history, there are also individuals in the taiko community who take these myths quite seriously and locate in them much of their inspiration. Though Mayumi probably did not realize it at the time, her interpretation of taiko performance as an evocation of martial spirit was likely closer to the mark than she ever would have imagined.

Epilogue

TAIKO AT HOME AND ABROAD

TAIKO IN PLACES FAMILIAR AND STRANGE

I have heard it said that, at some point in their training, medical students feel erroneously that they have come down with one or more of the rare illnesses they spend so much time studying. This propensity to see what you study emerge from the pages and, against all probability, appear suddenly in your everyday life is, I think, hardly limited to students of medicine. At some point, anyone who has invested countless hours researching and thinking about a subject is bound to see it pop up in unexpected places. Usually these experiences are illusory. Sometimes they are not.

On one of many days in graduate school that I spent writing about taiko, I decided to take a break for lunch at a nearby cafeteria. The campus cafeteria I chose has a wonderful view of the Pacific Ocean, which I always found a welcome respite for eyes sore from staring at a blank computer screen. Apparently, though, this sumptuous view was not sufficient entertainment for the undergraduates who lunched there each day, because the university had recently placed a giant projection television in the middle of the dining area. The television was set to play various Hollywood hits, and on this particular day students were enjoying *The Scorpion King,* a recent film starring the former professional wrestler Dwayne "the Rock" Johnson. The film is set in ancient Egypt, where our hero ("the Rock") does battle with an evil emperor and his minions. So it was, I thought, my weary eyes playing tricks on me when I looked away from my lovely ocean vista to see a group of ancient Egyptians playing taiko on the big screen.

I blinked a couple of times. Rubbing my eyes, I looked around to make sure I was not dreaming. Could it be? Taiko in *The Scorpion King?* I swore that I had seen something, but I could not shake the feeling that I was mistaken. It just seemed so odd. Sure enough, I later rented a copy of the film to watch, and there they were: a group of about ten drummers dressed in period costume, half standing up behind *chū-daiko,* the other half seated and pounding away on *shime-daiko.* The drums had been modified to blend with the period aesthetic, but they still looked (and definitely sounded) unmistakably like taiko.

What led to the decision to use taiko in a movie set in ancient Egypt? Probably the film's producers felt that the drums looked "exotic" enough and sounded primal enough (and were played mostly by Asian players who looked "foreign" enough) to fit in a story set several millennia ago. Then again, perhaps I should not have been so surprised to see taiko reappear in film. Earlier in this book, I noted the links between taiko and cinema, from the origins of Ondekoza's famous "Ōdaiko" in the film *The Rickshaw Man* to the ominous appearance of taiko in *Rising Sun.* Whereas in those cases the connection between taiko and Japan was readily apparent and purposeful, however, in *The Scorpion King* taiko drumming appeared as a loose signifier, unmoored from any national or cultural context. Its appearance at the turn of the millennium suggested that taiko was both familiar and unfamiliar to foreign audiences: familiar enough to producers to find its way into a film, but unfamiliar enough not to jolt audiences out of suspended disbelief. That the group featured in the film was, in fact, started in Los Angeles by an expatriate Japanese actor known for Hollywood portrayals of ninja assassins struck me as yet more evidence of how this intensely localized art form remained in motion, circulating through the spaces of media and community in Japan and beyond.

The unexpected appearance of taiko in the *The Scorpion King* brought to mind a story told to me by Tatsu, my first informant at Kodo, about the unexpected presence of taiko in another movie involving a king. After work one night, Tatsu was relaxing at home, reading the newspaper while his young daughter watched a video featuring two characters from *The Lion King:* Timon the meerkat and Pumbaa the warthog. He paid the video no mind until the unfamiliar sounds of African drumming in the background suddenly turned very familiar. The staff member heard the cartoon characters playing one of Kodo's own performance pieces. "Huh?" he thought to himself. "Did we approve this?" Alarmed, Tatsu called a manager at Kodo, Kenichi, who happened to be in Tokyo preparing to leave the next day for a meeting in New York with Kodo's American tour manager. Kenichi did not recall giving permission for use of this piece either and immediately went to a local store to buy the video. He confirmed that it was, indeed, a Kodo piece. After meeting with their tour manager in New York, Kenichi took the video with him and played it for a group of Sony executives (Kodo releases albums under a contract with Sony Music). Lawyers for Sony in turn called lawyers working for Disney in Los Angeles and threatened to file suit over the apparent violation of copyright. In the end, the two corporations settled the dispute out of court and Kodo received several thousand dollars in compensation.

Around the time my friend at Kodo encountered taiko in *The Lion King*, the taiko community in North America was also dealing with unanticipated allegations of copyright abuse. In 1999, Kobayashi Seidō, the leader of Oedo Sukeroku Daiko in Tokyo, accused the North American taiko community of playing Sukeroku pieces in Sukeroku style and on Sukeroku-designed equipment without acknowledgment or monetary compensation. Kobayashi sent a letter demanding that North American groups cease performing these pieces and using these items unless they received approval from Oedo Sukeroku Daiko and paid compensation. Kobayashi followed up with a second correspondence instructing North American groups to study with a Sukeroku lineage teacher in the United States or Japan and to join a Sukeroku "club" if they wanted to continue playing the pieces (Wong 2004, 223–224). Kobayashi's demands fell largely on deaf ears. Virtually all taiko groups in North American integrate elements of the Sukeroku Daiko repertoire in their performances. Many of the most influential groups had been refining their technique and repertoire for decades before Kobayashi's letter arrived. A number also felt that their styles of taiko were different enough from Oedo Sukeroku Daiko that they should not be confused. Kobayashi's demands especially irked many ethnic Japanese in the first North American taiko groups, who felt that their cherished cultural heritage was now being claimed as property by members of the ethnic homeland (223–224).

Some conciliatory gestures were made in response to Kobayashi's claims, but there were problems on the Japanese side as well. The four original members of Sukeroku Daiko had difficulty agreeing on who should actually receive money from North American groups, because the pieces had emerged out of group collaboration. In addition, the dancer Sanada Minoru and the *shamisen* player Kowase Susumu had made significant contributions to the earliest Sukeroku pieces, but they no longer had any association with the group. Tensions that have simmered among the original members since they each went their separate ways also contributed to a lack of consensus. Some of these original members of the group, with whom I spoke, saw the claim as a somewhat crass move by Kobayashi to obtain more money for Oedo Sukeroku Daiko. (A couple, perhaps in an effort to be diplomatic, blamed the whole affair on Kobayashi's wife.) There was also the inconvenient but significant fact that none of the pieces had actually been copyrighted. In the end, no financial result came of the controversy. North American groups, to my knowledge, never sent any money to the Japanese group, and the former members of Sukeroku Daiko eventually relented in their demands.

These three episodes illustrate two broad instantiations of taiko in the wake of the taiko boom: on the one hand, its status as a symbol of "exotica," "the Orient," and "Japan," open to incorporation by Hollywood studios or appropriation by diasporic Japanese; on the other hand, its status as a proprietary expression of local culture, carefully guarded by those partly responsible for its creation and concerned with its integrity (and financial incentives realized therein). As I have argued throughout this book, these two processes of emplacement and circulation are closely related. Parochial expressions of locality are facilitated by interaction with people and culture from outside territorially circumscribed areas. Centrifugal pressures toward exchange, circulation, and standardization have been met by centripetal pressures toward provincialism, hierarchy, and localization.

At the same time, if there has been any trend in this study, it has been toward greater inclusion and less parochialism. This is true for the efforts of the Nippon Taiko Foundation, clearly aimed at establishing the technical basis for a nationally standardized taiko performance. The trend toward inclusion is also reflected by increased numbers of women interested in taiko. Should women remain active in the taiko community in large numbers, they will very likely change its earlier masculine orientation in a more gender-egalitarian direction. Finally, this deparochialization is illustrated by the emergence in recent years of professional groups with less of an attachment to regional identity and more of an interest in developing taiko as a performing art on its own terms. To the extent that these groups express a new Japanese taiko culture, they participate as well in the performative construction of that place called "Japan," but in a manner much more diffuse than the kinds of emplacement that emerged in earlier drives toward localization.

Even more recently, new information technologies of the Internet age have contributed to the movement and incorporation of Japanese taiko both in Japan and abroad. Most old and new professional taiko groups in Japan now have a pronounced web presence. YouTube videos of taiko groups in Japan and beyond are abundant, despite the relative lack of advertisement for taiko performance in the popular media. Even Kodo, the group for which I helped to construct a rudimentary website at the start of my research, now has a Twitter feed, Facebook page, blog, email newsletter, YouTube channel, and much enhanced website. New technology has made watching, appreciating, criticizing, and even copying taiko more possible than ever before. From this perspective, the controversy that erupted between Oedo Sukeroku Daiko and North American taiko groups represents perhaps the last gasp of efforts to extend abroad the proprietary localism that still resonates so powerfully within Japan. Is Oedo Sukeroku Daiko really going to chase down groups in Brazil, Malaysia, Germany, Australia, or Finland that have integrated elements of its repertoire? (Incidentally, Kodo has aggressively protected its products from manipulation by corporations but, to my knowledge, has not told taiko groups that have appropriated elements of their signature pieces to cease playing them.) Taiko, as least in its audiovisual form, is accessible to and open to interpretation by more people than ever before, regardless of their proximity to or long-term interest in Japan.

This movement of taiko is mediated not just by the slick flow of technology but also by the stickiness of cultural context. While the superficial appreciation of taiko abroad can lead to odd appropriations in film or to a sense that the propriety of local culture is being violated, the associations of audiences in Japan continue to work against the establishment of taiko as a performing art independent from festivity. After nearly thirty years as a taiko soloist, former Ondekoza and Kodo member Hayashi Eitetsu made the following comments in a newspaper interview:

> Ultimately, I have no real cultural position in Japan. As a taiko soloist, I'm not a performer of traditional Japanese music, but I'm not a performer of orchestral music either. I'm not playing "Western" music, nor am I playing typically "Japanese" music. Consequently, it's often hard for [Japanese] audiences to make sense of what I'm doing. To the extent that foreign audiences have few preconceptions about taiko, they tend to take my performance for what it is. By contrast, in Japan, where taiko has long had a presence in festivity and ritual, people tend to look through the tinted lenses of their preconceptions. When I used to say that I was a taiko performer, people thought that I traveled around Japan playing taiko in festival processions. They'd ask, "What do you do for work?" Of course, I recognize that it's always hard to do something new in the arts. But in the process of trying to develop taiko as a performing art in Japan I've also had to fight against the prejudices of audiences in my own country.[1]

Even after several decades in which ensemble taiko has developed as a performing art, Hayashi still finds himself betwixt and between popular Japanese divisions of musical genres into Japanese and Western. He is also frustrated by the lingering association of taiko with festivity in Japan. Surely if a performer as successful as Hayashi Eitetsu has to struggle with the continued association of Japanese taiko with festivity, other Japanese groups have to as well, even if they desire only to be appreciated as artists. Yet, while one can understand Hayashi's exasperation, it comes as no surprise that Japanese audiences continue to imagine taiko performance as a festival entertainment. Festivals continue to be the sites where the majority of Japanese experience live taiko performance, even if the social character of these festivals has changed over time. As I have argued in this book, there has been a close relationship between local and national government support for festivals and the growth of ensemble taiko groups in Japan in past decades.

NATIONALIZING AND LOCALIZING TAIKO IN MUSIC EDUCATION

This governmental role in shaping the development of Japanese taiko did not end with the support of festivity in the 1980s and 1990s. More recently, reforms of education policy and local administration seem to be pushing the development of taiko in opposite directions: both toward standardization and toward localization. It is unclear whether these policies will accelerate the spread of a generic style of taiko throughout Japan or contribute instead to the emergence of new kinds of localized performance.

In curricular guidelines implemented in 2002, the national government for the first time required music classes in public junior high schools to include exposure to Japanese musical instruments. More specifically, the curricular guidelines directed teachers to introduce students to at least two Japanese instruments over the three years of junior high school music (Monbushō 1999a, 5). This requirement is significant given the lack of precedent in the history of Japanese public music education. Prior to this reform, Japanese musical instruments had never been formally included in public school music classes since the establishment of mass education in the 1880s.[2] Taiko was one of the Japanese musical instruments included in the government directives, along with *shamisen, shakuhachi, koto,* and *shinobue* (short bamboo flute). In fact, the government even encouraged the use of taiko in the middle primary school grades, given the apparent ease with which they believed children could approach the drum—touch it and it makes a sound—in contrast to other Japanese instruments like *shakuhachi* and *shamisen* (Monbushō 1999b, 43–44).

In practice, however, taiko have been far less utilized than instruments such as *koto* and *shinobue* (Bender, forthcoming). Schools find it difficult to provide students with the drums, given their high cost. (Even relatively small taiko can run into the thousands of dollars.) Even if they are able to purchase or rent taiko, teachers have trouble controlling the loud rumbling of the drums, which can easily distract other students in the tight quarters of Japanese public schools. In addition, a number of teachers feel that their formal educational training, which still leans heavily in the direction of Western classical music, leaves them ill equipped to teach students how to play the instruments. If teachers want to learn how to play taiko at workshops sponsored by organizations like the Nippon Taiko Foundation, they are responsible for paying any costs on their own. As a consequence, many choose not to do so.[3]

Despite their relatively infrequent use in the classroom, taiko appear alongside other Western and Japanese instruments in assigned textbooks. In a textbook series used in 2008 by middle schools in the Kansai region of Japan, for example, taiko are featured in both the regular textbook used by first-year middle school students and in a special reference text on instruments used over three years.[4] In a manner very similar to the Nippon Taiko Foundation textbook discussed in the previous chapter, the reference text describes different kinds of *wadaiko* (Japanese drums) and presents pictures showing the correct way to hold drum mallets, position one's body, and strike the *chū-daiko* and *shime-daiko* drums. It also includes two practice exercises and two short pieces for *chū-daiko* and *shime-daiko* (Kyōiku geijutsu-sha 2007a, 28–35). One piece is newly composed, while the other is a new arrangement of a folk pattern from northern Japan. Rhythm patterns and shorter exercises are written in an adapted form of staff notation that places notes above or below a staff line to indicate a right-hand or left-hand strike. Below these notes are onomatopoeic *kuchi-shōga* vocables (the same notational style that is used in the Nippon Taiko Foundation's *Japan Taiko Textbook,* discussed in chapter 7.) There is no mention of the stylistic differences among taiko groups in Japan, but the text does note that *kuchi-shōga* can differ in pronunciation (33). Additional explanatory sections describe the use of taiko in ritual and festivity as well as its emergence "in the 1950s" as a form of group performance that has gained popularity "worldwide" (28–29). These sections also tell students about the importance of the mass media in popularizing ensemble performance throughout Japan, especially the performance of Osuwa Daiko at the Tokyo Olympics and Osaka World's Fair (29). All together, these eight pages of description are the most elaborate of any Japanese instrument presented in the textbook.

In its generic approach to taiko instruction, the text can be considered the culmination of a process started much earlier by organizations like the Nippon Taiko Foundation. Indeed, the exigencies of mass instruction all but require that taiko be presented in a nationally inclusive and generic manner; hence these texts signal the continued "disembodiment" of taiko at the very moment of its complete nationalization. Now a part of the national curriculum, taiko has surely earned its "citizenship rights," as Nishitsunoi Masahiro once hoped. Yet, while nationalization and "disembodiment" imply delocalization, the new curriculum may help foster new kinds of localized taiko groups based around school communities.

In fact, the national curricular guidelines are replete with suggestions that teachers interpret their application with "respect for the needs of local youth" (Monbushō 1999a, 1999b). Nothing in the guidelines prevents teachers from focusing on a local approach to drum playing instead of the generic approach presented in the reference text. Moreover, in the first-year middle school textbook, taiko are featured in a section on "improvisation." In text on either side of a photo of Hayashi Eitetsu playing an ōdaiko solo, the book suggests that students "improvise" based on a few sample patterns (Kyōiku geijutsu-sha 2007b, 36–37).[5] The textbook encourages students to expand on the basis of onomatopoeic vocables by building rhythm patterns around everyday Japanese phrases.[6] The intent here is not to indoctrinate students in one generic style of taiko but to encourage them to adapt the patterns as they wish. Examples of taiko's localization are presented just a few pages later in a section introducing students to the diversity of Japan's "regional music." Of the twelve forms of regional music indicated by dots on a map of Japan, half feature taiko prominently.[7] Intriguingly, given its postwar emergence, Osuwa Daiko is included as one of these regional forms.

Taken together, these textbooks seem to be pushing in two directions. On the one hand, generic approaches to performance are presented as "Japanese taiko," but, on the other, students and teachers are encouraged to adapt these techniques and rhythms to their own "local" needs and purposes. This emphasis on culture and creation appears to indicate that schools are being called upon to assist in the maintenance of culture, a responsibility formerly taken up by community groups outside schools. In fact, the new Fundamental Law of Education, revised in 2006, makes this official. The law states that the Japanese public education system should aim to "pass on tradition while facilitating the creation of new forms of culture" (MEXT 2006). This view of the role of the education system reflects a fear that institutions outside schools in local communities are failing to ensure the preservation of inherited forms as much as a hope that schools may newly take up this responsibility. Education in "traditional" Japanese music, both regional and classical, may not lead inexorably toward homogenization but to the emergence of new heterogeneous groups of local performers based around school districts rather than residential areas.

KODO, SADO, AND THE GREAT HEISEI AMALGAMATION

National policy affecting local cultural transmission has not been limited to educational reform alone. Roughly coinciding with the implementation of the new curricular reforms, the national government undertook one of the most significant reconfigurations of administrative districts in recent decades. The Great Heisei Amalgamation (Heisei Dai Gappei), as this reform is called (*heisei* refers to the imperial era, from 1989 to the present), took place between 1999 and 2006, and shrank the number of Japanese municipalities from 3,232 to 1,820. Amalgamation, the government believes, will help local governments better manage declining tax revenue and growing welfare burdens resulting from depopulation and an aging citizenry (Rausch 2006; Thompson 2008, 367). Regional areas, where depopulation and aging have been most severe, were most significantly affected by this reform. One of the first and most comprehensive programs of amalgamation took place in Niigata Prefecture, the administrative district that includes Sado Island.

In 2004, the ten municipalities on Sado merged to form a new "Sado City" (Matanle and Sato 2010, 189). Municipal administration was newly centralized on the island, with the former municipal units (and administrators) ceasing to have any official function. Local residents supported the merger in the hope that the new municipal administration would be better equipped to handle their needs in the long run. In the short run, however, the merger has forced these residents to adapt to new forms of affiliation and identity on the island, as the districts to which they formerly belonged have now disappeared.

The merger has affected the relationship between Kodo and its neighbors on the island as well, but not in an entirely negative way. This contrasts with other parts of regional Japan where mergers have also taken place. Christopher Thompson argues, for example, that the Great Heisei Amalgamation has negatively affected folk performing arts in a northern Japanese region he studied. For local Shinto dancing groups in the Ishihatōka hamlet of Iwate Prefecture, the Great Heisei Amalgamation "undermines the social and financial support structure that has enabled small rural towns and their locally based folk performance traditions to thrive during the postwar period" (2008, 368). This has caused some Shinto dance groups to fear that they may not be able to continue their activities in the future. Kodo is, by contrast, what I have called a "new" folk performing arts group, and it has never been as dependent for its operations on local government support as the groups in Thompson's study. That said, over the thirty years since its establishment on Sado, it has worked hard to cultivate good relations with the town of Ogi in which its Kodo Village was located prior to the merger. Since Ogi no longer exists as an administrative unit, Kodo, like other Sado residents, has had to reestablish its place on the island. In this sense, Kodo is likely similar to other new taiko ensembles in parts of Japan where mergers have taken place. Despite the ground shifting beneath Kodo's feet, it seems that the process of amalgamation has worked in Kodo's favor, even contributing to the emergence of a new, Sado-wide folk culture.

Soon after the merger, though, it did not seem that the process would work smoothly. This is illustrated best by the development of Kodo's annual performing arts festival, "Earth Celebration" (EC). EC is the event in which the group cooperates most closely with its neighbors on Sado. Each year Kodo invites a world music group to join it in a series of performances that cap off several days of smaller concerts and festival activities. Since its inception and prior to the merger, the group hosted the festival in collaboration with an EC Executive Committee made up of official representatives from the ten communities on the island. The mayor of Ogi Town chaired the committee, and members of the Ogi Town government played a large part in helping it succeed, while the other representatives had mostly ceremonial roles. After the creation of Sado City, the mayor of Ogi no longer chaired the committee (since the local government of Ogi ceased to exist). Instead, the newly elected mayor of Sado City, who happened to come from the town of Hamochi, took over as EC committee chair, and EC became a citywide event.

Even though the official change happened immediately, city officials were slow to show support for the festival. The feeling that EC was primarily an Ogi affair persisted. Over the next few years, however, the attitudes of the mayor and other city officials began to change. City officials started to see how many tourists, Japanese and foreign, the festival brought to the island. They gradually began to take a more active role in the event as they came to realize how much it benefited the island. The city now cohosts the festival with Kodo, allocating a portion of its budget to the festival and helping to advertise the event. The municipal-level recognition of EC has shifted patterns of participation in the event as well. For example, the festival has always had a flea market featuring the sale of handicrafts from Ogi and itinerant vendors from outside Sado. Following amalgamation and the support of the city, EC organizers have noticed that the number of vendors from all parts of the island has increased significantly. EC has now become one of the two major events on the island (along with the Sado Marathon).

Cooperation between the group and the new municipal administration now also extends significantly beyond EC. Since 2006, the Kodo Cultural Foundation, Kodo's nonprofit institution, has overseen the management of the "Sado Island Taiko Centre" (Sado Taiko Taiken Kōryūkan), known in Japanese more informally as the Tatakōkan. The word *tatakōkan* combines Kodo's global EC theme of *tataku* ("to beat a drum") with the notion of local "exchange/interaction" (*kōkan*).[8] Construction of the Tatakōkan was supported by the city of Sado in the hope that greater access to Kodo's taiko would help attract visitors to the island at times other than the summer. Under the management of the Kodo Cultural Foundation, the center now hosts over ten thousand visitors per year for workshops and taiko demonstrations. This success has not gone unnoticed by municipal officials. Longtime members of Kodo (and residents of Sado) have been asked to advise government officials on tourism and to serve on committees organized by the municipal government to devise a long-term plan for the island. Prior to amalgamation, members of the group had never been asked to participate in any kind of planning committee beyond the local level of Ogi Town.

A central premise of this book is that localization is closely tied to flows of people, ideas, and culture from outside a local community. Although the changes outlined above have taken place on Sado Island alone, it is important to note that this new relationship between Kodo and the municipal government has been facilitated by flows of people and ideas from outside the island. By this I mean not just tourists traveling to the island for taiko fun but also central government bureaucrats interested in promoting regional tourism and the success of regional amalgamation. In the past, the central government handled rural economic woes primarily through the redistribution of tax revenue and the support of major public works projects. As tax revenues have fallen, however, central government bureaucrats have become increasingly interested in enlisting nongovernmental organizations like Kodo and its Kodo Cultural Foundation to help devise solutions to local problems.

More than municipal government officials did at first, central government bureaucrats quickly took notice of the success that Kodo has had in generating interest in Japanese culture abroad. They recognized as well that Kodo had always publicly identified its activities with Sado Island, not just Ogi Town. As a result, they worked with Kodo to help facilitate access to new sources of revenue for the island. For example, with the support of the Kodo Cultural Foundation, Sado Island was selected to participate in the Tourism Renaissance Project, a national initiative to support travel to regional areas. Kodo's participation was vital to Sado's receipt of these funds; in fact, bureaucrats initially suggested that Kodo apply for the funds directly, but in the end the decision was made to apply for funds instead through the Sado Tourism Association. Portions of the money received through this program have been distributed back to the Kodo Cultural Foundation to assist its activities and to recognize its contribution. In this way, the circulation of Kodo throughout Japan and around the world has not only helped to establish further its base on Sado Island but also facilitated relationships of exchange, touristic and financial, that are helping to ensure the economic viability of the island into the future. The dreams of Den Tagayasu and the members of Kodo's antecedent group, Ondekoza, thus seem to be edging closer to reality.

Unintentionally, perhaps, these new national policies have also contributed to the preservation of Sado's inherited culture and to the support of new folk culture as well. In stark contrast to the dire situation of the Shinto dancing preservation in Thompson's study, the *ondeko* groups that provided the namesake for Ondekoza have been relatively unaffected by the creation of Sado City. Sado has 125 *ondeko* groups distributed over approximately 150 hamlets. These groups have historically received support from hamlet communities, so the amalgamation of Sado's ten towns had little effect on their sources of revenue. In fact, a Kodo member suggested to me that the disappearance of the towns has actually helped renew recognition of hamlet identity. The Kodo Cultural Foundation, in cooperation with another non-profit organization, has begun to host an "Ondeko Forum" twice a year at the Sado Island Taiko Centre, which helps to stimulate the preservation of these forms of ritual performance. Surprisingly, it has been the relatively new "local festival traditions" organized by the former towns on the island that have been most affected by the merger. Former town administrators have found it in poor taste to participate officially in these festivals, thus depriving them of key sources of leadership and support.

As further testimony to the improved relations between Kodo and the island community, the municipal government on Sado has started to allocate funds for elementary school students on the island to visit the Sado Island Taiko Centre. Students visit the Taiko Centre as part of their music classes or "integrated studies" sections meant to encourage involvement with the surrounding community. According to Tatsu, this new allocation of funds is rooted in the belief that the youth of Sado should all experience Kodo's taiko before leaving the island. Municipal support for the ensemble taiko of Kodo (and now Sado?) demonstrates how changes to educational policy and regional administration that ostensibly push toward nationalization and consolidation have instead encouraged the attachment of local youth to a new folk performing art.

The discussion of the taiko boom in this book thus ends where it began. New folk forms of performance emerge through attempts to express affiliation with local community in a context of circulating people, capital, and ideas. National government policies toward local areas unintentionally (and sometimes quite intentionally) facilitate the development of these expressions of local culture—culture that is not, strictly speaking, merely an inheritance from the past but is generated anew in the communities of the present.

NOTES

INTRODUCTION

1. Officially, they were known as Sado no kuni—Ondekoza (Sado's Ondekoza). The change to the name Kodo occurred in 1981, when Ondekoza's founder and manager left the group. I discuss this name change and the group's history in chapter 3.

2. Although it is the most precise English translation of *kumi-daiko,* "ensemble taiko drumming" is a rather cumbersome way to refer to these groups. For this reason, I use the terms *taiko ensemble* and *taiko group* interchangeably throughout the book. I also use the term *taiko* to refer both to a specific kind of drum and to the performance genre in which it is used extensively. Japanese sometimes signify taiko groups by the term *wadaiko,* which can be directly translated as "Japanese drum or drumming." The term is less specific than *kumi-daiko,* however, and can include kinds of percussion performance in which taiko are used but are not the focus of performance. I therefore avoid using it in this text, except in cases where it is used by informants.

3. *Boom (būmu* in Japanese) is a term borrowed from English and used generally in Japanese to signify a fad or trend (Kelly 1990, 69).

4. This number is a conservative estimate derived from information provided by a senior manager at Asano Taiko, one of the largest taiko manufacturers in Japan. With no official method of counting groups, it is difficult to arrive at more accurate figures than the estimates of longtime observers. (Consider the difficulty of arriving at a firm count of the number of jazz ensembles or rock groups in a given country, for example.) Nevertheless, few individuals with whom I spoke seriously challenged these numbers. Most agree that taiko has dramatically increased in popularity since its early days. I discuss the reasons for this increase in chapter 4.

5. More recently, it also has been released as a game application for the iPhone.

6. Since record company executives devised the category of "world music" in the late 1980s (Frith 2000), it has seeped into the popular and professional lexicon while being subjected to considerable scholarly commentary and criticism. For more on debates over the category of world music, see Erlmann 1996; Feld 1988, 1994, 2000; Garofalo 1993; and Guilbault 2005.

7. See Stevens 2007 for a discussion of the meaning of the prefix *J-* in contemporary Japan.

8. The classic text on Japanese music is William Malm's *Japanese Music and Musical Instruments*. It is not surprising that this book, published in 1959, did not discuss taiko ensembles, because they had emerged only a few years earlier. That relatively recent emergence also likely accounted for the absence ten years later of any mention of taiko ensembles in Kishibe (1969). In a revised edition of his text published as *Traditional Japanese Music and Musical Instruments* in 2000, Malm does note the emergence of taiko ensembles like Kodo, which he terms a "fad" (60n17). De Ferranti dispenses with musical genres altogether and focuses on instruments and the context of their use in Japan. Here taiko ensemble groups are mentioned briefly at the start of a section on varieties of Japanese percussion (2000, 40). Taiko groups receive fuller but anecdotal mention in Wade's *Music in Japan* (2004, 58–61) in the form of a brief postconcert exchange between the author and a taiko performer. In the comprehensive *Ashgate Research Companion to Japanese Music* (Tokita, McQueen, and Hughes 2008), David Hughes notes the emergence of taiko groups in the context of a longer entry on Japanese folk music but does not discuss them in detail. The *New Grove Dictionary of Music and Musicians* also contains a short entry on ensemble taiko (Alaszewska 2001).

9. Anthologies include Befu and Guichard-Auguis 2001; Craig 2000; Hendry and Raveri 2002; Lent 1995; Linhart and Frühstück 1998; Martinez 1998; Powers and Kato 1989; Skov and Moeran 1995; Tobin 1992; and Treat 1996. A notable exception is the contribution by Hugh de Ferranti in Allen and Sakamoto (2006). De Ferranti's chapter in that volume, however, focuses primarily on the Australian taiko ensemble TaikOz.

10. I would argue that this applies to Japanese-language sources as well. The most comprehensive scholarly work in Japanese is Mogi 2003. Aside from instructional textbooks too numerous to cite here, three books on taiko written by prominent drummers and observers contain useful if more limited information (Asano Taiko Co. 1995; Hayashi 1992; Oguchi 1993). Nishitsunoi (1985) also provides an influential analysis of taiko that is referenced in chapter 7. The significant amount of published research on North American taiko includes Asai 1985; Izumi 2001; Konagaya 2001, 2005; Powell 2004, 2008; Terada 2001; Tusler 1995, 2003; Wong 2000, 2004, 2005, 2006; and Yoon 2001.

11. The subject of what constitutes "tradition" within taiko performance is a complicated one, as I discuss in this chapter and throughout the book. The popularity of exciting new taiko ensembles has led to the reappraisal of folk performances from which many of them take inspiration. Many of these folk performances have come to be classed with newer groups in an emergent genre of *wadaiko* ("Japanese drumming"), which is one reason why I find this term less analytically useful than *kumi-daiko*. The motivations of these preservationist groups differ substantively from postwar taiko ensembles as I have described them above.

For these reasons, I think that categorizing taiko as "invented tradition" (Hobsbawm and Ranger 1983) or as a "revival" (Livingston 1999) is inaccurate. While there are surely many elements of invention at work in taiko ensembles, the lack of a self-conscious identification with tradition among postwar groups means that the concept of "invented tradition," and the related notion of "neotraditional," do not account best for their aims or motivations. In addition, while they commonly borrow motifs from regional drumming styles, these groups rarely attempt to "revive" these styles without modification. In this sense, taiko performance pieces are not copies of a forgotten art form but constitute originals in themselves. I take up issues related to authenticity and tradition within taiko more fully in part 2 of this book.

12. I should point out that my account of taiko drumming is limited to mainland taiko groups. I do not discuss, for example, the popular style of *eisa* drumming native to the islands of Okinawa in southern Japan. *Eisa* groups often perform together with mainland groups at national festivals, but they have a history and style distinct from the groups on which I focus in this volume. For a discussion of Okinawan drumming as interpreted by the Tokyo-based performer Kawata Kimiko, see Konagaya 2007.

13. The voluminous scholarly literature on "globalization" examines constructions of community and culture among increasingly mobile populations, ideas, goods, and services (Mazzarella 2004, 346). For some scholars, flows of people, capital, and culture imply that the long dominant organizing force of the nation-state is waning, as international organizations intrude on the domain of state institutions (Gupta and Ferguson 2002; Ong 2005), "global cities" (Sassen 1991) chip away at its sovereignty, or it recedes to just another node in an expanding "network society" (Castells 1996). For others, the global movement of people, capital, and culture entails a gradual blending or "creolization" of national cultures in an emerging "global ecumene" (Hannerz 1992). In a now classic analysis, Arjun Appadurai (1996) argues that growing disjunctures between flows of people and culture cannot be accounted for within current anthropological models. Instead, by extending Anderson's (1983) analysis of "imagined" national communities, Appadurai proposes a framework of five "-scapes" (ethnoscapes, mediascapes, technoscapes, financescapes, and ideoscapes) through which people "imagine" their place in the world (1996, 33).

14. The result is a simultaneous deterritorialization of culture and *re*territorialization of culture, a "lifting of cultural subjects and objects from fixed spatial locations and their relocalization in new cultural settings," what Inda and Rosaldo call "de/territorialization" (Inda and Rosaldo 2002, 12). This does not imply the aggressive assertion of locality in the face of encroaching "cultural imperialism" (Barber 1995; Tomlinson 1991), for doing so implies that there existed a pristine local culture prior to the intensification of global interaction. Nor does it imply that globalization has effected a homogenization of diverse local cultures. Rather, it suggests that scholars consider seriously the mutual imbrications of culture near and far, how the local is constituted in interaction with global flows (Tsing 2005).

15. Atkins (2001) investigates how Japanese musicians have attempted to adapt and authenticate jazz in Japan from the 1920s into the 1990s. The consistent ambivalence with which Atkins tells us Japanese have understood jazz over the years hints

at the incompleteness of this process of incorporation. In Atkins's study, however, Japan remains a bounded locality into which the foreign art form of jazz must be adapted. It is not clear what is "creolized" or "syncretized" other than the desire of Japanese musicians to claim the music as their own. By contrast, Condry's study of hip-hop in Japan moves the analytical lens away from showing how "something like hip-hop in Japan 'really is Japanese'" (2006, 17) to investigate how hip-hop in the *genba* (actual sites) of nightclub performance actualizes "a global Japan" (18). Condry deemphasizes questions of Japanese hip-hop's authenticity in favor of analyzing how Japanese appropriate hip-hop to express their position at the nexus of global-local interaction. Jennifer Milioto Matsue (2009) pursues a similar angle in her study of the underground Tokyo hardcore scene. Matsue argues that present-day Tokyoites are less concerned with the foreign origins of the music and more interested in using it as a means of "playing" with identity and resistance in a way that ultimately, and ironically, affirms dominant social values (43–47).

16. This Japanese term has been translated into English as "hometown" (Yano 2002, 17) and "native place" (J. Robertson 1991, 13), each an attempt to get at the affective loading of the original Japanese word. The word connotes a sense of "the [typically rural] place whence my family descends," which makes it better approximate an "ancestral village" in English than a mere hometown.

17. This literature is significant and wide ranging, and I reference only a few key examples here. Jennifer Robertson (1991) examines how local officials reimagined the municipal area of suburban Kodaira along the lines of the "native place" it now thoroughly encompasses. In a related vein, Theodore Bestor (1989) analyzes how local elites, who themselves claim long residence in the Tokyo ward in which he conducted his research, use the rhetoric of "traditionalism" to shore up political authority and undercut the political power of newcomers. In a sophisticated and stimulating analysis, Marilyn Ivy (1995) unpacks the rhetoric of *furusato* in the context of popular tourist campaigns and in community development plans to effectively reconstitute rural Tōno as a national *furusato*. Kelly (1990) traces how the conversion of Noh into a tourist attraction has affected authority and patterns of succession among local performers in rural Kurokawa. Keiko Ikeda (1999) investigates the transformation of a rural festival into a tourist event that draws visitors from far away in Japan. Millie Creighton (1997) and John Knight (1994) elucidate how *furusato* rhetoric has been manipulated in the marketing of products from rural locations. D. T. Martinez (1990) describes how local female divers *(ama)* have been transformed into the exotic objects of urban tourists eager to see this vestige of ancient Japan.

18. In an important contribution, Jennifer Robertson (1998a) has noted the coeval emergence of the *furusato* trope and the discourse of "internationalization" in 1980s Japan ("internationalization" shifts to "globalization" in the 1990s). For Robertson, Japanese assimilation of the foreign for touristic purposes and attempted replications of the *furusato* are congruent: "Touristified farm villages, international and Japanese historical theme parks, Dutch-style residences, and idiosyncratic mini-

nations are all sites where both 'pure' and hybrid forms of Japanese culture are inventoried, reified, transformed, contested, commercialized, and reproduced" (127–128). Robertson echoes globalization theorists who argue that differentiating territory as local, national, foreign, or familiar entails a "production of differences in a world of culturally, socially, and economically interconnected and interdependent spaces" (Gupta and Ferguson 1997, 43). In globalized Japan, touristified farm villages should be considered no more natural than touristified Dutch-style residences. Robertson's argument recalls Marilyn Ivy's brilliant analysis of Japan National Railway's famous "Discover Japan" campaign to encourage domestic tourism. Ivy notes that this was in fact a copy of the American campaign "Discover America"—evidence, she argues, of Japan's position in an "entirely global, advanced capitalist economy" (1995, 42).

19. There are of course examples of pop music and classical music that are identified by area. Puppet theater emerged in Osaka and kabuki theater in Kyōto, for example, and there are approaches to performance in these and other classical genres that differ based on region. Even with regard to pop music in the United States, it is not unusual to speak of music by its local origin (for example, Detroit house, Seattle grunge, Memphis soul, West Coast and East Coast hip-hop, and so on). In these cases, though, it is not an organic connection to a locale that identifies the music but a style of music that distinguishes a local "scene."

20. The full name of the law is "Law concerning the revitalization of tourism and selected regional commerce and industry through the implementation of events that incorporate regional traditional performing arts, etc."

21. In using the term "new folk," I want to make clear that this is an analytical term of my creation, rather than one derived from Japanese usage. I did not hear anyone refer to taiko in this manner in Japan during my fieldwork. This is in contrast to Finland, for example, where the term "new folk" has come into common use, at least among intellectuals, to signify newly composed works of folk music (Ramnarine 2003, xii). My usage also differs from Hughes' discussion of "new folk songs" that emerged in Japan in the late nineteenth century. "New folk songs" were composed for rural communities and the urban masses by professional artists based on the structures of traditional folk songs (Hughes 1991).

22. The administrative districts of Sado Island have since been collapsed into Sado City (Sado-shi).

23. In fact, three months before I began my fieldwork with Kodo, a female apprentice from France left the program for precisely these reasons. However, a male Japanese-American apprentice continued on to become a featured member of the group.

24. I later realized that my sense of what constituted instruction was quite different from that which prevails in taiko circles, a point to which I shall return in chapter 5.

25. During my time at Sukeroku Daiko, one woman was told to leave the school after Imaizumi found out that she had performed with a group in a different part of Japan.

1. Following the usage of Japanese scholars, I take "Japanese drums" here to refer to the kinds of drums used in "indigenous Japanese music"—that is, music that existed in Japan prior to the introduction of Western musical forms. This does not mean that these genres developed solely in Japan. Rather, the usage evinces a tendency in Japanese and American scholarship to see Japanese musical forms derived from Western influence as less capable of expressing Japanese sentiments than those extending from Asian sources.

2. Scholars of Japanese music might quibble with this conflation of folk and ritual music. Malm (1959), for example, distinguishes native Shinto and Buddhist ritual music from folk music. By contrast, Kishibe (1969) places Buddhist chanting in a category of its own and identifies Shinto ritual music with that of the imperial court. Complicating matters further, the line between the two can become blurry for reasons of political expedience. In appealing to the national government for help with the cost of preservation, early folklore scholars presented the folk performing arts as cultural tradition, even though many of these folk forms had been used only in religio-communal festivals. Classifying them as "traditional" did not violate constitutional prohibitions against state support of religion (see Saisu 1997). In this chapter, I classify folk and ritual music together, as this categorization best reflects how my informants expressed the social location and origins of their drums.

3. I use *chū-daiko* throughout to refer to these drums.

4. In practice, these categories do overlap—that is, there are local performances of Noh theater. Nevertheless, these performances are usually of canonical plays, not local customs.

5. The name of the area has changed since the time of my study. Mattō has been amalgamated into a larger administrative unit called Hakusan City.

6. "Road of Human Rights and Taiko Completed," Buraku Liberation News *[Kaihō shimbun]*, January 24, 2004, http://blhrri.org/blhrri_e/news/new129/new129 –01.htm).

7. The stage costumes of the group continue to bear a close resemblance to those worn by Jishōya's former group, Ondekoza. They are also similar to the costumes worn by Kodo.

8. This movement in Japan echoes others investigated by anthropologists around the world (see Wilson 1997).

9. The zones are the following: Northern Entrance Zone; Eastern Entrance Zone; Seaside Entrance Zone; Taiko Road Concept Zone; History Road Zone; Reflecting on Human Rights Culture Zone; Taiko Festival Zone; Taiko Maker Zone; and Information Dissemination Zone.

10. The Japanese text on the sign reads: "Beyond superficial differences, we are all citizens of the same world. Let's work toward understanding differences of custom and culture. Create a community with respect for human rights and zero tolerance for discrimination."

11. The position of the drummer on the left in this statue is associated with a

generic taiko style derived from a piece called "Ōdaiko," which was created by the taiko group Ondekoza in the 1970s. I discuss the creation of this piece in chapter 3.

12. Interestingly, informational literature for the road notes that this section was originally named the "Wadaiko Zone" (Japanese Drumming Zone). This was changed, according to the literature, to the "Taiko Zone [taiko used here in its generic sense as "drum"] ... in consideration of our fellow minority populations in Osaka: ethnic Koreans and Okinawa-born residents" (Osaka City Naniwa Human Rights Culture Center 2006, 16).

TWO. GENEALOGIES OF TAIKO I

1. This is not the case for the whole of Japan: *Kokura gion daiko* in Kyushu and *Chichibu yatai-bayashi* in Saitama Prefecture are exceptions. Oguchi was likely not aware of these styles at the time. From what he knew of festival drumming in Nagano Prefecture, the one drummer per taiko standard tended to be the general rule.

2. *Kakegoe* are also a part of Noh and kabuki ensembles. The *kakegoe* in Osuwa Daiko are used similarly to signal starting and stopping when playing, but they sound much more like the intimidating yells of martial artists than the subdued vocalizations of theater musicians.

3. This is Osuwa Daiko's translation. The problematic aspects of this piece are examined in more detail in chapter 7.

4. Osuwa Daiko was categorized along with several other groups in the "traditional performing arts" section of the opening ceremonies.

5. It is not uncommon to see women playing *Bon-daiko* in Japan these days. Informants told me that in the 1950s and 1960s, however, women never played. This contributed to the location of *Bon-daiko* as a site for masculine display.

6. Former members suggested that the failure of their managers to distribute earnings equally also factored into the decision of some to leave.

7. It was also suggested to me that the "demon drumming" *(ondeko)* of Sado Island influenced the development of this piece. Of course, Sado's "demon drummers" also inspired the creation of Ondekoza, the influential taiko ensemble discussed next.

8. I was unable to interview Den during my time in Japan. Attempts to contact him never bore fruit. Shortly after I returned to the United States from my fieldwork in 2001, he was killed tragically in a car accident. Unable to utilize firsthand information, I have drawn liberally on the recollections of those who knew him and on interviews of Den by others.

9. I use the name Den Tagayasu throughout this section.

10. This can also be taken to mean an absence of hierarchy.

11. By chance, during my fieldwork in 2000, Nippon Hōsō Kyōkai (NHK) broadcast a documentary series on Miyamoto Tsuneichi. The series, *Miyamoto Tsuneichi ga mita nihon* (Miyamoto Tsuneichi's Japan), was narrated by the journal-

ist Sano Shinichi and chronicled the life and works of Miyamoto, including his visits to Sado, his contact with Den, and his role in the creation of Ondekoza. The only remaining member of Kodo who was also a founding member of Ondekoza, Ōi Yoshiaki, was interviewed for the series about his recollections of the itinerant scholar. A brief discussion of Ondekoza and Kodo appears in a supplementary text accompanying the broadcast.

12. In fact, a framed letter Miyamoto sent to Ondekoza still hangs in Kodo's main office complex.

13. Given the proximity to Taiwan and Okinawa, it is likely that the style of taiko the older man played is similar to that used in Okinawan *eisa-odori*. *Eisa-odori* is a style of drum dance in which drummers wear a small taiko fastened onto the front of their bodies.

14. He remembers it in Japanese as *Nōson bungei kōwa,* but I can find no book by Mao under this title. The closest source in English is a book entitled *Talks at the Yenan Forum on Literature and Art.*

15. Two young women from this group later joined Ondekoza.

16. From Sano's description, it is difficult to tell whether Den used this phrase, meaning "traditional performing arts," or a related phrase, *minzoku geinō,* that is used to refer specifically to the folk performing arts. Although common usage of the "traditional performing arts" frequently collapses the distinction between "classical performing arts" and "folk performing arts" when Japanese music is opposed to "Western music" or "pop music," the two can be distinguished (see chapter 1). With the distinctions between the two in mind, it becomes clear that Den meant a revitalization of folk performing arts, since it is unlikely that Den, whose travels took him to many different regional communities, would have had in mind a revitalization of Noh ensembles, kabuki *geza* music and the like. That is not to say that Den would cut off Ondekoza from all sources of musical inspiration outside the folk performing arts. In fact, many of Ondekoza's initial instructors came from the world of the traditional performing arts. Nevertheless, the folk performing arts remained the most important musical inspiration for the group's repertoire.

17. During this speech, Den also admitted that he was making this plea because he had been unsuccessful in attracting local young people to join the group. This is significant because Den's original idea was to form Ondekoza out of Sado's youth for their own benefit and as a means of helping Masahiko Honma keep the young people of Sado interested in its culture. Ultimately, although a few members of Ondekoza did come from Sado, the majority of Ondekoza members, and Kodo members as well, have come from outside the island.

18. Of the six attendees who stayed on with Den, I was able to interview three. Two joined soon after the workshop came to a close and one joined later, after being aggressively recruited by Den. These interviews provided me with a good sense of why most individuals joined, and it is primarily on the basis of these interviews that I have written this section.

19. This gendered division soon changed, with men helping out with the cooking and women helping out with the production of crafts.

20. One former member recalled how the group became friendly with merchants at a market held occasionally on the island. These merchants sold food items that were soon to go rotten at reduced prices, so, as one group member wrote, the group was always eating black bananas. He also recalled that the group would sometimes receive surplus produce from friendly neighbors, including one occasion when they received dozens of seedless pumpkins, which they made into various dishes and feasted on for several days (Kashiwagi 1994, 26). An ethic of not wasting food, even if it was on the verge of going bad, accorded well with an emerging appreciation of manual labor and skillful cultivation of the earth.

21. The selection that appears in *Taikology* (Shinoda 1994), from which this quotation is taken, is excerpted from Shinoda's original essay.

22. Den has explained this conflation as follows:

> The *on* of *ondeko* used to have two connotations, one meaning "big" *[ōkii]* and the other meaning "shadow" *[kage]*. Since *deko* means "carpenter" (*daiku* in standard Japanese, *dēko* in Sado dialect), putting them together makes *on-no-dēko*, that is, *ondēko*, or "carpenters of the shadows" . . . . In the past, this word referred to miners working in Sado's "Gold Mountain." They used whale-oil lanterns to light their way in and out of the tunnels, and upon emerging were covered black with soot. . . . Most were exiles who lacked access to baths and must have looked quite fearsome to the locals. Once a year they would imitate the dances of the summer O-Bon season, making them look like demons *[oni]* dancing. In this way, the "carpenters of the shadows" became known by the homonym "demon drummers." To this word, I added the suffix *-za* to create Ondekoza. (Den 1994, 3)

23. *Iemoto* literally means "origin of the house." In practice, it refers to the highest authority in a particular school of the classical performing arts. Every legitimate classical musician is affiliated with a particular *ie* branch. One becomes an officially recognized member of the *ie* through a ceremony called *natori* (literally, "name-taking"), where the apprentice assumes the last name of the *iemoto* and a new first name to be used onstage. The process of succession used to take place within the family only (that is, from father to son) but this has become less frequent in recent years as *iemoto* have increasingly taken on students from outside their own nuclear families. The apprenticeship period before *natori* usually takes at least ten years.

24. Briefly, these included *Tsugaru shamisen* and *te-odori* from Aomori Prefecture; *yamabushi kagura* from Ōtsugunai, Iwate Prefecture; *oni-kenbai* from Iwasaki, Iwate Prefecture; *Chichibu yatai-bayashi* from Chichibu, Saitama Prefecture; *Yumigahama taiko* from Yumigahama Island, Tottori Prefecture; *Hachijō daiko* from Hachijō Island, Tokyo; *Gojinjō daiko* from the Nōtō Peninsula, Ishikawa Prefecture; and *hi no taiko* from Mikuni, Fukui Prefecture.

25. Ondekoza's taiko thus differs from the avant-garde dance form *butoh,* which was started in the 1960s as an attempt to fuse Western forms of dance with traditional Japanese dance. It can also be distinguished from attempts by Japanese composers such as Miyagi Michiyo and Takemitsu Toru to combine Western and Eastern forms of music in the early and mid-twentieth century.

1. This word is not restricted to the folk performing arts. There are also *hayashi* for Noh and kabuki. As was mentioned earlier, Ondekoza studied the *shime-daiko* playing technique used in *kabuki hayashi.*

2. There appears to be no record of why Den chose this piece. None of the members I interviewed knew why. Presumably, it was one form of folk drumming about which he had heard before starting Ondekoza.

3. Having heard only the Kodo version of this piece and imitations thereof, I was surprised when I went to the Chichibu festival and heard the feel of the original piece. My immediate reaction was that the locals were not very skillful performers, since I could not understand why they kept getting off beat. I did not realize at the time that they were playing the "correct" pattern that Ondekoza had had difficulty mastering.

4. The film was translated variously into English over the course of its several releases.

5. One of the great directors of his age, Itami Mansaku is also the father of Itami Jūzō, whose comedic films *Tampopo, A Taxing Woman,* and *The Funeral,* among others, have proven exceptionally popular with foreign and domestic audiences.

6. I refer here to the first two versions of the film, which are very similar in construction.

7. The nickname takes the word *muhō,* which literally means "lawless," and places it behind the first Chinese character of his real name, which reads *matsu,* or "pine." "Lawless" may be too strong a translation, since it is not so much that Matsugorō breaks the law as that he flaunts authority. In this sense, a better translation may be "unrefined" or "untamed." Throughout the movie, he is referred to by this name or by the sobriquet *Ma'-chan (-chan* is an affectionate honorific suffix that is less formal than *-san*).

8. We never learn the widow's first name. Throughout the movie, she is referred to only as Yoshioka's "wife" *(okusan).* This is not unusual for the society of the time or, for that matter, for Japan today.

9. Yomota makes much of this last connotation in his analysis (1996, 18). In his conception, public education was established in Europe to make young men literate enough to be effective soldiers, founded as it was in the reforms of Napoleonic France. In the Meiji era of westernization, industrialization, and militarization, Japan adopted a similar approach. Public athletic competitions functioned together with this new system of public education to simulate the organized execution of military exercises. Later, school-based athletic competitions would extend to the community, prefectural, and national level. The effect, Yomota contends, was to consolidate more of the Japanese populace under the umbrella of imperialist Japanese society. This contention aside, it is clear that organized sporting events appear together with industrialization throughout Asia (see Morris 2004).

10. This applies to the 1943 version of the film. The rhythms in the 1943 and 1958 versions of the film are different, but I have not been able to find out who created the rhythms for the 1958 version.

11. It would be no exaggeration to restate this as "urban Japanese" who had become unfamiliar with folk culture. The fact that the film was much more popular in urban areas than in rural areas supports this minor terminological correction (Otsuki 1996, 25).

12. A caveat: this form of dress is popular in festival processions throughout Japan.

13. Oguchi has said that the name of this piece derives from the historical fact that the Suwa area used to be a training ground for military horses (*Taikology* 1996, 64). I am skeptical of this explanation: the name is just too close, the expression too uncommon, and the timing too odd for this to be chance.

14. The group calls this piece "Kokura," which is of course the name of the "real" place in which the film is set. The rhythmic pattern used is the second one that Muhōmatsu plays in the 1958 version of the film. Even though the group's founder told me of his fondness for this film, he did not inform me of the specific connection to this piece.

15. The film also proved influential outside Japan (see Bender 2010).

16. This ritual, common to the Hokuriku region of Japan that includes Fukui Prefecture and Ishikawa Prefecture, is called *mushi-okuri*. The ritual is meant to rid agricultural fields of harmful pests and disease. Community members gather together and descend into the fields carrying torches and a drum. Two drummers wind their way along with the procession and play to the melodic accompaniment of a *fue*. It appears that the *hi no taiko* drumming style that Ondekoza learned had already been adapted for stationary performance on stage (Hayashi 1992, 57n3).

17. *Shaku* and *sun* are old Japanese standards of measurements used to describe the size of taiko, specifically the diameter of their heads. One *shaku* is approximately 30.3 centimeters and one *sun* is one-tenth of that, or 3.03 centimeters. Archaic as they may be, they are still the standard units of measurement in the manufacture of taiko today.

18. There is no record of taiko being played on such a festival cart anywhere in Japan other than in this film (Mogi 2003, 145).

19. Kodo programs used to say that the piece is "traditional," which means that it was originally inspired by a folk performing art. Now they say that it is a "Kodo arrangement." There is no direct reference to Mikuni taiko or to Hayashi's innovations, which, for the latter at least, is a source of some irritation.

20. The fisherman would unfurl the long piece of fabric that was tied into the *fundoshi* so that it would float up to those still on board, who would then help the man up.

21. Hayashi, however, does not recall this conversation taking place.

22. Other former members dispute Den's account of the encounter and his contention that Cardin played a central role in the change in costume.

23. In my experience researching Kodo, this fact has been made abundantly clear. In general, upon hearing about my research interests, most non-Japanese people would respond by saying, "Oh yeah, those are the guys that run all the time. They even played at the Boston Marathon, right?" even if they had never seen a per-

formance by Ondekoza, Kodo, or any other taiko group for that matter. It made no difference that this event happened over twenty years before or that all the members of the Ondekoza of the time had since retired. This is likely due to the tendency of journalists to continue to mention this fact in their articles about the two groups. Den was certainly prescient, but it is unlikely that even he considered how legendary the event would become.

24. I qualify this because the actual position of the drum is different than the one used in "Yatai-bayashi," in which the drums are placed sideways with the shell of the drum facing the audience. By contrast, in "Monochrome," the drums are placed so that their top heads face the audience. The position of the drummer at the drum is the same in both pieces. The shift in position and removal of clothing highlights the drummers' musculature.

25. These movements are so scripted, in fact, that they are pantomimed even during practice and dress rehearsal when *happi* are not worn.

26. The televised documentaries include *Moeru Ondekoza* (Ondekoza burns); *Hashiru, tataku, odoru jūgonin no wakamono* (Fifteen young people who run, drum, dance), which aired on Nippon TV on February 13, 1977; and *Seinen sasurai-bashi* (Song of a wandering youth), which aired on the TBS network on March 13, 1978. The documentary films include the aforementioned *Sado no kuni—Ondekoza* and *Ondekoza ni seishūn wo kaketa wakamono-tachi* (Coming of age in Ondekoza), which was completed in March of 1977. I have not been able to see any of these except for the Shinoda and Kato films. I am not aware whether copies of them are in circulation, but neither Kodo nor any other group mentioned them to me so it is unclear how much impact they had.

The second televised documentary was produced by the assistant director of *Sado no kuni—Ondekoza,* who, together with a three-man crew, traveled along with the group during its overseas tour in 1976. The second documentary film focused on the experience of Ondekoza members who had joined the group (or had been recruited by Den) primarily to run marathons. The group invited the American marathon runner Bill Rodgers to Sado, sponsored a marathon, and then filmed it in an effort to create a coming-of-age film. The third televised documentary followed Hayashi Eitetsu to the Tsugaru region of northern Japan during his journey to study folk *shamisen* with the master Yamada Chisato.

27. If not for a generous emergency equipment loan from the group's instrument supplier, Asano Taiko Corporation, the original group would not have been able to meet any of their performance obligations.

28. In its first few years of activity, the group went by the official name of Sado no kuni—Kodo (Sado's Kodo). Although the group name should technically have a macron over the second *o* when written in English, I have left it off in keeping with the group's preferred style of romanization.

29. While this may have been the case, it is also the case that an elaborate map of a prospective "Ondekoza Village" appears on the penultimate page of a promotional brochure produced by the group sometime in 1979 or 1980. While no informant could tell me definitively when it was made, it includes a history of Ondekoza run-

ning through the end of October 1980 as well as a short mission statement by Den Tagayasu, which suggests that the document was created during the period before he left the group. Despite Hayashi's suggestions, it seems unlikely that the concept of a "village" arose only in the period following Den's departure.

30. This is more intuitive in Japanese, where the word Hayashi created out of the Chinese characters for "drum" *(ko)* and "child" *(dō)* is homonymous with the word for "heartbeat" in Japanese *(kodō)*. Hayashi's recollection is also the only gendered reference to motherhood and femininity that emerged in the predominantly masculine recollections of former Ondekoza members.

31. The Chinese characters for this ship's name are the same as those used in the name of the company. The pronunciation is all that differs.

32. This style of playing has become nearly as ubiquitous in Japan as the form of *ōdaiko* performance that emerged earlier out of Ondekoza.

33. In a nod to the legacy of the native ethnologist Miyamoto Tsuneichi, one of Ondekoza's early supporters, Otodaiku also handled the sale of rice and persimmon varieties local to Sado until 2008.

FOUR. PLACING ENSEMBLE TAIKO IN JAPAN

1. Japanese scholars distinguish touristic festivals lacking the sanction of a particular "shrine spirit" from shrine-based festivals by referring to the former as "events" *(ibento)* and to the latter as "festivals" *(matsuri)* (Komatsu 1997). In practice, however, a firm distinction between the two is hard to maintain, as shrine-based festivals increasingly metamorphose into large-scale events. The everyday use of *matsuri* to refer to both kinds of celebration further confuses matters. In some cases, the word *matsuri* is written in the Japanese script used to represent foreign loanwords, thus connoting a sense of novelty or foreignness, but this custom is not standardized. Without background knowledge, therefore, it is often difficult to separate out communal festivals from newer events. Nevertheless, in my conversations with taiko drummers, the distinction between event-festivals *(ibento)* and shrine-festivals *(matsuri)* had considerable salience.

2. This is likely due to a functionalist bias that runs through this literature, making the focus the "collective effervescence" of participants rather than the dynamics of inclusion and exclusion.

3. In her important study of a citizens' festival *(shimin matsuri)* in suburban Kodaira, Jennifer Robertson describes how the festival is utilized as a means of improving relations between longtime residents, mostly former residents of the old village encapsulated by the urban neighborhood, and neighborhood newcomers, who migrated to the city from other regions in search of economic opportunity. As part of the city's "native-place making" projects the festival is "modeled after shrine *matsuri,* with the ostensible purpose of creating an 'old village' ambience within the suburban bedroom town" (1991, 38–39). However, these efforts to cultivate good

relations have been mostly unsuccessful. Rather than leading to more intimate ties, Robertson remarks, "this social interaction provokes and reinforces sectoral differences" between natives and newcomers (39).

Like Robertson, Theodore Bestor (1989) depicts the strife caused by the implementation of a new ward festival in a Tokyo community. As part of its "community-building" activities, the ward office started a "ward festival" *(kumin matsuri)* to encourage conviviality among the many administrative divisions of the ward. This "new" O-Bon festival was of a much grander "event"-like scale than those held in the ward's subneighborhoods, complete with dance troupes, a high drum tower, a miniature steam railroad, children's sumo, fireworks, and pony rides, among other events (Bestor 1989, 115). Although the office had hoped to instill a sense of solidarity among residents of the ward, many felt that the new festival needlessly duplicated and even intruded on annual festival customs already in its subneighborhoods. These two studies strongly suggest that new city or ward festivals not only are likely to be unsuccessful, but may even cause tension in the very communities they intend to serve.

4. For example, Scott Schnell (1999) mentions that the festival music–dance group he studied was formerly an organization composed of male residents who were household heads or household heirs in a delimited section of the town. In recent years, however, "the number of young people has declined to such an extent that practically any *resident male* who desires to join may do so" (121, my emphasis). Participation in the grand procession of taiko through this community has also shifted as a result of depopulation, especially the departure of young men. Whereas in the past, a participant in the taiko procession was required to be "a native of the town, unmarried, and the eldest son and designated heir of his household," the criteria have recently shifted to include those men "who were born and raised in the neighborhood and who have committed themselves to remaining there for the rest of their lives, or at least returning after a period of educational training or employment in some other area" (135). Ashkenazi (1993, 84) describes how festival participation in his field site in northern Japan demonstrates a "significant pattern of change from an exclusive and hierarchical form based on lineage to an egalitarian one based on neighborhood residence." Similarly, in a move that recalls the efforts of Masahiko Honma to preserve *ondeko* on Sado Island, some groups in southern Japan have broadened the criteria for inclusion even further by developing ties with local schools to train future generations of participants: "The roles of the dancers who perform *Yoron Jūgoya Odori* [in southern Kagoshima Prefecture] have reportedly been passed from father to son within certain families for four hundred and fifty years [but] . . . the community is now allowing certain dance roles to be taken by school students outside of the hereditary families" (Thornbury 1997, 64). These studies indicate that, while in some community festivals the emphasis on being a native-born, male member of the community remains, participation has begun to shift away from hereditary inheritance toward egalitarianism.

5. Schnell (1999) remarks that population decrease has led to the integration of girls into the festival procession: "Since there are no longer a sufficient num-

ber of boys to perform the festival music while riding the *yatai* [festival carts], two of the neighborhoods have had to open participation to girls as well. Though girls were traditionally prohibited from riding the vehicles, these two districts have opted for greater flexibility over the complete demise of their erstwhile traditions" (279). Folk performing arts groups in other parts of Japan have similarly seen the entry of women into festival folk ensembles (Thornbury 1997, 64). Christopher Thompson describes how, in the northernmost reaches of mainland Japan, one deer-dance (*shishi odori*) troupe, although previously composed exclusively of older male residents of the community, began accepting women as performers in 1990 and later "actively recruited boys and girls from all [neighboring] hamlets and neighboring cities. In 1994, membership in the troupe . . . and the Preservation Association were opened to anybody . . . whether or not they were born and raised in Ochiai" (2006, 140). In nearby Tōno, Marilyn Ivy finds that the traditional male inheritors of lion-deer dancing (also *shishi odori*) are being replaced: "The role of the sword-wielding warriors who dance opposite the masked lion-deer is now most often played by junior high school girls; not enough boys are interested to form the all-male troupes demanded by convention" (1995, 131).

6. In a footnote to his discussion of shrine-based festivals in the Tokyo ward in which he conducted his study, Bestor mentions that women, who were in the past customarily prevented from carrying the *mikoshi* (the shrine palanquin in which the deity resides during the festival) over concerns about the "ritual pollution of women," became able to carry the *mikoshi* in 1980 (1989, 310n11). Significant as this is, Bestor does not elaborate on why such a shift took place. Yet, because he also mentions that until the neighborhood obtained a new *mikoshi* two years later "almost no men in their teens or early twenties participated [in the festival]," (311n11) women's participation was likely due to a lack of available men. As if confirming the vector of change, Bestor notes that the new *mikoshi* attracted not only young men interested in joining the festival but young women in their teens and twenties as well.

7. With some resignation, Thornbury remarks that at an annual performance of folk performing arts held in conjunction with the National Youth Convention, which is divided between performances of "well-established" and "newly created" folk performing arts, the performances in the latter category "are almost exclusively drum (*taiko*) performances" (1997, 79). She also mentions that one seemingly exasperated Japanese folklore scholar noted, in his review of the 1994 National Youth Convention Performance, that "he would like to see something other than drums in the new performance category" (177n3). Without intending to, these two anecdotes confirm the thesis presented here—namely, that ensemble taiko groups have become pervasive expressions of a new folk performance culture in Japan.

8. In fact, research by the folklore scholar Yagi Yasuyuki found that there were at least four towns that planned to put Takeshita's grant toward the creation of ensemble taiko groups (1994, 40). Furthermore, Yagi found that grants to aid in the creation of taiko groups in the period from 1985 to 1993 averaged nearly two million yen per group (38–39), an amount more than sufficient to start a small group.

9. Nevertheless, in response to the increase in the number of groups, some orga-

nizations have produced instructional manuals that use staff notation to represent taiko performance.

10. In its popularity, especially with young people, taiko is similar to *Tsugaru shamisen,* a dynamic form of folk *shamisen* performance that originated in the Tsugaru region of northern Japan. Like ensemble taiko, *Tsugaru shamisen* increased dramatically in popularity during the 1990s when exciting young stars like the Yoshida Brothers and Agatsuma Hiromitsu generated mass interest in the folk form (Johnson 2006; Peluse 2005). Still, there are significant differences between the two popularized folk forms. While it can be as thrilling as taiko performances, *Tsugaru shamisen* tends to be performed by individuals or pairs, not ensembles. Furthermore, the lack of an association between *Tsugaru shamisen* and community festivity also differentiates it from the new folk performing art of ensemble taiko. Still, the widespread interest in *Tsugaru shamisen,* and the large numbers of new, nonlocal *Tsugaru shamisen* players, reflects a growing appreciation for folk instruments like taiko.

FIVE. (DIS)LOCATING DRUMMING

1. There are some international referents as well. One example is the *samul nori* drumming of Korea. A modern interpretation of Korean drumming styles, *samul nori* incorporates synchronized movements and dance-like hops with drumming (Hesselink 2004). Farther away, in South America, Brazilian *capoeira* mixes drumming, dancing, and martial arts in a kind of dance-music-sport combination.

2. Although I do not develop the gendered elements of these ideas here, this "Japanese body" should be understood as a masculine one. I discuss the implications of development of taiko aesthetics around male bodies in the following chapter.

3. For an analysis of taiko discourse and practice that draws on Pierre Bourdieu's (1977, 1990) concept of *habitus,* see Bender 2005.

4. This is the case for the mallets used to play mid-size *chū-daiko* and large *ōdaiko* drums. Smaller, tightly strung *shime-daiko* drums are played with "sticks" that are approximately the same size as Western drumsticks (about half an inch in diameter or smaller).

5. The Chinese character for this word is used differently in two locales in Japan, Kyoto and Tokyo, to reflect the stereotypical character of each place. The reading of the character of the word in Kyoto, *sui,* comes from the Chinese reading of the character and connotes the effete sensibility of courtly life and aristocratic privilege, whereas the Japanese reading of the character as *iki* that is common in Tokyo evokes the urbane sophistication of the merchants and artisans of old Edo. The word is thus related to feudal distinctions between Kyoto as the seat of imperial court culture and Edo as the bastion of the shogunal authority, and gender differences, with the former connoting masculinity and the latter femininity. Today, the term extends beyond the regional distinction between eastern Japan and western Japan to encompass the metropolitan area of Tokyo, with its new "high" city (Yamanote) and

older "low" city *(shitamachi),* the former representing cosmopolitanism and super-ficial westernization and the latter representing rustic tradition and autochthonous authenticity (cf. Kondo 1990; Kuki 1979; Seidensticker 1983). The topographical distinction here between "high" and "low" city maps onto the distinctions between foreigner and Japanese as well.

6. *Gaijin,* which literally means "outside person," is often translated as "for-eigner." The word is a shorter form of *gaikokujin,* which literally means "outside country person." In common parlance, *gaijin* tends to refer (somewhat pejoratively) more to white, Euro-American foreigners than to those of Asian or African ancestry.

7. The reverse of this logic holds as well. As informants often told me, Japanese people face difficulties when they try to mimic non-Japanese genres of performance. While a Japanese person's attempt to learn how to play Latin percussion or African drums may be an endeavor worthy of respect, it is believed that a Japanese person will never be able to perform those styles as well as a native. By implication, a for-eigner will never be able to play ensemble taiko, despite its novelty and regardless of experience, as well as a Japanese person.

8. Much like Hayashi's anecdote, after my teacher told me the story of the *gai-jin yukata* (summer kimono), he realized there was a problem with his story. Rich-ard and I were both foreigners, but of different physical types. He thought about it a moment more, and then looked at me again and said: "But, you know, you don't look like the typical *gaijin.*" He then glanced over at another student in the class, Hayashi, who was about the same height as Richard, and said: "You look more Japa-nese than Hayashi." Alas, my similarity in stature to an average Japanese man did nothing to accelerate the pace with which I acquired Sukeroku technique, nor did it lessen the frequency of comments about my foreignness in future lessons. His correction, however, speaks to the way in which notions of national difference are reproduced even in the face of obvious challenges to their validity.

9. This was the cost of the program during my fieldwork with Kodo in 2000–2001.

10. The relationship between the Apprentice Centre and the local community is symbolic on a number of levels. For one, idealistic former urbanites, like the manag-ers of Kodo, newly populate spaces—such as this abandoned schoolhouse—that are material representations of depopulated rural communities. At the same time, the relationship of landlord and tenant, which replicates that of native and newcomer, affirms the persistence of attitudes toward land ownership and a reluctance to sell to newcomers in provincial areas like Sado. In effect, the Apprentice Centre itself speaks to Kodo's larger project to (re)establish community and culture in rural areas like Sado and the resistance of locals to realization of this goal.

11. The idea that an apprentice must "steal" a set of skills from a master is not uncommon in Japan or elsewhere (see Herzfeld 2004; Singleton 1989).

12. Kodo is also legendary for the long runs (approximately ten kilometers) that apprentices embark on every morning. While long-distance running obviously requires intense physical and mental discipline, it also helps apprentices develop the leg and hip strength necessary to perform the folk dances and drumming in the

apprentice program. In this sense, long-distance running is conceived as a contemporary method of building the physical strength formerly wrought through daily physical labor.

13. The apprentices were in charge of maintaining two vegetable fields, one adjacent to their living/working space and one on the grounds of Kodo Village, to which they shuttled as needed.

14. Informants explained the reason for this practice variously. One rationale emphasized the ability of this practice to help develop ambidexterity. A few senior members mentioned that it was a trick learned from a *shamisen* player who did it for the very same reason. Another explanation, offered by a supervisor of the program, was that increased use of the left hand stimulates the right side of the brain, where creative faculties are believed to be concentrated. Regardless of which is correct, eating with the left hand has been a group custom for a long time, and it is yet another way that the bodies of the apprentices are disciplined in a distinctive manner. In fact, one enthusiastic apprentice went so far as to write his daily entries in the Apprentice Centre diary with his left hand instead of his right.

15. Of course, this is a statement of considerable generality, but it is true that many apprentices told me that they had not sat in *seiza* much before coming to the Apprentice Centre and did find it a difficult adjustment.

16. Kodo's stage performance features pieces inspired by the folk performing arts, pieces written for the group by outside composers, and pieces created by performing members themselves.

17. I put the word "original" in quotation marks because the version of Miyake Daiko that Kodo learned—*Kamitsuki kiyari daiko*—differs from the version performed by the local preservation society.

18. In the case of drum pieces built on the aforementioned folk drumming of Miyake Island and Chichibu City, native practitioners from these local areas have granted Kodo permission to use elements of their folk drumming in performance.

19. In accordance with Japanese law, Kodo's copyrights do not extend to pieces in their repertoire originally inspired by the folk performing arts. In essence, they are shared, not owned.

SIX. WOMAN UNBOUND?

1. While this is true in the realm of myth, some folklore scholars have claimed on the basis of historical evidence that female shamans and Shinto shrine maidens were among the first taiko drummers on the Japanese archipelago (Nishitsunoi 2001, 2–3; Konagaya 2007, 82–84).

2. While to my knowledge there is no data on the gender distribution of taiko groups nationwide, the claim regarding the relatively equal number of male and female drummers proved true in my own observations and in those of others I encountered in my research. In addition, older drummers confirmed that this gen-

der balance was a recent (post-1980s) phenomenon. More comprehensive data is obviously needed to strengthen these anecdotal claims. At this point, though, it is important to stress that equality of gender representation within groups does not mean equality of participation.

3. The gender ideology of "good wife, wise mother" *(ryōsai kenbo)* symbolized the stance of the Meiji government toward women. Women were expected to serve the state by being supportive wives and nurturing mothers. While women were unable to participate actively in the public sphere, the Meiji state newly appreciated the importance of women's literacy and education. Meiji leaders believed that only with education could women effectively rear the next generation of soldiers and civil servants (see Gordon 2009, 111–112).

4. The fear of a slippage between onstage persona and offstage personhood has been less of an issue for kabuki theater. In some cases, such a slippage was encouraged (J. Robertson 1992b, 424).

5. This is particularly surprising in the case of Takarazuka, because the majority of its audience and fan base is women (J. Robertson 1998b).

6. To be precise, Yumi is referring here to the role that men have in playing the three *chū-daiko* in "Miyake." These drums are typically played by men clad only in loincloths. Women do play the smaller, high-pitched *shime-daiko* that provide a steady underlying rhythm for the players on the larger taiko.

7. The piece "Hana Hachijō" is an exception. In this piece, a female taiko drummer dressed in a kimono plays solo on a medium-sized taiko that is mounted horizontally on a stand at eye level. The piece derives from a folk performing art native to the island of Hachijō, where historically a woman and a man would play the drum together. Even though the contemporary inheritors of Hachijō drumming are mainly men, it remains as the only recent example of folk taiko drumming where women traditionally played as often as, if not more than, men. One reason for this is the performance context. In contrast to most types of folk drumming, Hachijō drumming was never a part of any religious occasion. Instead, people played it for fun at parties in their homes, where concerns over pollution or purity did not apply. Still, even though it had been practiced by women in the group for a couple of decades, "Hana Hachijō" was not added as a performance number until 2000–2001.

8. Amanojaku's website, accessed June 25, 2009, at http://amanojaku.info.

9. Honō Daiko's website, accessed June 25, 2009, at http://www.asano.jp/hono.

10. Other new groups featuring female performers, such as Gocoo and Wappa Daiko, similarly look to use the drum in new ways, borrowing from Western drum techniques and mixing taiko with electronic drum music and other percussion instruments.

11. During my fieldwork, none of the actively performing male members of Kodo or Ondekoza lifted weights to help build their bodies for taiko performance. To my knowledge, supplemental weight lifting is rare for men in other taiko groups as well.

12. This reflects a mixture of gender and status. "Ōdaiko" tends to be particularly valued in a performance. Playing it is a sign of seniority and status within a taiko group, and it is still the case for most groups that senior members tend to be men.

13. Women also play taiko alongside male members of the group in another piece entitled "Zoku." However, from the beginning, "Zoku" was intended as a piece that featured all members of the group playing together. In contrast, "Chonlima" formerly had been played only by men, and only the better male players of the group at that. Still, since Tomomi's debut, opportunities for women to drum alongside men have increased.

14. Tomomi's experiment with this new small group was relatively short-lived. She has since left the group to start a family, affirming the maternal ideology of cocon and conforming to the patterns of women in other taiko groups. With her departure, cocon ceased its performance activities.

SEVEN. THE SOUND OF MILITARISM?

1. The difference in meaning between *wadaiko* and *Nihon no taiko* is subtle. *Nihon* is the word for "Japan" in Japanese. The phrase *Nihon no taiko,* therefore, expresses something akin to "the taiko of Japan," a phrase with a more modern nuance than the contrastive *wa-,* which connotes timeless, essential aspects of contemporary Japanese society. *Wa-* was also a part of the name for Japan—*Wa no kuni*—before it became *Nihon* (though the former uses a different Chinese character for *wa-* than is used in *wadaiko*), giving it a more archaic feel.

2. I borrow the concept of "disembodiment" from the anthropologist John Traphagen's (2000) work on the social consequences of mental and physical decline in rural Japan. Traphagan argues that succumbing to *boke*—preventable mental and physical decline—leads to an individual's disengagement from the cycles of obligation and reciprocity that are fundamental to the smooth operation of rural society. Proper behavior within the often fraught relations among neighbors is cultivated over many years and expressed through embodied action and patterns of speech. However, this changes once a person begins to suffer from *boke.* Having lost personal control over mental and physical functions, Traphagan argues, "the *boke* person *disembodies* basic Japanese notions of how people should interact" (155; emphasis added). The social implications of physical decline among Traphagan's informants correlate well with the interest of taiko drummers in the social meaning of physical movement and bodily comportment. In each case, physical control over movement indexes the incorporation of local values. Much like the *boke* individual, the textualization of taiko *disembodies* taiko in a manner that undercuts the expression of localized meanings exemplified in performance and direct instruction. Given these implications, the process of disembodiment and textualization seemed destined to provoke tension among the taiko drummers it intends to serve.

3. In analyzing the emergence of "Japan Taiko" as a cultural category, I draw on the work of the French philosopher-historian Michel Foucault (1980, 1995), who argues that the rendering of new categories into discourse is always bound up with relations of power. The ability to define, classify, and analyze—that is, to create and

manipulate "knowledge"—is inextricably tied to the power to inscribe this knowledge in texts and on bodies. In brief, the power to define reality and to authorize knowledge about it is always founded on the power to control. While the authoritative power to control has traditionally been assigned to state institutions (what Foucault calls "macro-power"), Foucault's thinking suggests instead that relationships between power and knowledge permeate through society beyond the state. Ostensibly apolitical knowledge produced by natural and social scientists does not merely reflect a preordained reality but in fact constructs the very "objective" world it seeks to explain. The inscription of this generative process in texts, the marking of black script on a white background, effectively mirrors how representation slices the world up into new units of analysis. For these reasons, it should not be surprising that the transformation of a wide diversity of drumming styles into "Japan Taiko" engaged scholarly research, well-financed national organization, and textual production.

4. Incidentally, the taiko group featured in *Rising Sun* is the San Francisco Taiko Dojo, a group started by Seiichi Tanaka, a Japanese expatriate and former student of Oguchi.

5. Misha Schubert, "Veterans Win Fight to Silence Drums of War," *The Weekend Australian*, August 7, 1999.

6. In addition to the Bon festival, Mayumi and Makoto also organized a "Peace Concert" for that summer. It is possible that pacifistic beliefs also factored into her appraisal of taiko performance.

7. Written records indicate that one of these drummers was an ancestor of Oguchi's, Oguchi Seidayū.

8. There is really no convincing explanation for this. Oguchi blames the cessation on the decrease in qualified drummers resulting from the wars of the time.

9. The same English pamphlet explains the origin of "Thunder at Suwa" (their translation) as follows:

> The awe-inspiring, ominous sounds of thunder in the Suwa area, which is surrounded by mountains and hence has the form of a bowl, reverberate through the entire area with great force. This composition reproduces the effects of that thunder as music for drums. The original piece was used in prayers for rain and for a bountiful harvest, and later was performed in prayers for victory in battle, including one of the most famous battles in the history of Japan's Middle Ages, the battles of Kawanakajima between Takeda Shingen and Uesugi Kenshin. When the shells are blown, and all percussion instruments are mustered for the performance, we can well imagine the way the music engendered fighting spirit among warriors before a battle.

10. One caveat: In its original formulation (Nishitsunoi 1985), the name "Osuwa Daiko" does not actually appear on the typology Nishitsunoi created. Instead, in the place where "Osuwa Daiko" appears in later versions of the typology (for example, in taiko textbooks discussed later in this chapter), Nishitsunoi writes "Okaya Daiko." This perhaps reflects Nishitsunoi's initial recognition of Osuwa Daiko's complicated origins.

11. The composer Maki Ishii, who composed Ondekoza's "Monochrome" (see

chapter 3), has also referred to the type of drumming performed by "new" ensemble taiko groups such as Ondekoza as *Nihon taiko,* rather than *wadaiko,* because, in his opinion, it represents a new kind of taiko performance, different from either classical or regional types. Although it differs in formulation from Nishitsunoi's, Ishii's nomenclature demonstrates a similar aversion to the use of *wadaiko* (see Ishii 1994).

12. This is now the Ministry of Land, Infrastructure, Transport, and Tourism.

13. The Imperial Rescript on Education was a fixture of classrooms from the late nineteenth century until the end of the war. It pledges filial piety and undying loyalty to the Japanese emperor.

14. The word *kokusui* is usually translated as "ultranationalism." Here my informant may also be making reference to the prewar political party Sasakawa led, which was called the Ultranationalist People's Party.

15. Interview on March 22, 2001.

16. "Yamato" is the name of a clan that took political control of Japan in the fourth or fifth century. During the various wars of the early twentieth century, the "Soul of Yamato" was believed to be carried in the blood of all Japanese, uniting soldiers with their ancestors and their imperial authority. The term "Soul of Yamato" evokes the nationalist sentiments of wartime Japan.

17. An *iemoto* is the founder of an artistic lineage. An *iemoto system* refers to the dominance of hierarchical control over instruction and performance in classical theatrical ensembles, among other traditional arts.

18. The members of Dengakuza have posted their correspondence with Oguchi about this issue online. The documents can be accessed at www.matsuri-kobo.com/texto2/body.html.

EPILOGUE

1. Interview with Hayashi Eitetsu, *Asahi Shimbun* [Asahi newspaper], October 25, 2010, http://doraku.asahi.com/hito/interview/html/101025.html.

2. In 2008 there was another revision to the 1998 reforms. These had the effect of furthering, rather than curtailing, the reforms of 1998.

3. Over a seven-month period in 2008, I observed music classes at fifteen schools in western Japan to investigate the implementation of these new guidelines for public music education. I have based the arguments in this section on data collected in these observations, interviews with music teachers, and analysis of key documents and texts relating to music education.

4. The Ministry of Education, Culture, Sports, Science and Technology must approve all textbooks used in Japanese schools. Even though this is just one of many possible textbooks, it is representative of the kinds of texts that the national government promotes.

5. The inclusion of Hayashi playing taiko is perhaps complimentary, but it is also ironic, since most performances of "Ōdaiko" are not improvisational.

6. Kodo and other taiko groups use this technique in workshops as well. It helps beginners coordinate the movement of their bodies with the kinds of sounds and rhythms that they hope to make.

7. These include many of the drumming forms introduced in this book, such as *ondeko* (Sado Island), *gion daiko* (Kokura, Kyushu), *sansa-odori* (Iwate Prefecture), and *eisa-odori* (Okinawa Prefecture).

8. A literal translation of this name might be something like "let's learn about each other by playing taiko together."

REFERENCES

Alaszewska, Jane
2001 "Kumi-daiko." In *The New Grove Dictionary of Music and Musicians* 14:21–22. Albany: State University of New York Press.

Allen, Matthew, and Rumi Sakamoto, eds.
2006 *Popular Culture, Globalization and Japan.* New York: Routledge.

Allison, Anne
2006 *Millennial Monsters: Japanese Toys in the Global Imagination.* Berkeley: University of California Press.

Ames, Walter
1981 *Police and Community in Japan.* Berkeley: University of California Press.

Anderson, Benedict
1983 *Imagined Communities: Reflections on the Origin and Spread of Nationalism.* London: Verso Editions.

Aoyagi, Hiroshi
2005 *Islands of Eight Million Smiles: Idol Performance and Symbolic Production in Contemporary Japan.* Cambridge, MA: Harvard University Asia Center.

Appadurai, Arjun
1996 *Modernity at Large: Cultural Dimensions of Globalization.* Minneapolis: University of Minnesota Press.

Asai, Susan
1985 "Horaku: A Buddhist Tradition of Performing Arts and the Development of Taiko Drumming in the United States." *Selected Reports in Ethnomusicology* 6:163–172.

Asano Taiko Co., ed.
1995 *Wadaiko ga wakaru hon* [Understanding taiko]. Mattō-shi, Japan: Asano Taiko.

Ashkenazi, Michael
1993 *Matsuri: Festivals of a Japanese Town.* Honolulu: University of Hawaii Press.

Atkins, E. Taylor

2001   *Blue Nippon: Authenticating Jazz in Japan*. Durham: Duke University Press.

Barber, Benjamin

1995   *Jihad vs. McWorld: How Globalism and Tribalism Are Reshaping the World*. New York: Times Books.

Befu, Harumi

2001   *Hegemony of Homogeneity: An Anthropological Analysis of "Nihonjinron."* Melbourne, Australia: Trans Pacific Press.

Befu, Harumi, and Sylvie Guichard-Auguis, eds.

2001   *Globalizing Japan: Ethnography of the Japanese Presence in Asia, Europe, and America*. New York: Routledge.

Ben-Ari, Eyal

1992   "Uniqueness, Typicality, and Appraisal: A 'Village of the Past' in Contemporary Japan." *Ethnos* 57 (3–4): 201–218.

Bender, Shawn

2005   "Of Roots and Race: Discourses of Body and Place in Japanese Taiko Drumming." *Social Science Japan Journal* 8 (2): 197–212.

2010   "Drumming from Screen to Stage: Ondekoza Ōdaiko and the Reimaging of Japanese Taiko." *Journal of Asian Studies* 69 (3): 843–867.

Forthcoming   "Making Music-Making Kids: Japanese Music Education in the Twenty-First Century."

Bestor, Theodore

1989   *Neighborhood Tokyo*. Stanford, CA: Stanford University Press.

Bondy, Christopher

2010   "Understanding Buraku Inequality: Improvements and Challenges." *Contemporary Japan* 22 (1/2): 99–113.

Bourdieu, Pierre

1977   *Outline of a Theory of Practice*. Translated by Richard Nice. Cambridge, UK: Cambridge University Press.

(1980) 1990   *The Logic of Practice*. Translated by Richard Nice. Stanford, CA: Stanford University Press.

Brumann, Christoph

2009   "Outside the Glass Case: The Social Life of Urban Heritage in Kyoto." *American Ethnologist* 36 (2): 276–299.

Castells, Manuel

1996   *The Rise of the Network Society*. Cambridge, UK: Blackwell.

Chung, Erin Aeran

2006   "The Korean Citizen in Japanese Civil Society." In *Japan's Diversity Dilemmas*, edited by Soo im Lee, Stephen Murphy-Shigematsu, and Harumi Befu, 125–149. New York: iUniverse.

Coaldrake, A. Kimi

1997   *Women's* Gidayū *and the Japanese Theatre Tradition*. New York: Routledge.

Condry, Ian
   2006   *Hip-Hop Japan: Rap and the Paths of Cultural Globalization.* Durham: Duke University Press.

Connell, R. W.
   1995   *Masculinities.* Berkeley: University of California Press.

Craig, Timothy J., ed.
   2000   *Japan Pop! Inside the World of Japanese Popular Culture.* Armonk, NY: M. E. Sharpe.

Creighton, Millie
   1997   "Consuming Rural Japan: The Marketing of Tradition and Nostalgia in the Japanese Travel Industry." *Ethnology* 36 (3): 239–254.

Cresswell, Luke, and Steve McNicholas
   2002   *Pulse: A Stomp Odyssey.* Los Angeles: Walden Media.

Dale, Peter
   1986   *The Myth of Japanese Uniqueness.* New York: St. Martin's Press.

Daventry, Paula, ed.
   1981   *Sasakawa: The Warrior for Peace, the Global Philanthropist.* Oxford, UK: Pergamon Press.

De Ferranti, Hugh
   2000   *Japanese Musical Instruments.* New York: Oxford University Press.
   2006   "Japan Beating: The Making and Marketing of Professional Taiko Music in Australia." In *Popular Culture, Globalization and Japan,* edited by Matthew Allen and Rumi Sakamoto, 75–93. New York: Routledge.

Den Tagayasu
   1994   "Oni-tachi no ruzan" [Exile of the demons]. Interview with Den Tagayasu. *Taikology* 10:2–10.

DeVos, George, and Hiroshi Wagatsuma
   1966   *Japan's Invisible Race.* Berkeley: University of California Press.

Donoghue, John
   1978   *Pariah Persistence in Changing Japan: A Case Study.* Washington, DC: University Press of America.

Endo, Kenny
   1999   "Yodan Uchi: A Contemporary Composition for Taiko." MA thesis, University of Hawaii.

Erlmann, Veit
   1996   "The Aesthetics of the Global Imagination: Reflections on World Music in the 1990s." *Public Culture* 8:467–487.

Feld, Steven
   1988   "Notes on World Beat." *Public Culture* 1 (1): 31–37.
   1994   "From Schizophonia to Schismogenesis: On the Discourses and Commodification Practices of 'World Music' and 'World Beat.'" In *Music Grooves: Essays and Dialogues,* edited by Charles Keil and Steven Feld, 257–289. Chicago: University of Chicago Press.
   2000   "Sweet Lullaby for World Music." *Public Culture* 12:145–171.

Foreman, Kelly

2005   "Bad Girls Confined: Okuni, Geisha, and the Negotiation of Female Performance Space." In *Bad Girls of Japan,* edited by Laura Miller and Jan Bardsley, 33–48. New York: Palgrave Macmillan.

Foucault, Michel

(1977) 1995   *Discipline and Punish: The Birth of the Prison.* Translated by Alan Sheridan. New York: Vintage Books.

1980   *Power/Knowledge: Selected Interviews and Other Writings, 1972–1977.* Edited by Colin Gordon. Translated by Colin Gordon, Leo Marshall, John Mepham, and Kate Soper. New York: Pantheon Books.

Frith, Simon

2000   "The Discourse of World Music." In *Western Music and Its Others: Difference, Representation, and Appropriation in Music,* edited by Georgina Born and David Hesmondhalgh, 305–322. Berkeley: University of California Press.

Fujie, Linda

2001   "Japanese Taiko Drumming in International Performance: Converging Musical Ideas in the Search for Success on Stage." *World of Music* 43 (2–3): 93–101.

Garofalo, Reebee

1993   "Whose World, What Beat: The Transnational Music Industry, Identity, and Cultural Imperialism." *World of Music* 35 (2): 16–32.

Gordon, Andrew

2009   *A Modern History of Japan.* New York: Oxford University Press.

Guilbault, Jocelyne

2005   "On Redefining the 'Local' through World Music." In *Ethnomusicology: A Contemporary Reader,* edited by Jennifer C. Post, 137–146. New York: Routledge.

Gupta, Akhil, and James Ferguson

1997   "Beyond 'Culture': Space, Identity, and the Politics of Difference." In *Culture, Power, Place: Explorations in Critical Anthropology,* edited by Akhil Gupta and James Ferguson, 33–51. Durham: Duke University Press.

2002   "Spatializing States: Toward an Ethnography of Neoliberal Governmentality." *American Ethnologist* 29 (4): 981–1002.

Hannerz, Ulf

1992   *Cultural Complexity: Studies in the Social Organization of Meaning.* New York: Columbia University Press.

Harootunian, H. D.

1998   "Figuring the Folk: History, Poetics, and Representation." In *Mirror of Modernity: Invented Traditions of Modern Japan,* edited by Stephen Vlastos, 144–159. Berkeley: University of California Press.

Hart, Mickey

1991   *Planet Drum: A Celebration of Percussion and Rhythm.* Petaluma, CA: Acid Test Productions.

Harvey, David
1989 *The Condition of Postmodernity: An Enquiry into the Origins of Cultural Change.* Cambridge, UK: Blackwell.
Hashimoto, Hiroyuki
1998 "Re-Creating and Re-Imagining Folk Performing Arts in Contemporary Japan." Translated by David Ambaras. In "International Rites." Special issue, *Journal of Folklore Research* 35 (1): 35–46.
Hayashi Eitetsu
1992 *Ashita no taiko-uchi e* [For tomorrow's taiko player]. Tokyo: Shobunsha.
1999 "Hayashi Eitetsu: zenshi 1970–2000" [Hayashi Eitetsu—a history: 1970–2000]. Series of interviews with Hayashi Eitetsu. *Taikology* 17: 4–79.
Hendry, Joy, and Massimo Raveri, eds.
2002 *Japan at Play: The Ludic and Logic of Power.* London: Routledge.
Henshall, Kenneth
1999 *Dimensions of Japanese Society: Gender, Margins, and Mainstream.* New York: St. Martin's Press.
Herd, Judith
2008 "Western-influenced 'Classical' Music in Japan." In *The Ashgate Research Companion to Japanese Music,* edited by Alison Tokita and David Hughes, 363–382. Burlington, VT: Ashgate.
Herzfeld, Michael
2004 *The Body Impolitic: Artisans and Artifice in the Global Hierarchy of Value.* Chicago: University of Chicago Press.
Hesselink, Nathan
2004 "Samul Nori as Traditional: Preservation and Innovation in a South Korean Contemporary Percussion Genre." *Ethnomusicology* 48 (3): 405–439.
Hill, Peter B. E.
2003 *The Japanese Mafia: Yakuza, Law, and the State.* Oxford: Oxford University Press.
Hobsbawm, Eric, and Terence Ranger, eds.
1983 *The Invention of Tradition.* Cambridge: Cambridge University Press.
Honma Masahiko
1994 "Ondekoza-goto hajime" [The beginning of Ondekoza]. *Taikology* 10:11–13.
Hughes, David
1991 "Japanese 'New Folk Songs,' Old and New." *Asian Music* 22 (1): 1–25.
Igarashi, Yoshikuni
2000 *Bodies of Memory: Narratives of War in Postwar Japanese Culture, 1945–1970.* Princeton, NJ: Princeton University Press.
Ikeda, Keiko
1999 "Kenka Matsuri: Fighting with Our Gods in Postindustrial Japan." In *Lives in Motion: Composing Circles of Self and Community in Japan,*

edited by Susan Orpett Long, 119–136. Ithaca, NY: Cornell University East Asia Program.

Inagaki Hiroshi

1943   *Muhōmatsu no isshō* [The life of Muhōmatsu]. Tokyo: Daiei Motion Picture Co.

1958   *Muhōmatsu no isshō* [The rickshaw man]. Tokyo: Toho Company, Ltd.

Inda, Jonathan Xavier, and Renato Rosaldo, eds.

2002   *The Anthropology of Globalization: A Reader.* Malden, MA: Blackwell.

Ishii, Maki

1994   "'Nihon taiko'— Ondekoza kara no hirogari" [Japan taiko— spreading out from Ondekoza]. *Taikology* 10:35–37.

Ivy, Marilyn

1995   *Discourses of the Vanishing: Modernity, Phantasm, Japan.* Chicago: University of Chicago Press.

Izumi, Masumi

2001   "Reconsidering Ethnic Culture and Community: A Case Study on Japanese Canadian Taiko Drumming." *Journal of Asian American Studies* 4 (2): 35–36.

Johnson, Henry M.

2006   "Tsugaru Shamisen: From Region to Nation (and Beyond) and Back Again." *Asian Music* 37 (1): 75–100.

Kaplan, David E., and Alec Dubro

2003   *Yakuza: Japan's Criminal Underworld.* Berkeley: University of California Press.

Kashiwagi Kaoru

1994   "Ondekoza shodai zachō no ki" [Notes from Ondekoza's early leader]. *Taikology* 10:24–28.

Katayama, Hans

1994   "The Man Who Tried to Buy Respect." *Asia-Inc.,* March, 34–37.

Kaufman, Philip.

1993   *Rising Sun.* Los Angeles: Twentieth Century Fox.

Kawano, Satsuki

2005   *Ritual Practice in Modern Japan: Ordering Place, People, and Action.* Honolulu: University of Hawaii Press.

Kelly, William

1990   "Japanese No-Noh: The Crosstalk of Public Culture in a Rural Festivity." *Public Culture* 2(2): 65–81.

Kishibe, Shigeo

1969   *The Traditional Music of Japan.* Tokyo: Kokusai Bunka Shinkōkai.

Kitaguchi, Suehiro

1999   *An Introduction to the Buraku Issue: Questions and Answers.* Translated by Alastair McLaughlan. Richmond, UK: Japan Library.

Knight, John

1994 "Rural Revitalization in Japan: Spirit of the Village and Taste of the Country." *Asian Survey* 34 (7): 634–646.

Komatsu Kazuhiko

1997 *Matsuri to ibento* [Festival and event]. Tokyo: Shogakukan.

Konagaya, Hideyo

2001 "Taiko as Performance: Creating Japanese American Traditions." *The Japanese Journal of American Studies* 12:105–123.

2005 "Performing Manliness: Resistance and Harmony in Japanese American Taiko." In *Manly Traditions: The Folk Roots of American Masculinities,* edited by Simon J. Bronner, 134–153. Bloomington: Indiana University Press.

2007 "Performing the Okinawan Woman in Taiko: Gender, Folklore, and Identity Politics in Modern Japan." PhD diss., University of Pennsylvania.

Kondo, Dorinne

1990 *Crafting Selves: Power, Gender, and Discourses of Identity in a Japanese Workplace.* Chicago: University of Chicago Press.

Kuki Shōzō

1979 *Iki no kōzō: Hoka nihen* [The structure of *iki*]. Tokyo: Iwanami shoten.

Kuwahara Mizuki

2005 "Sōsaku wadaiko to jendā—josei sōsha no ichi-zuke wo megutte" [Ensemble taiko and gender—the place of women drummers]. *Toshi bunka kenkyū* [Studies of urban cultures] 6:2–17.

Kyōiku geijutsu-sha

2007a *Chūgakusei no ongaku* [Musical instruments for middle school students]. Tokyo: Kyōiku geijutsu-sha.

2007b *Chūgakusei no ongaku,* 1 [Music for middle school students, 1]. Tokyo: Kyōiku geijutsu-sha.

Lancashire, Terence

2003 "World Music or Japanese—The Gagaku of Tōgi Hideki." *Popular Music* 21 (1): 21–39.

Lee, Soo im

2006 "The Cultural Exclusiveness of Ethnocentrism: Japan's Treatment of Foreign Residents." In *Japan's Diversity Dilemmas,* edited by Soo im Lee, Stephen Murphy-Shigematsu, and Harumi Befu, 100–124. New York: iUniverse.

Lent, John A., ed.

1995 *Asian Popular Culture.* Boulder, CO: Westview Press.

Linhart, Sepp, and Sabine Frühstück, eds.

1998 *The Culture of Japan as Seen through Its Leisure.* Albany: State University of New York Press.

Livingston, Tamara

1999 "Music Revivals: Towards a General Theory." *Ethnomusicology* 43 (1): 66–85.

Luvaas, Brent
　2009　"Dislocating Sounds: The Deterritorialization of Indonesian Indie Pop." *Cultural Anthropology* 24 (2): 246–279.

Malkki, Lisa
　1992　"National Geographic: The Rooting of Peoples and the Territorialization of National Identity among Scholars and Refugees." *Cultural Anthropology* 7 (1): 24–44.

Malm, William
　1959　*Japanese Music and Musical Instruments.* Tokyo: Tuttle.
　2000　*Traditional Japanese Music and Musical Instruments.* New York: Kodansha International.

Marcus, George
　1995　"Ethnography in/of the World System: The Emergence of Multi-Sited Ethnography." *Annual Review of Anthropology* 24:95–117.

Martinez, D. T.
　1990　"Tourism and the Ama: The Search for a Real Japan." In *Unwrapping Japan: Society and Culture in Anthropological Perspective,* edited by Eyal Ben-Ari, Brian Moeran, and James Valentine, 97–116. Manchester, UK: Manchester University Press.

Martinez, D. T., ed.
　1998　*The Worlds of Japanese Popular Culture: Gender, Shifting Boundaries, and Global Cultures.* New York: Cambridge University Press.

Matanle, Peter, and Yasuyuki Sato
　2010　"Coming Soon to a City Near You! Learning to Live 'Beyond Growth' in Japan's Shrinking Regions." *Social Science Japan Journal* 13 (2): 187–210.

Mathews, Gordon
　2000　*Global Culture/Individual Identity: Searching for Home in the Cultural Supermarket.* London: Routledge.

Matsue, Jennifer Milioto
　2009　*Making Music in Japan's Underground: The Tokyo Hardcore Scene.* New York: Routledge.

Mazzarella, William
　2004　"Culture, Globalization, Mediation." *Annual Review of Anthropology* 33:345–367.

McCargo, Duncan
　2004　*Contemporary Japan.* 2nd ed. New York: Palgrave Macmillan.

MEXT [Japanese Ministry of Education, Culture, Sports, Science and Technology]
　2006　*Kyōiku kihon hō* [Fundamental law of education]. Accessed November 15, 2010, www.mext.go.jp/b_menu/kihon/about/06121913/002.pdf.

Misumi Kenji
　1965　*Muhōmatsu no isshō* [The wild one]. Tokyo: Daiei Motion Picture Co.

Mitsuya Motoshiro
　1994　"Long Interview with Den Tagayasu." *Mainichi Club—Amuse* 14:59–64.

Mogi Hitoshi

    2003   *Nyūmon nihon no taiko: Minzoku dentō soshite nyūwēbu* [An introduction to Japanese drums: Folklore, tradition, and the new wave]. Tokyo: Heibonsha.

    2010   *Taiko no minzokugaku: Oedo sukeroku taiko* [Taiko folklore: Oedo Sukeroku Taiko]. *Taikology* 36:34–41.

Monbushō [Japanese Ministry of Education]

    1999a *Chūgakkō gakushū shidō yōryō kaisetsu: Ongaku-hen* [Course of study for middle schools: Music guidelines and explanation]. Tokyo: Kyōiku geijutsusha.

    1999b *Shōgakkō gakushū shidō yōryō kaisetsu: Ongaku-hen* [Course of study for primary schools: Music guidelines and explanation]. Tokyo: Kyōiku geijutsusha.

Moriarty, Elizabeth

    1972   "The Communitarian Aspect of Shinto Matsuri." *Asian Folklore Studies* 31 (2): 91–140.

Morris, Andrew

    2004   *Marrow of the Nation: A History of Sport and Culture in Republican China*. Berkeley: University of California Press.

Neary, Ian

    1997   "Burakumin in Contemporary Japan." In *Japan's Minorities: The Illusion of Homogeneity*, edited by Michael Weiner, 50–78. London: Routledge.

Nippon Taiko Foundation

    1999   *Nippon taiko jittai chōsa hōkoku-sho* [Report on the current state of Japanese taiko]. Tokyo: The Nippon Taiko Foundation and the Nippon Foundation.

    2001   *Nihon taiko kyōhon* [Japan taiko textbook]. Tokyo: The Nippon Taiko Foundation and the Nippon Foundation.

Nishitsunoi Masahiro

    1985   *Sairei to furyū* [Festival and spectacle]. Minzoku-mingei sōsho [Folklore-folk art series] 99. Tokyo: Iwasaki Bijutsusha.

    2001   "Onna ga utsu taiko" [Women play taiko— interview]. *Taikology* 18:2–9.

Ogasawara, Yuko

    1998   *Office Ladies and Salaried Men: Power, Gender, and Work in Japanese Companies*. Berkeley: University of California Press.

Oguchi Daihachi

    1993   *Tenko* [Heavenly drum]. Nagano, Japan: Ginga Shobō.

    1994   *Nihon no taiko: Fuku-shiki fuku-da hō kyōhon: Kumi daiko* [Japan taiko: Textbook for multiple-drum, multiple-player ensemble taiko]. Okaya, Japan: Osuwa Daiko Rakuen.

    1995   "Wadaiko ongaku no reimeiki" [The dawn of Japanese drum music]. Interview with Oguchi Daihachi. *Taikology* 14:5–15.

Ong, Aihwa

1999   *Flexible Citizenship: The Cultural Logics of Transnationality.* Durham, NC: Duke University Press.

2005   "Graduated Sovereignty in South-East Asia." In *Anthropologies of Modernity: Foucault, Governmentality, and Life Politics,* edited by Jonathan Xavier Inda, 83–104. Malden, MA: Blackwell.

Osaka City Naniwa Human Rights Culture Center

2006   "Jinken taiko rōdo, jinken ishiki kanban, chiiki kōryū jōhō-shiryō." [Informational literature for the road of human rights and taiko, human rights awareness bulletin boards, and community interaction], November 15.

Osuwa Daiko Preservation Society

n.d.   "Japanese Drums of Suwa Shrine." Unpublished pamphlet.

Otsuki Takahiro

1996   "Muhōmatsu, sengo ni iki-nobite, minshu-shugi ni te wo musubu koto" [Muhōmatsu lives into the postwar, joining hands with democracy]. Interview in *Taikology* 13:24–29.

Peluse, Michael S.

2005   "Not Your Grandfather's Music: Tsugaru Shamisen Blurs the Lines Between 'Folk,' 'Traditional,' and 'Pop.'" *Asian Music* 36 (2): 57–80.

Powell, Kimberly

2004   "The Apprenticeship of Embodied Knowledge in a Taiko Drumming Ensemble." In *Knowing Bodies, Moving Minds,* edited by Liora Bresler, 183–195. Boston: Kluwer Academic Publishers.

2008   "Drumming Against the Quiet: The Sounds of Asian American Identity in an Amorphous Landscape." *Qualitative Inquiry* 14 (6): 901–925.

Powers, Richard Gid, and Hidetoshi Kato, eds.

1989   *Handbook of Japanese Popular Culture.* New York: Greenwood Press.

Priestly, Ian

2009   "Breaking the Silence on Burakumin." *Japan Times.* January 20, 2009, accessed December 17, 2010, http://search.japantimes.co.jp/cgi-bin/fl20090120zg.html.

Ramnarine, Tina K.

2003   *Ilmatar's Inspirations: Nationalism, Globalization, and the Changing Soundscapes of Finnish Folk Music.* Chicago: University of Chicago Press.

Rausch, Anthony

2006   "The Heisei Dai Gappei: A Case Study for Understanding the Municipal Mergers of the Heisei Era." *Japan Forum* 18 (1): 133–156.

Robertson, Jennifer

1991   *Native and Newcomer: Making and Remaking a Japanese City.* Berkeley: University of California Press.

1992a   "The 'Magic If': Conflicting Performances of Gender in the Takarazuka Revue of Japan." In *Gender in Performance: The Presentation of Difference in the Performing Arts,* edited by Lauren Senelick, 46–67. Hanover, NH: University Press of New England.

1992b   "The Politics of Androgyny in Japan: Sexuality and Subversion in the Theater and Beyond." *American Ethnologist* 19 (3): 419–442.

1998a   "It Takes a Village: Internationalization and Nostalgia in Postwar Japan." In *Mirror of Modernity: Invented Traditions of Modern Japan,* edited by Stephen Vlastos, 110–129. Berkeley: University of California Press.

1998b   *Takarazuka: Sexual Politics and Popular Culture in Modern Japan.* Berkeley: University of California Press.

Robertson, Roland

1995   "Glocalization: Time-Space and Homogeneity-Heterogeneity." In *Global Modernities,* edited by Mike Featherstone, Scott Lash, and Roland Robertson, 25–44. London: Sage.

Saisu Yumiko

1997   "Soshite minzoku geinō wa bunka-zai ni natta" [And then the folk performing arts became cultural properties]. *Taikology* 15:26–32.

Sano Shinichi

2000   Miyamoto tsuneichi ga mita nihon [The Japan Miyamoto Tsuneichi saw]. Program notes for NHK Ningen Kōza (January–March). Tokyo: Nippon Hōsō Kyokai.

Sassen, Saskia

1991   *The Global City: New York, London, Tokyo.* Princeton, NJ: Princeton University Press.

Sato Kazumasa

1994   "Ondekoza wa dō umare, dō sodatta ka?" [How was Ondekoza born and raised?]. *Taikology* 10:15–23.

Schade-Poulsen, Marc

1997   "Which World? On the Diffusion of Algerian Raï to the West." In *Siting Culture: The Shifting Anthropological Object,* edited by Karen Fog Olwig and Kirsten Hastrup, 59–85. New York: Routledge.

Schnell, Scott

1999   *The Rousing Drum.* Honolulu: University of Hawaii Press.

Seidensticker, Edwin

1983   *Low City, High City: Tokyo from Edo to the Earthquake.* New York: Knopf.

Shinoda Masahiro

1994   "Ondekoza— sono shisō to saisei" [Ondekoza— its running and rebirth]. *Taikology* 10:32–34.

Shirai Yoshio

1996   "Muhōmatsu no taiko wa naze bakuhatsu-teki ni taka-natta no ka?" [Why did Muhōmatsu's taiko have such a powerful impact?]. *Taikology* 13:12–16.

Shively, Donald

    1978   "The Social Environment of Tokugawa Kabuki." In *Studies in Kabuki: Its Acting, Music, and Historical Context,* edited by James R. Brandon, William P. Malm, and Donald H. Shively, 1–61. Honolulu: University of Hawaii Press.

Singleton, John

    1989   "Japanese Folk Craft Pottery Apprenticeship: Cultural Patterns of an Educational Institution." In *Apprenticeship: From Theory to Method and Back Again,* edited by Michael Coy, 13–30. Albany: State University of New York Press.

Skov, Lise, and Brian Moeran, eds.

    1995   *Women, Media, and Consumption in Japan.* Honolulu: University of Hawaii Press.

Sterling, Marvin

    2010   *Babylon East: Performing Dancehall, Roots Reggae, and Rastafari in Japan.* Durham, NC: Duke University Press.

Stevens, Carolyn

    2007   *Japanese Popular Music: Culture, Authenticity, and Power.* New York: Routledge.

Suzuki Tadashi

    1996   *The Way of Acting: The Theatre Writings of Tadashi Suzuki.* Translated by J. Thomas Rimer. New York: Theatre Communications Group.

Taikology

    1996   "Daijūsan maku no uchi-dashi" [Notes on our thirteenth issue]. *Taikology* 13:64.

Taira, Koji

    1997   "Troubled National Identity: The Ryukyuans/Okinawans." In *Japan's Minorities: The Illusion of Homogeneity,* edited by Michael Weiner, 140–175. London: Routledge.

Takada Tsuyoshi

    1995   "Sengo wadaiko shōshi" [A brief history of postwar wadaiko]. In *Wadaiko ga wakaru hon* [Understanding Japanese taiko], edited by Asano Taiko Co., 42–45. Mattō-shi, Japan: Asano Taiko.

Taylor, Melanie

    2008   "P. P. C and cocon Tour." *Kodo Beat* 83:1–2.

Terada, Yoshitaka

    2001   "Shifting Identities in Taiko Music." In *Transcending Boundaries: Asian Musics in North America,* edited by Yoshitaka Terada, 37–59. Osaka, Japan: National Museum of Ethnology.

    2008   "Angry Drummers and Buraku Identity: The Ikari Taiko Group in Osaka, Japan." In *The Human World and Musical Diversity: Proceedings from the Fourth Meeting of the "Music and Minorities" Study Group in Varna, Bulgaria, 2006,* edited by Rosemary Sialeiova, Angela Rodel,

Lozanka Peycheva, Ivanka Vlaeva, and Venlsislav Dimo, 309–315, 401. Sofia, Bulgaria: Bulgarian Academy of Science, Institute of Art Studies.

Thompson, Christopher

2006 "Preserving the Ochiai Deer Dance: Tradition and Continuity in a Tōhoku Hamlet." In *Wearing Cultural Styles in Japan: Concepts of Tradition and Modernity in Practice,* edited by Christopher Thompson and John Traphagan, 124–150. Albany: State University of New York Press.

2008 "Population Decline, Municipal Amalgamation, and the Politics of Folk Performance Preservation in Northeast Japan." In *The Demographic Challenge: A Handbook about Japan,* edited by Florian Coulmas, Harald Conrad, Annette Schad-Seifert, and Gabriele Vogt, 361–386. Boston: Brill.

Thornbury, Barbara

1997 *The Folk Performing Arts: Traditional Culture in Contemporary Japan.* Albany: State University of New York Press.

Tilly, Christopher

1997 "Performing Culture in the Global Village." *Critique of Anthropology* 17 (1): 67–89.

Tobin, Joseph J., ed.

1992 *Re-made in Japan: Everyday Life and Consumer Taste in a Changing Society.* New Haven, CT: Yale University Press.

Tokita, Alison McQueen, and David W. Hughes, eds.

2008 *The Ashgate Research Companion to Japanese Music.* Burlington, VT: Ashgate.

Tomlinson, John

1991 *Cultural Imperialism.* Baltimore, MD: Johns Hopkins University Press.

Traphagan, John

2000 *Taming Oblivion: Aging Bodies and the Fear of Senility in Japan.* Albany: State University of New York Press.

Treat, John Whittier, ed.

1996 *Contemporary Japan and Popular Culture.* Honolulu: University of Hawaii Press.

Tsing, Anna

2005 *Friction: An Ethnography of Global Connection.* Princeton, NJ: Princeton University Press.

Tusler, Mark

1995 "The Los Angeles Matsuri Taiko: Performance Aesthetics, Teaching Methods, and Compositional Techniques." MA thesis, University of California, Santa Barbara.

2003 "Sights and Sounds of Power: Ensemble Taiko Drumming (Kumi Daiko) Pedagogy in California and the Conceptualization of Power." PhD diss., University of California, Santa Barbara.

Wade, Bonnie

2004   *Music in Japan: Experiencing Music, Expressing Culture.* New York: Oxford University Press.

Wilson, Richard, ed.

1997   *Human Rights, Culture, and Context: Anthropological Perspectives.* Chicago: Pluto Press.

Wong, Deborah

2000   "Taiko and the Asian/American Body: Drums, Rising Sun, and the Question of Gender." *The World of Music* 42 (3): 67–78.

2004   *Speak It Louder: Asian Americans Making Music.* New York: Routledge.

2005   "Noisy Intersection: Ethnicity, Authenticity and Ownership in Asian American Taiko." In *Diasporas and Interculturalism in Asian Performing Arts: Translating Traditions,* edited by Hae-kyung Um, 75–90. New York: RoutledgeCurzon.

2006   "Asian/American Improvisation in Chicago: Tatsu Aoki and the 'New' Japanese American Taiko." *Critical Studies in Improvisation/Études critiques en improvisation* 1 (3): 1–33.

Yagi Yasuyuki

1994   "Furusato no taiko: Nagasaki-ken ni okeru kyōdo geinō no sōshutsu to chiiki bunka no yukue" [The drum troupe boom as folklorism: Inventing local cultures for whom?]. *Jinbun chiri* 46 (6): 23–45.

Yano, Christine

2002   *Tears of Longing: Nostalgia and the Nation in Japanese Popular Song.* Cambridge, MA: Harvard University Press.

Yomota Inuhiko

1996   "Yuigonjo wa okuri-todokerareta no ka?" [Were his last wishes heard?] *Taikology* 13:17–23.

Yoon, Paul Jong-Chul

2001   "'She's Really Become Japanese Now!' Taiko Drumming and Asian American Identifications." *American Music* 19 (4): 417–438.

Yoshino, Kosaku

1992   *Cultural Nationalism in Contemporary Japan: A Sociological Enquiry.* London: Routledge.

1998   "Culturalism, Racialism, and Internationalism in the Discourse on Japanese Identity." In *Making Majorities: Constituting the Nation in Japan, Korea, China, Malaysia, Fiji, Turkey, and the United States,* edited by Dru C. Gladney, 13–25. Stanford, CA: Stanford University Press.

INDEX

Page numbers in italics indicate illustrations.

acrobatic choreography, 56, 58–60, 120, 144

advertising, 5, 194; and Asano Taiko Corporation, 34, 47; and Earth Celebration (EC), 200

aesthetics, 6; and bodily discipline, 120–23, 126, 141, 218n2; and women taiko drummers, 22, 144–45, 166, 169

Africa, 156; African drums, 219n7; tree trunks imported from, 35

Agatsuma Hiromitsu, 218n10

Agency for Cultural Affairs, 177–78

aging citizenry, 198

Ainu of Hokkaido, 46

Akioka Yoshio, 70

Akira (pseud.), 46–47

Akita Prefecture, 65

ama (female divers), 206n17

amalgamation, 198–202

Amanojaku, 157, 159–61, 161, 162–64, 169

Ama-no-uzume (goddess), 143–44

Amaterasu (Japanese sun goddess), 142–44, 143, 145

amateur ensemble taiko, 7, 18–20, 73, 87, 108; and bodily discipline, 127; and festival performances, 104–5, 108; and nationalism, 173; and taiko as new folk performance, 112–15; and women taiko drummers, 144, 163–66. See also names of groups

ancestors, 31, 50, 53, 206n16

Anderson, Benedict, 205n13

anthropology, 8–10, 15, 205n13; cultural anthropology, 13, 15; and festival performances, 22, 107

Aomori Prefecture, 211n24

Appadurai, Arjun, 205n13

apprentice programs, 211n23; for gidayū (musician-singers), 148; for hōgaku (music of the homeland), 31; of Kodo, 1–2, 7, 13–17, 103, 127–41, 138, 165, 207n23, 219nn9–12, 220nn13–15; of Sukeroku Daiko, 18–19; and women taiko drummers, 19, 140, 150–56, 165, 207n23, 207n25

arm movements. See furi (arm movements)

artisans (shokunin), 61, 69–71, 77–78, 87, 98, 101, 129, 144; artisan academy (shokunin daigaku), 7, 60, 67, 70, 97, 101, 103, 214n29; and Asano Taiko Corporation, 35–36

Asako (pseud.), 152–55

Asano Akitoshi, 157

Asano Taiko Corporation, 34–37, 38, 41, 44, 47, 203n4; and Good Design Award, 47; and Ondekoza, 214n27; and women taiko drummers, 157–59

Asano Taiko Village, 35–36; drum museum at, 35; national tax office certificates at, 36–37; taiko culture research institute at, 35

Ashgate Research Companion to Japanese Music (Tokita, McQueen, and Hughes), 204n8
Ashiharabashi Station, 42
Ashkenazi, Michael, 216n4
Asian Americans, 97
assimilation areas, 38
atarigane (small brass gongs), 32
Australian taiko, 3, 173, 194, 204n9
authenticity, 7, 50, 204n11, 205n15; and bodily discipline, 120, 127, 134, 218n5; and festival performances, 22, 107; and Kodo, 127, 134; and nationalism, 187; and Ondekoza, 70, 77; in *The Rickshaw Man* (film), 85–87; and taiko as new folk performance, 112–13
authority, 54, 68; and bodily discipline, 140; and festival performances, 108; and Izumo no Okuni (Shinto shrine maiden), 146; and *kabuki-mono* (bizarre people), 146; and Kodo, 140; and Muhōmatsu (in *The Rickshaw Man*), 84; and nationalism, 179, 184; and taiko as new folk performance, 114–16; and women taiko drummers, 146–47, 150, 169

Bandō Tsumasaburō, 79
Bantsuma, 86
Bestor, Theodore, 107–8, 206n17, 215n3, 217n6
bicycle racing, 181
blacksmiths, 50, 69
blisters, 121
bodily discipline, 6–7, 20–22, 119–41; and Japanese theater, 124–25; and Kodo, 98–99, 120, 127–41, *138*, 159–62, 164, 219n12, 220nn14–16, 221n11; and "new-style" Japanese, 126–27, 140; and Nihon Taiko Dōjō, 124, 136, 138, 140; and Ondekoza, 64–65, 67–70, 77, 90–94, 120, 159, 161–62, 213n23, 221n11; and place, 22, 120–23, 131, 133–36, 141, 145, 150; and race, 119–20, 123–27, 134, 136, 141, 150, 219nn6–8; in *The Rickshaw Man* (film), 83, 212n9; and Sukeroku Daiko, 121–24, 133, 136–38, 140, 218n1, 219n8; and upper/lower body strength, 121–23, 126, 129, 132, 138, 219n12; and

women taiko drummers, 124, 140, 145, 150, 153–63, *160*, *161*, 168–69, 221n11
boke (preventable mental and physical decline), 222n2
Bolshoi Ballet, 16
Bon-daiko, 53–54, 56, 58–59
Bon festivals, 32, 53–54, 56, 123–24, 144, 211n22; *Bon-odori* (Bon-dancing) groups, 32, 53, 58, 110; and nationalism, 171, 223n6; recorded music at, 53–54; ward festival *(kumin matsuri)*, 215n3. See also *Bon-daiko*
Boston Marathon, 2, *89*, 94, 213n23, 214n26
Boston Symphony Orchestra, 8, 94
Bourdieu, Pierre, 218n3
Brazil, 57, 194; Brazilian *capoeira*, 218n1; Brazilian samba, 57
Buddhism: Buddhist chanting, 27, 110; Buddhist rituals, 32, 53, 110, 208n2; Buddhist temples, 32, 53; and *buraku* people, 37; and nationalism, 182; Nichiren sect of, 32. *See also* Bon festivals
bugaku (dance music), 26
buk (Korean percussion instrument), 45
Bungakuza (theater troupe), 78–79
bunraku (puppet theater), 65, 67–68, 146–48, 207n19
Buraku Liberation League (BLL), 38–40
burakumin/buraku people, 36–47, *43*
butoh, 211n25

calluses, 121
capitalism, 5, 82, 85
Cardin, Pierre, 91–93, 95, 213n22
carpenter's apron *(haragake)*, 83, 87, 95, 106, 213n12
categorizations of music, 4–6, 204n11
Center of the Study of Folk Culture, 62
certification, 185–86
chappa (small hand cymbals), 80
Chichibu City (Saitama Prefecture), 20, 73–77, 114, 134–36, 139, 211n24, 212n3, 220n18; Shitagō Ward, 74
Chichibu yatai-bayashi, 74–77, 114, 184, 209n1, 211n24, 212nn2–3
chiiki dentō geinō (regional traditional performing arts), 116

children, 53–54, 56, 74, 165–66, 172; children's festivals, 105–6, 166; in *The Rickshaw Man* (film), 83–84
Chinese court music, 26–27
Chinese literature, 61
"Chonlima," 166–67
chopsticks, 128–29, 132, 220n14
Christianity, 146
chū-daiko drums, *29*, 32, *33*, 34, 191, 208n3; and bodily discipline, 137, 218n4; and Kodo, 98–99, 137, 154, 156, 221n6; and music education, 196; and Ondekoza, 74–75, 95; and Osuwa Daiko, 50–51, 53; in *The Rickshaw Man* (film), 80; and Sukeroku Daiko, 58; and Taiko Ikari, 44; and women taiko drummers, 154, 156, 167, 221n6
citizens' festival *(shimin matsuri)*, 215n3
classical performing arts, 5, 25, 33–34, 112, 207n19; and bodily discipline, 132–33, 136, 139; drums of, 27–31, 33–34, 59; and Kodo, 132–33, 136, 139; and music education, 198; and nationalism, 178, 183, 187; and Ondekoza, 70–72, 211n23; and women taiko drummers, 142, 148, 150, 159. *See also* kabuki; Noh
class relations, 8, 11; in *The Rickshaw Man* (film), 79–85
coal mine strikes, 65
cocon, 167–68, *168*
communal lifestyle, 10–12, 34; and Kodo, 99, 130, 220n13; and Ondekoza, 66–68, 77, 99, 210n19, 211n20; and Warabiza, 65. *See also* religio-communal celebrations
communism, 65, 181
community festivity, 6, 22, 33, 83, 104–10, 205n13, 206n17, 215n1; governmental support of, 22, 53; increasing egalitarianism of, 105, *109*, 216nn4–5; and Kodo, 8, 101–2; and nationalism, 171; and new festivals, 107–8, 215n3; and Ondekoza, 60–61, 69, 104; and taiko as new folk performance, 60–61, 112, 115–16; and *Tsugaru shamisen*, 218n10. *See also* festival performances; local culture
composers, 8, 33, 220n16, 223n11
concerts/concert halls, 5–6, 13, 20; and *buraku* groups, 39–40; "Japan Taiko," 178;

and Kodo, 101–2, 199; and nationalism, 176–78, 184; and Ondekoza, 91–93, 96–97, 214n27; "Peace Concert," 223n6; "Taiko of Japan" (Nihon no Taiko), 142; "Women Play Taiko," 142–44, *143*, 145, 169. *See also* stage performances
cooking, 17, 67, 130–33, 220n13
corporate taxes, 36
cosmopolitanism, 8, 49, 54, 116, 133–34, 218n5
court music performances, 25–28, 30–31, 34, 208n2; drums of, 26–28, 30; and imperial music bureau, 26
craftsmanship, 64, 67, 69–70, 210n19
creativity, 5, 12, 49, 56, 107
Creighton, Millie, 206n17
creolization, 9, 205n13
Crichton, Michael, 172–73
crime, 37, 152
cross-dressing, 146–47, 149, 156

dadaiko (largest *gagaku* drum), 26–27
dai (horizontal drum platform), 88
daibyōshi, 30, *31*. See also *okedō-daiko* drums
Daisho Elementary School, 99–100
Daisuke (pseud.), 140–41, 152
dance, 2–3, 15, 26, 32; and bodily discipline, 120, 125, 129, 135–36, 218n1, 219n12; and festival performances, 110, 216n4; and Great Heisei Amalgamation (Heisei Dai Gappei), 199; and Kodo, 99, 129, 135–36, 154–55, 219n12; and nationalism, 171; and Ondekoza, 68, 88, 211n25; in *The Rickshaw Man* (film), 80; and Sukeroku Daiko, 57, 192; and Warabiza, 65; and women taiko drummers, 154–55, 167
deer dance *(shishi idori)*, 99, 216n5
De Ferranti, Hugh, 204n8, 204n9
delocalization, 22, 76, 114, 197
demon drumming *(ondeko)*, 64–66, 69, 78, 128–30, 201–2, 209n7, 211n22, 216n4, 225n7
demons *(oni)*, 97, 100
dengaku (rice-planting dances of peasants), 27
Dengakuza, 188–89, 224n18

Den Tagayasu, 60–71, 201, 209nn8–9, 209n11, 210nn16–18; and artisans *(shokunin)*, 60–61, 69–71, 77–78, 87, 97, 101, 214n29; departure of, 93, 96–100, 137, 214n29; and filmmaking, 96, 214n26; and *fundoshi* (Japanese loin-cloths), 91–93, 213n22; and marathon running, 69, 94, 213n23, 214n26; and "new" Ondekoza, 157; and "Ōdaiko," 77–78, 88, 90–94; and *ondeko* (demon drumming), 64–66, 69, 78, 209n7, 211n22; as protestor, 61–62, 64–65; and *The Rickshaw Man* (film), 78, 80–81, 87–88, 90–91, 96; and women taiko drummers, 157; and "Yatai-bayashi," 74, 92, 94, 212n2
Department of Public Morals, 147
depopulation, 16, 107, 109, 128, 180, 198, 216nn4–5, 219n10
diasporic communities, 9, 193
"Directive on Developing Basic Plans in Accordance with the Festival Law" (1993), 12
disabled persons, 46
discrimination, 37–41, *43*, 44–46, 208n10; occupational, 37
disembodiment, 21–22, 171, 187, 197, 222n2
Disney, 192
dora (gong), 95
drum makers, 21, 25–26, 34–47; Asano Taiko Corporation, 34–37; heritage of, 34, 42, 44–45, 47; and Road of Human Rights and Taiko, 38, 41–46; and Taiko Ikari, 38–45, 47
drums, types of: folk and religious music, 31–34; *gagaku* (music of imperial court), 26–27; kabuki (classical performing arts), 29–31; Noh (classical performing arts), 27–29
drum sets, 49–51, *51*, 174
Dutch-style residences, 206n18

Earth Celebration (EC), 8, 101–2, 108, 199–200; Executive Committee, 199
Edo, 18, 58, 72, 123, 147, 218n5. *See also* Tokyo
Edo (dandy), 58
Edo period (1603–1868), 100

education, music, 195–98, 202, 224nn2–5, 225n6; and curricular reforms, 195–98
Ei Rokusuke, 66
eisa drumming, 45, 205n12; *eisa-odori*, 210n13, 225n7
electronic drum music, 221n10
elites: and *furusato* (old village) projects, 10, 38, 206n17; in *The Rickshaw Man* (film), 79, 82–85; and Taiko Ikari, 39; and women taiko drummers, 147
Emancipation Edict (1871), 37
embodiment, 21–22, 127, 170–71; and defeat of Japan, 119–20; and Kodo, 127–30, 133, 136, 140–41, 155; and Muhōmatsu (in *The Rickshaw Man*), 93; and Ondekoza, 93, 95; and Sukeroku Daiko, 58, 72; and women taiko drummers, 145, 147, 155. *See also* bodily discipline
enka singing, 5, 148–50
ensemble taiko groups *(kumi-daiko)*, 2–8, *3*, *4*, 10, 12, 104, 203n2, 203n4, 204nn8–10; characteristics of, 111–16; increase in number of, 3, 105, 110–11, 115, 144–45, 217–18nn8–9, 220n2; as new folk performance, 12–13, 60–61, 111–16, 126, 177–78, 199, 207n21, 217nn7–8, 218n10, 223n11; openness to change, 12, 106–7, 109–10, *109*, 116; popularization of, 3–7, 13, 21–22, 25, 41, 46–48, 51–54, 105, 172, 197 (*see also* taiko boom); surveys of, 110–11; typology of, 176–79, 184–85, 187–88, 223nn10–11. *See also* instruction in ensemble taiko; *names of ensemble groups*
eroticism, 92–93, 145, 150, 156, 159, 162, 164
Espace Pierre Cardin (Paris), 91–93
eta (great filth), 36
ethnic heritage/identity, 45–46, 97
exclusion, social, 10, 106–8, 215n2, 216n4

Facebook, 194
farming, 31, 128–30, 132–33, 144, 172, 220n13
fascism, 180
Federation of Prefectural Associations of Motorboat Racing, 181
females. *See* gender ideologies; *entries beginning with* women

feminine/femininity, 21, 215n30, 218n5; and kabuki, 147, 149; and women taiko drummers, 145, 147, 149, 156–57, 162–64, 167–68, *168*

Festival Law (1992), 11–12, 116, 207n20

festival performances, 2–3, 6, 10, 12–13, 20, 22, 105–16, 194–95; and bodily discipline, 129, 134–35; children's festivals, 105–6; citizens' festival *(shimin matsuri)*, 215n3; drums of, *29*, 31–32; and *eisa* drumming, 45, 205n12, 210n13; and *furusato* (old village) projects, 10, 206n17; increasing egalitarianism of, 105, *109*, 216nn4–5; and Kodo, 8, 101–2, 105, 129, 134–35, 199–202; and *Kokura gion daiko*, 80–81, 83–88, *89*, 90, 209n1, 212n10, 213n12; and Miyamoto Daiko, 105–6; and music education, 196; and nationalism, 171–72, 177–80; night festivals, 20, 135; and Ondekoza, 73–77, 91–93, 104–5, 212nn2–3; and Osuwa Daiko, 49–52, 60, 104–5, 174–75, 209n1; in *The Rickshaw Man* (film), 80–81, 83–88, 90, 209n1, 212n10, 213n18; shrine-based festivals, 31–32, 53–54, 73–74, 105, 108–10, *109*, 128, 215n1, 217n6; and Sukeroku Daiko, 48, 53–54, 56, 58, 104–5; summer festivals, 53, 56, 109, *109*, 158; and taiko as new folk performance, 112–16, 177–78; ward festival *(kumin matsuri)*, 215n3; winter festivals, 73–74; and women taiko drummers, 109, 142, 151, 158, 216n5; and *yatai* (festival carts), 73–74, 216n5; and *yatai-bayashi* (festival-cart drumming), 20, 74–77, 209n1, 211n24, 212nn2–3

FIFA World Cup (2002), 3

Finland, 194, 207n21

fishermen, 62, 91, 213n20

folk performing arts, 2, 5–12, 22, 25, 34, 48, 111, 204n8, 204n11, 208n2; and bodily discipline, 126–29, 133–36, 139–41, 220nn17–19; and *buraku* groups, 42; as "cultural properties," 115–16, 176; difficulty of transmission of, 74, 77, 83; drums of, 18, 25, 28, 30–34, 46; and *furusato* (old village) projects, 10; and Great Heisei Amalgamation (Heisei

Dai Gappei), 199, 202; inheritors of, 7, 12–13, 17, 22, 73, 83, 109, 111–12, 127, 134, 136, 141, 216n5; and Kodo, 15, 17, 63, 77, 98–99, 102–4, 127–29, 133–36, 139–41, 199, 202; and Miyamoto Daiko, 18; and "Monochrome," 95; and music education, 196; and nationalism, 171–72, 177–78, 180, 186–87; and native ethnology, 62–64, 78, 85–86, 212n10; and "Ōdaiko," 77–78, 87, 91, 93, 213n19; and *ondeko* (demon drumming), 64–66, 69, 78, 128–30, 209n7, 211n22, 216n4; and Ondekoza, 48, 61–66, 69–75, 77–78, 87, 91, 93, 95, 98, 104, 144, 210n16, 213n19; and Osuwa Daiko, 75, 104; and *The Rickshaw Man* (film), 78, 85–87, 212n10, 213n11; and Sukeroku Daiko, 53–54, 57, 104; and taiko as new folk performance, 12–13, 60–61, 111–16, 126, 177–78, 199, 207n21, 217nn7–8, 218n10, 223n11; and Taiko Ikari, 42; and Warabiza, 65; and women taiko drummers, 109, 144, 159, 216n5, 221n7; and "Yataibayashi," 74–75, 77

foreigners *(gaijin)*, 123–24, 126, 134, 140–41, 219nn6–8

foreign influence, 4–6, 9, 21, 205n15, 206n18; and bodily discipline, 123–25, 219n6; and festival performances, 215n1; and Kodo, 102; and Ondekoza, 71–72; and Osuwa Daiko, 57, 72; and Sukeroku Daiko, 57, 72. *See also* Western influence

Foucault, Michel, 222n3

Foundation for the Promotion of Japanese Music (Nippon Kokumin Ongaku Shinkō Zaidan), 182

"free solo"/"freestyle," 56

fue (Japanese flute), 32, 53, 70–71, 74, 76, 213n16

Fukui Prefecture, 73, 88, 211n24, 213n16

Fundamental Law of Education, 198

fundoshi (Japanese loincloths), 91–93, *94*, 213nn20–22, 221n6

The Funeral (film), 212n5

furi (arm movements), 51, 88, 90, 113

furusato (old village), 9–10, 38, 206nn16–18; *furusato* boom, 10 *gagaku* (music of imperial court), 25–28, 47, 208n2; drums of, 26–27; strict regulation of, 27

gaijin (foreigners), 123–24, 126, 134, 140–41, 219nn6–8

gaikokujin (outside country person), 219n6

gaku-daiko (gagaku drum), 26, 30

Gakudan Umi-tsubame, 65

gambling, 181–82

gangs, 152

gays, 46, 92–93

genba (actual sites), 205n15

gendai ongaku (modern music), 94

gender ideologies, 6, 11, 21–22, 142–69, 193; and apprentice programs, 19, 140, 150–56, 207n23, 207n25; and bodily discipline, 145, 150, 218n2, 218n5; and cross-dressing, 146–47, 149, 156; and eroticism, 92–93, 145, 150, 156, 159, 162, 164; and femininity, 21, 145, 147, 149, 156–57, 162, 164, 167–68, *168*, 215n30, 218n5; and gender difference, 150, 153–54, 160–62, 165, 169, 218n5; and gender representation within groups, 144, 166, 220n2; and history of women's stage performance, 146–50, 221n3; and masculine performance norms, 6, 21–22, 46, 115, 144–45, 147, 149, 169, 209n5, 215n30, 218n2, 218n5; and *otokoyaku* ("male"-gender specialists), 149; and ritual pollution of women, 115, 144, 156, 217n6; and taiko as new folk performance, 115; and Takarazuka Revue, 149. *See also entries beginning with* women

Germany/Germans, 8, 62–63, 92, 194

geza (offstage area), 29–30, 32, 210n16

gidayū (musician-singers), 147–48, 150, 156

Ginza Crown (Tokyo club), 56–57

gion daiko. See Kokura gion daiko

globalization, 8, 10, 13, 171, 205nn13–14; and *furusato* (old village) projects, 10, 206n18; global-local articulation of, 8–10, 13, 22, 205–6nn14–15; and Kodo, 17, 48

global performance, 5, 7–9, 205n14; global ecumene, 205n13; and Kodo, 7–8, 15, 98, 101–2; and Ondekoza, 95

Gocoo, 221n10

Gojinjō daiko, 211n24

Golden Lion award (Venice Film Festival), 79

gongs, 32, 74, 95

governmental support: of *buraku* groups, 38, 41; of community festivity, 6, 22, 53, 105, 195; of folk performing arts, 11–12, 208n2; and "Grants for the Creation of Native-Places" program, 111, 217n8; of music education, 195–98, 202, 224nn2–3; and nationalism, 188; and taiko as new folk performance, 111, 115–16, 217n8

Great Heisei Amalgamation (Heisei Dai Gappei), 198–202

habitus, 218n3

Hachijō daiko, 113–14, 184, 211n24, 221n7

Hachijō Island, 20, 113–14, 211n24, 221n7

Haida Haruhiko, 49

Hakusan City, 208n5

Hamochi, 199–200

Hana (pseud.), 155–56

"Hana Hachijō," 221n7

hanchō (leader), 98

happi (kimono-like topcoats), 95, 106, 213n25

haragake (carpenter's apron), 83, 87, 95, 106, 213n12

Hara Tarō, 65

Hart, Mickey, 7

Hashiru tataku, odoru jūgonin no waka-mono (Fifteen young people who run, drum, dance; documentary), 214n26

hayashi (ensemble), 28, 74, 212n1

hayashi-daiko, 46

Hayashi Eitetsu, 74–77, 90–93, 95, 97–99, 103–4, 194–95, 213n19, 214n26, 214n29, 215n30; and bodily discipline, 126–27, 219n8; and *fundoshi* (Japanese loincloths), 91–93, *94*, 213nn21–20; and music education, 197, 224n5

headbands, 165

heisei (imperial era), 202

hierarchies, 11–12, 54, 193, 209n10, 216n4; and bodily discipline, 120, 141; and *iemoto* system, 183, 224n17; and Osuwa Daiko, 114

hinin (non-persons), 36–37

hi no taiko, 73, 88, 91, 211n24, 213n16

hip-hop, 205n15, 207n19

Hirano Village, 49
Hirohito, Emperor, 119–20, 141
Hiroshima Prefecture, 85, 110–11
HIV/AIDS, 46
hōgaku (music of the homeland), 30–31; strict regulation of, 31
Hokkaido, 100, 128, 151
Hokuriku region, 213n16
homeless people, 38, 46
homoeroticism, 92–93
Honma, Masahiko, 64–66, 210n17, 216n4
Honō Daiko, 157–60, *160*, 161–64, 168–69
"Hōrōsha no techō" (From a vagabond's notebook; Den), 65
horse racing, 181
Hughes, David, 204n8, 207n21
humanism, universal, 98, 102, 125
human rights, 41–42, *43*, 44, 46, 208n8, 208n10

ibento (events), 215n1
Ide Magoroku, 119
iemoto (grand master), 70, 211n23; iemoto system, 183, 224n17
Ikeda, Keiko, 206n17
iki, 58, 123, 218n5
imagined communities, 205n13
Imaizumi Yutaka, 18–19, 59, 207n25
imitation, 9, 22, 70, 212n3; and bodily discipline, 125, 135–36, 159; and women taiko drummers, 159, 164
Imperial Rescript of Education, 182, 224n13
improvisation, 74, 197, 224n5
Inagaki Hiroshi, 79
Indian court music, 26–27
indigenous Japanese music, 32; and Hachijō daiko, 113; and Osuwa Daiko, 33, 52, 208n1
industrialization, 83, 87, 212n9
industrial pollution, 46
inherited folk performances, 5–7, 12–13, 21–22, 54; and bodily discipline, 22, 122, 127, 134, 136, 141; and Bon-daiko, 54; and Festival Law (1992), 11–12, 116, 207n20; and festival performances, 6, 108–9, 111–12, 216nn4–5; and furusato (old village) projects, 10; and Great Heisei Amalgamation (Heisei Dai Gap-

pei), 201; and Kodo, 17, 60, 102, 127, 134, 136, 141, 201; and music education, 198; and nationalism, 187; and Ondekoza, 73; and *The Rickshaw Man* (film), 83; and Sukeroku Daiko, 19, 58; and taiko as new folk performance, 12–13, 21, 114–15
innovation, 5, 12, 27, 48–49, 174; and Ondekoza, 91, *94*; and Osuwa Daiko, 52; and Sukeroku Daiko, 54, 57; and taiko as new folk performance, 112, 116
instruction in ensemble taiko, 21–22, 25, 54; and bodily discipline, 22, 120–26, 133–38, *138*, 219n8; and certification, 185–86; and Kodo, 114, 133–38, *138*; and Miyamoto Daiko, 19; and music education, 196–97; and nationalism, 171, 174, 179–80, 183–85, 188, 222nn2–3, 223n10; and Ondekoza, 66, 70–71, 73, 115; and Osuwa Daiko, 52, 114; standardization of, 22, 113, 171, 179, 185–87, 193–95; and Sukeroku Daiko, 19, 59, 120–24, 207n24; and taiko as new folk performance, 112–15, 217n9; textualizing of, 21–22, 171, 174, 179–80, 183–89, 196–97, 204n10, 217n9, 222nn2–3, 223n10, 224n4, 225n6; and women taiko drummers, 158
international performance, 2–3, 6–8, 10, 12, 194, 206n18; and bodily discipline, 218n1; and drum makers, 41; and furusato (old village) projects, 10; and Kodo, 17, 48, 102–3, 201; and Ondekoza, 57, 60, 68, 73, 95, 214n26; and Sukeroku Daiko, 57. See also tours
International Theater (Kokusai Gekijō; Tokyo), 57–58
Internet, 16–17, 193–94
"Irodori," 102
"Isami-goma," 87, 213n13
isami-goma, 80–81, 87, 213n13
Ishihatōka, 199
Ishii, Maki, 8, 94–96, 223n11
Ishikawa Prefecture, 158, 163, 211n24, 213n16
Ishikura Yoshihisa, 54, 57, *59*
Ishizuka Yutaka, 54, 56–57, *59*
Itami Jūzō, 212n5
Itami Mansaku, 79, 212n5
Ivy, Marilyn, 206nn17–18, 216n5

Iwasaki, 211n24
Iwashita Shunsaku, 78, 85–86
Iwate Prefecture, 199, 211n24, 225n7
Izumo no Okuni (Shinto shrine maiden), 29, 146

janggo (Korean percussion instrument), 45–46, 102
Japan Australia Professional Exchange Programs (JAPEP) Wadaiko Drummers, 173
Japanese Americans, 13, 49, 144
"The Japanese Drums of Suwa Shrine" (pamphlet), 175
Japanese flag, 142, 188
Japanese Music and Musical Instruments (Malm), 204n8
Japaneseness, 9, 99; *nihonjinron* (discourses of Japaneseness), 124
Japan National Railway: "Discover Japan" campaign, 206n18
Japan Sea, 100
Japan Shipbuilding Industry Association (Nippon Senpaku Shinkōkai), 180
Japan Shipbuilding Industry Foundation (JSIF), 181–82
Japan Taiko Textbook. See Nihon Taiko Kyōhon (Japan taiko textbook)
Japan Times, 43
jazz, 205n15; jazz clubs, 9; jazz drumming, 49–51, *51*, 58, 121, 174
JEUGIA, 4
jing (Korean percussion instrument), 45
Jishōya Ichiro, 40–41, 208n7
Johnson, Dwayne ("the Rock"), 190
J-Pop (Japanese pop music), 4–5

kabuki, 11, 31, 47, 86, 207n19, 210n16; drums of, 29–33; and *geza* (offstage area), 29–30, 32, 210n16; *kabuki hayashi*, 58, 70–71, 212n1; and Sukeroku Daiko, 56, 58; and women taiko drummers, 146–50, 221n4
kabuki-mono (bizarre people), 146
Kagoshima Prefecture, 61, 63, 216n4
kagura (god music), 31–32
kakegoe (drum calls), 29, 51, 209n2
Kaki-no-ura, 16, 128–29

kakko (*gagaku* drum), 27
kami (spirits), 31, 50, 53, 73–74
Kamitsuki kiyari daiko, 220n17
Kamitsuki Village (Miyake Island), 98–99
Kamo River (Kyoto), 146
Kana (pseud.), 153–54
Kanagawa Prefecture, 62
kane (small brass gong), 74
Kaneko Ryūtarō, 102
kangen (instrumental music), 26
Kannami Kiyotsugu, 27
Katō Shun, 96, 214n26
Kawata Kimiko, 205n12
Kawauchi Toshio, 97–98, 100–101, 103
keigō (polite language), 62, 209n10
Kelly, William, 206n17
kendō (Japanese sword-fighting) masters, 84
Kenichi (pseud.), 191–92
Kimiko (pseud.), 151
kimonos, 80–81; and *enka* singing, 148–50; and *gidayū* (musician-singers), 147–48; and *happi* (kimono-like topcoats), 95, 106, 213n25; and kabuki, 147; and race, 123–24; and women taiko drummers, 140, 147–50, 155–60, 168, 221n7; *yukata* (summer kimonos), 155, 157–60
Kimura, Mr. (pseud.), 134, 136
Kineya Sasazō, 57
Kishibe, Shigeo, 204n8, 208n2
Kishi Nobusuke, 181
kitae-ageta erosu wo dishitakatta (eroticism through intense training), 159
Kitamaebune (ship), 100, 215n31
Kitamaesen Corporation, 99–100, 103, 215n31
kkwaenggwari (Korean percussion instrument), 45
Knight, John, 206n17
knowledge, 22, 222n3
ko-bai (drummer), 88
Kobayashi (male founder of Takarazuka Revue), 149
Kobayashi Seidō, 18, 54, 56–57, 59, 192–93
Kobayashi Seikō, 56–58, *59*
Kobe, 62
Kodama Yoshio, 181
Kodo, 2, 4, 7–8, 10, 13–17, 20–22, 46, 48, 65, 72, 94–103, 194, 204n8, 207n23,

208n7, 209n11, 210n12, 210n17, 213n23, 214n26; Apprentice Program of, 1–2, 7, 13–17, 103, 127–41, *138*, 207n23, 219nn9–12, 220nn13–15; and artisans/artisan academy, 98, 101, 103, 129; and bodily discipline, 98–99, 120, 127–41, *138*, 153–55, 159–62, 164, 219n12, 220nn14–16, 221n11; copyrights of, 192, 220n19; creation of, 60, 94–98; and Earth Celebration (EC), 8, 101–2, 108, 199–200; and *furusato* (old village) projects, 10; and Great Heisei Amalgamation (Heisei Dai Gappei), 199–202; and "Hana Hachijō," 221n7; and "Irodori," 102; and Kitamaesen Corporation, 99–100, 103, 215n31; and "Lion," 102; and *The Lion King* (film), 191–92; and "Miyake," 98–99, 102, 134, 137–38, 154–55, 220n17, 221n6; and "Monochrome," 1, 8, 94–98, 102; and music education, 225n6; name change of, 97–98, 101, 103, 203n1, 214n28, 215n30; and native ethnology, 63, 215n33; and "Ōdaiko," *94*, 98, 102, 137, 152, 155, 213n19; and *ondeko* (demon drumming), 128–30; and Otodaiku Ltd., 103, 215n33; probationary program of, 14–15, 17, 135, 140; and romantic relationships, 99; and salaries, 100; and taiko as new folk performance, 112–13, 199; three decades of, 98–103; and women taiko drummers, 14–15, 108, 140, 150–57, 159–62, 164–68, 207n23; and "Yatai-bayashi," *76*, 77, 98, 102, 135, 137, *138*, 139, 154, 212n3, 221n6; and "Zoku," 102, 156
Kodo Cultural Foundation, 103, 200–202
Kodo Village, 7, 14–16, 20, 101–3; administrative center, 14, 100–101
Kōetsushin-sen scroll, 176
kōkan (exchange/interaction), 200
"Kokura," 213n14
Kokura (Kyushu), 79–81, 83–86, 114, 213n14, 225n7; Kokura Gion Festival, 80–81, 86
Kokura gion daiko, 80–81, 83–88, *89*, 90–91, *94*, 114, 209n1, 212n10, 213n18; *abare-uchi*, 81; *isami-goma*, 80–81, 87, 213n13; *kaeru-uchi*, 80; and music education, 225n7; *nagare-uchi*, 80

kokusui (ultranationalism), 182, 224n14
koma-gaku (music of Korean and Manchurian origin), 26–27
Korea/Koreans: court music, 26–27; drumming, 45–46, 58, 99, 102, 209n12, 218n1; ethnic Koreans, 45–46; folk music, 45; percussion instruments, 45
koten geinō, 11, 25. *See also* classical stage performances
koto (thirteen-string zither), 4, 71, 172, 195–96
ko-tsuzumi (Noh drum), 28, 59
Kowase Susumu, 57, 192
kuchi-shōga (onomatopoeic patterns), 74, 76, 139, 186, 196; *Do-Ko*, 139; *Do-Ko-Do-Ko*, 139; *Do-Ko-Don*, 139
kumi-daiko (ensemble taiko), 2, 49, *51*, 203n2, 204n11. *See also* ensemble taiko groups *(kumi-daiko)*
kumin matsuri (ward festival), 215n3
Kurokawa, 135–36, 206n17
Kurokawa sansa odori dance, 135–36, 225n7
kuromaku (influential figures), 180
Kurosawa, Akira, 79
kuse (habits), 132
kyōgen (classical comic theater), 132–33
Kyoto, 27, 172, 207n19, 218n5; Kyoto shrine maiden, 29, 146
Kyushu, 61, 63, 78–79, 114, 209n1

Latin percussion, 219n7
leatherwork, 34, 36–38, 43–44
Leonard Eto, 102
leprosy, 46
lesbians, 46
Liberal-Democratic Party (LDP), 181
Liberal Party, 181
Liberty Osaka. *See* Osaka Human Rights Museum
"Lion," 102
lion-deer dancing *(shish idori)*, 216n5
The Lion King (film), 191–92
local culture, 6–7, 9, 11–13, 20–21, 34, 104, 193–95, 207n19; and bodily discipline, 120, 123, 127, 129–31, 133–36, 138–41, 219n10, 220nn17–19; and delocalization, 76–77; disembodiment of, 170–71, 187, 197, 222n2; and festival performances, 22,

local culture *(continued)*
107–8, 110–11, 215n3; and *furusato* (old village) projects, 9–10, 206nn17–18; global-local articulation of, 8–10, 12–13, 22, 205–6nn14–15; and Great Heisei Amalgamation (Heisei Dai Gappei), 198–202; and Kodo, 7–8, 17, 77, 100, 103, 127, 129–31, 133–36, 138–41, 151, 199–202, 219n10, 220nn17–19; and music education, 197–98; and *namari* (local nuance), 139; and nationalism, 171–72, 180, 185–87; and Ondekoza, 72–73, 76–78, 95; and Osuwa Daiko, 72; in *The Rickshaw Man* (film), 79, 83–87; and Sukeroku Daiko, 54, 72, 133; and taiko as new folk performance, 112–16, 199; and Taiko Ikari, 40, 44; and women taiko drummers, 142, 151, 158
loincloths. See *fundoshi* (Japanese loincloths)

MacArthur, Douglas, 119–20, 141
Makoto (pseud.), 171–73, 223n6
Malaysia, 194
mallets, 4, 25–26, 30, 56, 70, 88, 91, 113; and bodily discipline, 121, 129, 137–38, 218n4; and music education, 196; and nationalism, 184–86; and women taiko drummers, 158, 165
Malm, William, 204n8, 208n2
Mano, 99
Mao Zedong, 64, 71, 78, 210n14
marathon running, 68–69, 96, 219n12; Boston Marathon, 2, *89*, 94, 213n23, 214n26; Sado Marathon, 200
marginalization, 4–6, 12, 21–22, 187; of drum makers, 26, 37, 41, 47; of Muhō-matsu (in *The Rickshaw Man*), 84; of nonhereditary performers, 12; of women, 6, 147
marriage, 37, 39–40, 147, 149, 163, 165–66, 221n3; and family register checks, 37; and Kodo, 99; and marriage agencies, 37
Martinez, D. T., 206n17
masculine performance norms, 6, 21–22, 46, 169, 215n30; and bodily discipline, 160–63, 218n2, 218n5; and *Bon-daiko*, 209n5; "hegemonic masculinity," 145, 161; and taiko as new folk performance,

115; and women taiko drummers, 144–45, 147, 149, 161–63, 166, 218n2, 218n5
Masuda Takashi Dance Troupe (Masuda Takashi Buyōdan), 57
Matsue, Jennifer Milioto, 205n15
Matsugorō Tomishima. *See* Muhōmatsu (in *The Rickshaw Man*)
matsuri (festivals), 106–7, 215n1, 215n3. *See also* festival performances
"Matsuri Daiko," 60
Mattō City (Ishikawa Prefecture), 34, 208n5
Mayumi (pseud.), 171–73, 189, 223n6
"meat-eating animals" *(nikushoku dōbutsu),* 124
media: and *gidayū* (musician-singers), 148; and Kodo, 100; and music education, 197; and Ondekoza, 68, 213n23; and Osuwa Daiko, 52
Meiji period (1868–1912), 34, 79, 82, 147–50, 156, 163, 212n9, 221n3
"Midare-uchi," 60
Mifune Toshirō, 79
mikoshi (shrine palanquin), 109, *109*, 217n6
Mikuni (Fukui Prefecture), 88, 211n24, 213n19
militarism of wartime Japan, 170, 172–76, 184–85, 188–89, 223nn8–9
Minamata disease, 46
Ministry of Education, 147
Ministry of Education, Culture, Sports, Science and Technology, 224n4
Ministry of Land, Infrastructure, Transport, and Tourism, 224n12
Ministry of Transport, 181, 224n12
minority groups, 36–47; Ainu of Hokkaido as, 46; *burakumin/buraku* people, 36–47, *43*; ethnic Koreans as, 45–46, 209n12; Okinawans as, 45–46, 209n12
minyō (recorded folk songs), 53–54
minzokugaku, 62–63
minzoku geinō (folk performing arts), 10–11, 25, 210n16. *See also* folk performing arts
mitsudomoe pattern (yin-yang symbol with extra teardrop), 26
Mitsui Company (Miike), 65
miya (shrine), 32
miya-daiko, 32, *33*. See also *chū-daiko* drums
Miyagi Michiyo, 211n25

"Miyake," 98–99, 102, 134, 137–38, 154–55, 220n17, 221n6
Miyake Island, 20, 98–99, 113, 134, 136, 220n18
Miyako Music Market, 4
Miyamoto Daiko, 18–19, 105–6; state costume of, 106
Miyamoto Tsuneichi, 62–64, 66, 78, 209n11, 210n12, 215n33
Miyamoto Tsuneichi ga mita nihon (Miyamoto Tsuneichi's Japan; TV documentary), 209n11
Miyamoto Unosuke Taiko Company, 19
modernity, 11–12, 79; and bodily discipline, 127, 132; and *enka* singing, 148–49; and festival performances, 107; and *The Rickshaw Man* (film), 81–84; and Takarazuka Revue, 149; and women taiko drummers, 147–49, 159
Moeru Ondekoza (Ondekoza burns; documentary), 214n26
"Monochrome," 1, 8, 94–98, 102, 214nn24–25, 223n11
motherhood, 97, 147–49, 163, 165–67, 215n30, 221n3
motorboat races, 181–82
muhō (lawless), 212n7
Muhōmatsu (in *The Rickshaw Man*), 78–88, 96, 144, 191, 212n7; and folklore studies, 85–88, 93; and *Kokura gion daiko*, 80–81, 83–88, *89*, 90–91, *94*, 212n10, 213n18; meaning of, 81–85, 212n9; story of, 78–81
Muhōmatsu no kage (Muhōmatsu's shadow; Otsuki), 86
mushi-okuri, 176, 213n16
Music Department of the Imperial Household Agency, 27
Mussolini, 180
mythology, Japanese: and folk performing arts, 11, 136; and nationalism, 184, 189; and women taiko drummers, 142–44, *143*, 145, 169, 220n1

Nagano Prefecture, 49–52, 72, 176, 209n1
Nagano Winter Olympics (1998), 3
Nagasaki Prefecture, 96, 111
Naito Testurō, 102

Naked Festival (Hadaka Matsuri), 91–93
namari (local nuance), 139
Namco, 4
naname-uchi (playing style), 88
Naniwa Human Rights Cultural Center, 42
Naniwa Ward (Osaka City), 37–47; and Road of Human Rights and Taiko, 38, 41–46
Nara shrine, 27
national culture, 6–8, 10, 21–22, 34; and bodily discipline, 119–20, 125, 219n8; creolization of, 205n13; and drum makers, 41; and *furusato* (old village) projects, 10, 206n18; and *The Rickshaw Man* (film), 84; and taiko as new folk performance, 115, 177–78, 223n11. *See also* nationalism
nationalism, 170–89; and disembodiment, 21–22, 171, 187, 197, 222n2; and Imperial Rescript of Education, 182, 224n13; and Japanese flag, 142, 188; and militarism of wartime Japan, 84, 170, 172–76, 180–81, 183–85, 188–89, 223nn8–9; and music education, 196–97, 224n4; and national anthem, 188; and Nippon Taiko Foundation (Nippon Taiko Renmei), 3, 110–11, 166, 174, 179–89, *183*, 193; and "Soul of Yamato," 182, *183*, 224n16; and typology of taiko, 177–79, 188, 223nn10–11; and Western staff notation, 33–34, 115; and women taiko drummers, 142, 164, 169
national tax office, 36–37
National Theater (Tokyo), 115, 142, 163–64, 176–78, 184
National Youth Convention, 217n7
native ethnology, 62–64, 78, 85–86, 212n10, 215n33
natives, 6, 21, 87; and bodily discipline, 120, 124–25, 135–36, 219n7, 219n10, 220n18; and festival performances, 108, 115, 135, 216n4; and nationalism, 187; native place, 10, 111, 120, 206nn16–17; and taiko as new folk performance, 115
nativism, 63
natori (name-taking), 211n23
neotraditional Japanese music, 204n11
New Grove Dictionary of Music and Musicians, 204n8

"Nidan-uchi," 58, 209n7
Nihon Dokusho Shinbun, 65
nihonjinron (discourses of Japaneseness), 124. *See also* Japaneseness
Nihon taiko, 223n11
Nihon Taiko Dōjō, 18–19, 124, 136, 138, 140
Nihon Taiko Kyōhon (Japan taiko textbook), 170–71, 177–78, 183–89, 196, 222n1, 222n3
Nihon Taiko Seinen Grūpu (Japan Taiko Youth Group), 56
Niigata Prefecture, 56, 60, 103, 198
Nikkei newspaper, 46–47
Nippon Foundation (Nippon Zaidan), 180, 182
Nippon Hōsō Kyōkai (NHK; TV network), 52, 65, 209n11, 214n26
Nippon Music Foundation, 182
Nippon Taiko Foundation (Nippon Taiko Renmei), 3, 110–11, 166, 174, 179–89, *183*, 193; and music education, 196–97; and *Nihon Taiko Kyōhon* (Japan taiko textbook), 170–71, 177–78, 183–89, 196, 222n1, 222n3; Skills Committee, 183
Nishitsunoi Masahiro, 163, 176, 184, 197; typology of, 176–79, 184–85, 187–88, 223nn10–11
Noh, 11, 31, 47, 132–33, 206n17, 208n4, 210n16, 212n1; drum makers of, 34; drums of, 27–30, 33–34; and *kakegoe* (drum calls), 29, 51, 209n2; Noh masks, 16; and women taiko drummers, 148
noh-kan (flute), 28
noh taiko, 28–29
nongovernmental organizations, 41, 201
North American taiko, 3, 13, 59–60, 192–94, 204n10
North American taiko conference (1997, Los Angeles), 13
notation, 33–34, 43, 217n9; and Kodo, 113; and *kuchi-shōga* (onomatopoeic patterns), 74, 76, 139; and music education, 196; and Ondekoza, 94–96; Western, 33–34, 115, 139. *See also* scores, taiko
Nōtō Peninsula (Ishikawa Prefecture), 211n24

ō-bai (drummer), 88
obi (belts), 124

O-Bon (Buddhist festival), 32, 53, 171, 211n22, 215n3, 223n6. *See also* Bon festivals
Ochiai, 216n5
"Ōdaiko," 77–93, *89*, 97–98, 102, 137, 208n11; and bodily discipline, 126; creation of, 88–91, *89*; and *fundoshi* (Japanese loincloths), 91–93, *94*, 213nn20–22; and Muhōmatsu (in *The Rickshaw Man*), 78–88, 191; and music education, 197, 224n5; and women taiko drummers, 152, 155, 157, 160, 163, 165, 221n12
ōdaiko drums, 29–30, *30*, 32, 35; and bodily discipline, 124, 126, *161*, 218n4; and *fundoshi* (Japanese loincloths), 91–93, 213nn20–22; and music education, 197, 224n5; and nationalism, 182; and Ondekoza, 88, *89*, 90–93, 215n32; and Sukeroku Daiko, 57–58, 60; and Taiko Ikari, 40; and women taiko drummers, *161*
Oedo Sukeroku Daiko, 59, 192–94, 218n1
Oedo Sukeroku Kai. *See* Sukeroku Kai
O-funa matsuri (festival), 49
Ogi Town, 99, 101, 199–201
Oguchi Daihachi, 7, 49–52, *51*, 57, 75, 144, 209n1; and nationalism, 174–77, 179–80, 182–86, 188–89, 223n4, 223nn7–8, 224n18; and *The Rickshaw Man* (film), 87, 213n13
Oguchi Seidayū, 223n7
"Oi-uchi Daiko," 60
Ōi Yoshiaki, 209n11
Okaya City (Nagano Prefecture), 49
Okaya Daiko, 223n10. *See also* Osuwa Daiko
Okayama, 91–93
okedō-daiko drums, 29–30, *31*, 46; and Kodo, 99, 102; and Ondekoza, 88; and Osuwa Daiko, 51; and women taiko drummers, 167
Okinawa/Okinawans, 63, 128, 210n13; Okinawan drumming, 39, 41, 45–46, 205n12, 209n12, 210n13, 225n7
Okuni (Kyoto shrine maiden), 29, 146
ondeko (demon drumming), 64–66, 69, 78, 128–30, 201–2, 209n7, 211n22, 216n4, 225n7
"Ondeko Forum," 202

Ondekoza, 2, 21–22, 40, 48, 60–72, 104, 112, 203n1, 208n7, 208n11, 209n11, 210n12, 211n25, 215n32; and artisans/ artisan academy, 7, 60–61, 67, 69–71, 77–78, 87, 97, 129, 144, 214n29; and bodily discipline, 64–65, 67–70, 77, 90–94, 120, 159, 161–62, 213n23, 221n11; and Boston Marathon, 2, *89*, 94, 213n23, 214n26; and craftsmanship, 64, 67, 69–70, 210n19; creation of, 66–72, 210nn16–19, 211nn20–22; and Den Tagayasu, 60–70, 93, 96–99, 209nn8–9, 209n11, 210n16, 214n29; documentaries about, 69, 96, 214n26; and *fundoshi* (Japanese loincloths), 91–93, 213n22; mission of, 60, 76, 95, 103, 201, 214n29; and "Monochrome," 1, 8, 94–98, 214nn24–25, 223n11; and native ethnology, 62–64, 78; "new" Ondekoza, 157; and "Ōdaiko," 77, 88, *89*, 90–93, 97, 160, 191, 208n11, 213n16, 213n22; and *ondeko* (demon drumming), 64–66, 69, 78, 128, 201–2, 209n7, 211n22, 216n4, 225n7; and physical training, 67–70, 77, 94, 213n23; and *The Rickshaw Man* (film), 78, 87–88; and romantic relationships, 99; and taiko as new folk performance, 60–61, 112, 115; and women taiko drummers, 144, 155, 157, 159–62; and "Yatai-bayashi," 73–77, 94–95, 97, 212nn1–3, 214n24. *See also* Kodo
Ondekoza ni seishūn wo kaketa wakam onotachi (Coming of age in Ondekoza; documentary), 214n26
oni (demons), 97, 100
oni-kenbai, 211n24
Onozato Motoe, 19, 54, 57, *59*
openness, 12, 106–7, 109–10, *109*, 116, 180
oral transmission, 6, 8, 21; and folk performing arts, 11–12, 33; and nationalism, 183, 186
orchestral percussion section, 2, *4*, 49–51, *51*, 174, 176
Orikuchi Shinobu, 63, 85
Osaka, 100, 108–9, 152, 166; Naniwa Ward, 37–41, 47; Taishō Ward, 45; Tsuruhashi district, 45
Osaka Human Rights Museum, 38, 42, 44, 46

Osaka theater, 207n19
Osaka World Expo (1970), 3, 52, 197
Osuwa Daiko, 7, 21–22, 48, 49–52, 72, 104, 112, 114, 197, 209nn2–4; and bodily discipline, 120; and music education, 197; and nationalism, 174–78, 182, 184–86, 223n10; Ondekoza compared to, 75; and *The Rickshaw Man* (film), 87, 213n13; Sukeroku Daiko compared to, 57, 59; and women taiko drummers, 144
Osuwa Daiko Group of Twenty-One (O-suwa daiko ni-jū-isshū), 174–76, 184, 223n7
"Osuwa Drum Group," 175
"Osuwa Ikazuchi" (Thunder at Suwa), 51, 176, 209n3, 223n9
"other," 125, 127
Otodaiku ("sound carpenter"), 103, 215n33
otokoyaku ("male"-gender specialists), 149
Ōtsugunai (Iwate Prefecture), 211n24
Otsuki Takahiro, 86–87
ō-tsuzumi (Noh drum), 28
outcast groups, 36–37
outsiders, 40, 54, 116; and bodily discipline, 123, 219n6, 220n16; and festival performances, 107, 109; and Kodo, 220n16; and Ondekoza, 74, 94–95
Ozawa, Seiji, 8, 94

pākasshon (percussion), 126
pacchi (snug-fitting pants), 83, 106
pacificism, 223n6
Pacific War, 53. *See also* World War II
palanquin holders, 109, *109*, 217n6
Paris (France), 91–93
parochialism, 134, 193
"Peace Concert," 223n6
peasantry, 27, 64, 66, 144, 175
pedagagy, taiko. *See* instruction in ensemble taiko
physical discipline. *See* bodily discipline
Pia (magazine), 4
place making, 22, 120–23, 131, 133–36, 141, 150; and bodily discipline, 145; and nationalism, 171; native place, 10, 111, 120, 206nn16–17
Planet Drum (Hart), 7
polluting occupations, 26, 36–37

popular culture, Japanese, 6, 9, 11, 22, 207n19; anthologies on, 5, 204n9; pop groups, 5, 112; pop music, 139, 148, 162–64

popularization of taiko, 3–7, 13, 21–22, 25, 41, 46–48, 51–54, 105, 172, 197. *See also* taiko boom

power, 22, 172, 222n3

prejudice, 37, 39, 164

preservation societies *(hozonkai)*, 5, 11–12, 204n11, 208n2; and Great Heisei Amalgamation (Heisei Dai Gappei), 201–2; and Kodo, 134, 220n17; and music education, 198; and nationalism, 180, 186–87; and Osuwa Daiko, 175; and Sukeroku Daiko Hozonkai, 18–19, 123

professional ensemble taiko, 3–5, 7, 16, 18–20, 35, 41, 127, 193; and nationalism, 173; and taiko as new folk performance, 114–15; and women taiko drummers, 142, 144–45, 164–65. *See also names of groups*

prostitution, 146–47

Pulse: A Stomp Odyssey (2002 film), 7

punk bands, 140–41, 167

puppet theater *(bunraku)*, 65, 67–68, 146–48, 207n19

race: and bodily discipline, 119–20, 123–27, 134, 136, 141, 150, 219nn6–8; and women taiko drummers, 124, 145

Raijin (thundergod), 142, 184

Rashomon (film), 79

recessions, 38, 182

record stores, Japanese, 4–5; "world music" section of, 4, 203n6

refugee communities, 9

regional culture, 7, 12, 21, 34, 48, 54, 193; and bodily discipline, 120, 128–29, 139; and *chiiki dentō geinō* (regional traditional performing arts), 116; and drum makers, 46; and festival performances, 108–9; and Great Heisei Amalgamation (Heisei Dai Gappei), 198–99, 201–2; and Kodo, 128–29, 139, 198–99, 201–2; and Miyamoto Daiko, 18; and music education, 197, 225n7; and nationalism, 170, 177, 179, 185–87; and Ondekoza, 60, 64, 70, 72–73, 210n16, 211n24; and

Osuwa Daiko, 60, 72; and Sukeroku Daiko, 72; and taiko as new folk performance, 113–14, 116

religio-communal celebrations, 6, 208n2; drums of, 31–34; and festival performances, 22, 106–7, 110; and *fundoshi* (Japanese loincloths), 91. *See also* rituals, religious

Returned Soldier's League (Melbourne, Australia), 173

revitalization projects, 53; and festival performances, 111; and *furusato* (old village) projects, 10; and Kodo, 15–17, 101, 151; and Ondekoza, 63, 66; and women taiko drummers, 151

Richard (pseud.), 123–24, 219n8

The Rickshaw Man (film), 78–88, 191, 212nn4–10, 213nn14–15; and folklore studies, 85–88, 212n10, 213n11; meaning of, 81–85, 212n9; nationalistic militarism in, 84–85; story of, 78–81; taiko display scene in, 80–81, 83–88, *89*, 90–91, *94*, 212n10, 213n18; theater scene in, 81–82; track meet scene in, 82–83

right-wing causes, 180–82, 188–89

Rising Sun (1993 American film), 172–73, 191, 223n4

rituals, religious: and bodily discipline, 120; drums of, 2, 25, 27, 31–34, 208n2; and festival performances, 106–7, 110, 217n6; *mushi-okuri* ritual, 176; and music education, 196; and Ondekoza, 64, 73–74, 88, 213n16; and Osuwa Daiko, 50, 144, 176; and ritual pollution of women, 115, 144, 156, 217n6; and Sukeroku Daiko, 53–54; and taiko as new folk performance, 116

Road of Human Rights and Taiko (Jinken Taiko Rōdo), 38, 41–47; bronze statues of drummers on, 44–46, 208n11; bus shelters on, 42–43; clock tower on, 43–44; information kiosks on, 42; and Naniwa Human Rights Cultural Center, 42; nine zones of, 42, 46, 208n9, 209n12; and Osaka Human Rights Museum, 38, 42, 44, 46; Taiko Maker Zone on, 42–46, 209n12; and Tamahime Park, 43; ward posters on, 44, 208n10

Robertson, Jennifer, 107–8, 206nn17–18, 215n3

Rodgers, Bill, 214n26

roots/rootlessness, 8, 114, 120, 123, 127, 132–33, 140–41

running. *See* marathon running

rural periphery, 10–11, 34, 47, 206n16; and bodily discipline, 127, 133–34, 219n10; and festival performances, 107; and Great Heisei Amalgamation (Heisei Dai Gappei), 199, 201; and Kodo, 134, 199, 201; rural-urban migration, 9–10; and taiko as new folk performance, 115–16

ryōsai kenbo ("good wife, wise mother"), 149, 163, 221n3

Ryōtsu City, 16, 128

sadō (tea ceremony), 132–33

Sado City (Sado-shi), 198–202, 207n22

Sado Island, 1–2, 7–8, 13–17, 20, 60, 72–73, 91, 98, 207n22, 209n7, 214n26; Apprentice Centre on, 16–17, 20, 101, 128–33, 135–36, 140–41, 153, 219n10, 220n14; and bodily discipline, 127–28, 133, 141; Daisho Elementary School, 99–100; and Den Tagayasu, 63–70, 209n11, 210n17; Earth Celebration (EC) on, 8, 101–2, 108, 199–200; ferry service to, 14; "Gold Mountain," 211n22; and Great Heisei Amalgamation (Heisei Dai Gappei), 198–202; Hamochi, 199–200; and *Kitamaebune* (ship), 100; Kodo Cultural Foundation, 103; Kodo Village, 1–2, 7–8, 13–17, 20, 101–3, 130–31, 199, 220n13; Ogi Town, 99, 101, 199–201; Sado Agricultural High School, 64, 66; and Sado Marathon, 200; and Tatakōkan, 200, 225n8; water on, 130

"Sado Island Taiko Centre" (Sado Taiko Taiken Kōryūkan), 200, 202

Sado no kuni—Kodo (Sado's Kodo), 214n28. *See also* Kodo

Sado no kuni—Ondekoza (documentary), 214n26

Sado Tourism Association, 201

Saidaiji Temple (Okayama), 91–93

Saitama Prefecture, 18, 20, 73–74, 114, 134–36, 139, 152, 209n1, 211n24, 220n18

Sakai Chikuhō, 70

Samul Nori, 102

samul nori playing style, 45–46, 218n1

samurai, 146, 173, 184

Sanada Minoru, 56–58, 192

San Francisco Taiko Dojo, 223n4

sangaku (Chinese acrobatics), 27

San Jose Taiko, 13

san-no-tsuzumi (gagaku drum), 27–28

Sano Shinichi, 209n11, 210n16

sansai (wild vegetables), 131; *sansai tempura*, 131

sansa-odori, 135–36, 225n7

sarugaku (monkey music), 27, 29

sarugaku-no-noh, 27–28. *See also* Noh

Sasakawa Ryōichi, 180–83

sato-kagura (music that accompanies Shinto festivals), 31–32

Schade-Poulsen, Marc, 9

Schnell, Scott, 216nn4–5

scores, taiko, 8, 43, 49–51, 74, 94–95, 174–76, 209n1

The Scorpion King (film), 190–91

"Seafarer's Festival" (O-funa matsuri), 175

Seiichi Tanaka, 223n4

Seinen sasurai-bashi (Song of a wandering youth; documentary), 214n26

seiza (correct way to sit), 131–33, 140, 220n15

self-transformation, 128, 141

semiprofessional ensemble taiko, 18–19, 104, 167

senmin (outcast group), 36

The Seven Samurai (film), 79

shaku (standard of measurement), 88, 213n17

shakuhachi (Japanese long bamboo flute), 4, 70, 172, 195–96

shamans, women, 220n1

shamisen (three-stringed Japanese lute), 4, 29, 53, 57–58, 69, 99, 148, 172, 192, 195–96, 214n26, 218n10, 220n14

Shibusawa Keizō, 62, 78

Shimazaki Makoto, 66

shime-daiko drums, 1, 28–29, *29*, 32, 44–45, 191; and bodily discipline, 136–37, 218n4; and Kodo, 136–37, 221n6; and Miyamoto Daiko, 106; and music education, 196; and Ondekoza, 70, 74–75, 95, 212n1; and Osuwa Daiko, 51; and

shime-daiko drums *(continued)*
  Sukeroku Daiko, 57–58; and women taiko drummers, 167, 221n6
shimin matsuri (citizens' festival), 215n3
Shimomura Keiichi, 73
Shinobazu Pond near Ueno, 54
shinobue (short bamboo flute), 195–96
Shinoda Masahiro, 69, 211n21, 214n26
Shin-On Taiko (New Sound Taiko), 57–58, 209n6
Shinto: and mi-kagura, 31; and mikoshi (shrine palanquin), 109, *109*, 217n6; and nationalism, 174–76, 182; and ritual pollution of women, 115, 144, 156, 217n6; and sato-kagura, 31–32; Shinto dancing groups, 199, 201; Shinto festivals, 31–32, 53–54, 73–74, 105, 108–10, *109*, 128, 215n1, 217n6; Shinto priests, 49–52; Shinto rituals, 27, 64, 110, 208n2; Shinto shrine maidens, 29, 146, 168, 220n1; Shinto shrines, 27, 31–32, 51–54, 56, 73–74, 105–6, 108–10, *109*, 129, 174–76, 215n1, 217n6. *See also* rituals, religious
Shizuoka Prefecture, 151
shokunin. *See* artisans *(shokunin)*
shōmen-uchi, 91
shōmyō chants, 32
Shrine of Remembrance (Melbourne, Australia), 173
Soga reforms, 26
solidarity, 46–47, 170
Sony Music, 192
"Soul of Yamato," 182, *183*, 224n16
South American taiko, 3, 218n1
Southeast Asia, 3, 15, 102
Special Measures Law for Assimilation Projects (1969), 38
spectacle, 54, 184
spirits *(kami)*, 31, 50, 53, 73–74, 174–75, 182
sporting events, 3, 83, 212n9
stage performances, 2–3, 5, 7, 11, 21–22, 25, 31, 33; and bodily discipline, 122, 127, 129, 132–35; and fundoshi (Japanese loincloths), 91–93, 221n6; and Kodo, 99, 102, 127, 129, 132–35, 150–56; and Miyamoto Daiko, 105–6; and nationalism, 186; and Ondekoza, 60, 67–68, 70, 72, 74, 76–78, 91–93, 97–98, 213n16; and

stage costumes, 91–93, *94*, 106, 145–50, 155–56, 159–60, *160*, 162, 165, 168–69, *168*, 213nn20–22; and taiko as new folk performance, 112–13; and women taiko drummers, 145–56, 158–60, 162. *See also* concerts/concert halls
standardization, 22, 113, 171, 179, 185–87, 193, 195
strikes, 61, 65
student demonstrations, 62
Sugamo Prison (Tokyo), 181
Sukeroku Daiko, 18–19, 21–22, 48, 52–60, *55*, *59*, 61, 72, 104, 112, 144, 157, 192–93, 207n25, 209nn6–7; and acrobatic choreography, 56, 58–60, 120, 144; and bodily discipline, 120–24, 133, 136–38, 140, 218n1, 219n8; and nationalism, 178, 184
Sukeroku Daiko Hozonkai (Sukeroku Daiko Preservation Society), 18–19, 123
Sukeroku Kai, 18, 56–58
Sukeroku Seimen (noodle shop), 56
Sukeroku Yukari Edo-zakura (kabuki play), 56, 58
sumo wrestling, 93
sun (standard of measurement), 213n17
Susanō (god of the sea), 143
sutōbu (gas heater), 14
Suwa Grand Shrine, 174–76
Suwa region, 51, 72, 213n13, 223n9
Suzuki Tadashi, 124–25

taigen *(embody)*, 93. *See also* embodiment
taiko, 2, 25, 34, 203n2, 208n1; and music education, 195–96; origin of, 48; standards of measurements for, 88, 213n17. *See also* ensemble taiko groups *(kumi-daiko)*
taiko boom, 3, 20–21, 25–26, 47, 104, 193, 203nn3–4; and drum makers, 37, 41; and Great Heisei Amalgamation (Heisei Dai Gappei), 202; and Ondekoza, 61
Taiko Dojo (San Francisco), 223n4
Taiko Ikari (Taiko Rage), 38–45, 47; mission of, 38–40, 47; stage costumes of, 208n7
Taikology (Asano Taiko journal), 35

taiko makers. *See* drum makers

"Taiko no Tatsujin" (Taiko Master), 4, 203n5

"Taiko of Japan" (Nihon no Taiko; concert series), 142

Taiko Road. *See* Road of Human Rights and Taiko (Jinken Taiko Rōdo)

Taikoya Matabē, 44

TaikOz, 204n9

Taishō Ward (Osaka City), 45

Taiwan, 63, 210n13

Tajikarao-no-kami (god of strength), 143–44

Tajiri Kōzō. *See* Den Tagayasu

Takakubo Yasuko, 157, 160

Takarazuka Revue, 149–50, 221nn4–5

Takeda Shingen, 174–76, 184, 223n9

Takemitsu Toru, 211n25

Takeshita, Noboru, 111, 217n8

Tamahime Park (Jeweled Princess Park), 43

Tampopo (film), 212n5

Tanaka Denji, 86

Tanaka Densaemon, 70, 86

Tanaka Seiichi, 60

tango, 49–50

Tatakōkan, 200, 202, 225n8

tataku (beating of a drum), 101–2, 200

Tatsu (pseud.), 13–15, 17, 20, 191, 202

A Taxing Woman (film), 212n5

Tazawako Town (Akita Prefecture), 65

TBS network, 214n26

tea ceremony *(sadō)*, 132–33

textbooks of taiko instruction, 21–22, 171, 174, 179–80, 183–89, 204n10, 217n9, 222nn2–3, 223n10; and music education, 196–97, 224n4, 225n6; *Nihon Taiko Kyōhon* (Japan taiko textbook), 170–71, 177–78, 183–89, 196, 222n1, 222n3

Thompson, Christopher, 199, 201, 216n5

Thornbury, Barbara, 116, 217n7

Thunder at Suwa. *See* "Osuwa Ikazuchi" (Thunder at Suwa)

tōgaku (music of Indian and Chinese origin), 26–27

Tokugawa period (1603–1867), 34, 36–37, 146–47

Tokyo, 18–20, 109; Asakusa District, 19, 61; Bunkyō Ward, 18; Hongō area, 56; Ikebukoro Station, 18; International Taiko Contest (2005), 144; International Theater (Kokusai Gekijō), 57–58; Metropolitan Police Department, 147; National Theater, 115, 142, 163–64, 176–78, 184; *shitamachi* section of, 18–19, 53–54, 55, 56, 58, 61, 72, 123, 218n5; Sugamo Prison, 181; Yamanote, 218n5

Tokyo College of the Arts, 171

Tokyo Olympics (1964), 3, 7, 52, 177, 197, 209n4

Tomihisa (pseud.), 151

Tomishima Matsugorō (The story of Tomishima Matsugorō; Iwashita), 78

Tomomi (pseud.), 167

Tōno, 206n17, 216n5

Tōsha Roetsu, 70

Tōsha Suihei, 70

Toshio (in *The Rickshaw Man*), 79–80, 82, 84–85

Tottori Prefecture, 211n24

tourism, 10–12; and Asakusa District (Tokyo), 61; cultural tourism, 7; domestic tourism, 10–12, 48, 200; and Earth Celebration (EC), 200; and festival performances, 107, 111, 215n1; foreign tourism, 10, 200–201; and *furusato* (old village) projects, 10, 206nn17–18; international cultural tourism, 12; and Kodo, 200–201; and Ondekoza, 66; and Osuwa Daiko, 52; and Road of Human Rights and Taiko, 38; and taiko as new folk performance, 113, 116

Tourism Renaissance Project, 201

tours: American tours, 2–3, *89*, 94–95, 97, 213n23, 214n26; European tours, 3, 91–93, 96. *See also* international performance

Tower Records, 4

trade secrets, 35

Traditional Japanese Music and Musical Instruments (Malm), 204n8

traditional performing arts *(dentōteki na geinō)*, 4–6, 11–12, 22, 47, 204n11, 206n17, 208n2; and bodily discipline, 127–28, 132, 139; and drum makers, 37; and festival performances, 107; and Kodo, 15, 127–28, 132, 135–36, 139, 152,

traditional performing arts *(dentōteki na geinō) (continued)*
213n19; and music education, 198; and nationalism, 177–78, 182, 186–87; and "new folk songs," 207n21; and Onde-koza, 74, 77, 210n16, 211n25; and Osuwa Daiko, 209n4; in *The Rickshaw Man* (film), 83; and taiko as new folk performance, 112, 115–16; and women taiko drummers, 144, 152, 159, 162

transcendence, 125–26

Traphagen, John, 222n2

tsu (rest), 139

Tsugaru region, 214n26, 218n10

Tsugaru shamisen, 211n24, 218n10

Tsuruhashi district (Osaka City), 45

tsuzumi drums, 28, 70

Twitter, 194

typology of taiko, 176–79, 184–85, 187–88, 223nn10–11

uchiwa-daiko (fan drum), 30, 32

Uesugi Kenshin, 174–75, 184, 223n9

ujigami (tutelary deity), 106

ujiko (children of the shrine), 106

Ultranationalist People's Party, 180, 224n14

Umi ni ikiru hitobito (The people who live on the sea; Miyamoto), 62

United Nations, *43*

University of Tokyo, 18, 54, 105, 171

U.S.-Japan security treaty (1960), 65

Venice Film Festival, 79

video games, 3–4; "Taiko no Tatsujin" (Taiko Master), 4

violence, 37

wadaiko (Japanese drums), 44–46, 196, 203n2, 204n11, 222n1, 223n11

Wappa Daiko, 221n10

Warabiza, 65, 114

ward festival *(kumin matsuri)*, 215n3

war drumming, 173–76, 184–85, 223nn8–9

Waseda University, 61–62

Watanabe Shōichi, 157

Watanabe Village, 38, 42, 44

weight lifting, 161–62, 221n11

Western influence, 4–5, 208n1, 218n5; and bodily discipline, 126–27, 132, 139, 220n15; and drum sets, 49–51, *51*; and Kodo, 139; and music education, 196; and nationalism, 184; and notation, 33–34, 115, 139; and Ondekoza, 71–72, 95–96, 210n16, 211n25; and Osuwa Daiko, 52, 72; and Sukeroku Daiko, 72; and taiko as new folk performance, 112, 115; and women taiko drummers, 148, 159, 164, 221n10. *See also* foreign influence

Winston, George, 4

women, Japanese, 142–69; *ama* (female divers), 206n17; at Asano Taiko Village, 36; and *Bon-daiko*, 54, 144, 209n5; and festival performances, 109, 216–17nn5–6; and Ondekoza, 67–68, 93, 210n19; in *The Rickshaw Man* (film), 79–80, 82, 84, 212n8; and Sukeroku Daiko, 54, 144. *See also* gender ideologies; women taiko drummers

"Women Play Taiko" (concert), 142–44, *143, 145*, 164, 169

women taiko drummers, 12, 21–22, 193; and Amanojaku, 157, 159–61, *161*, 162–64, 169; Ama-no-uzume (goddess) as first taiko drummer, 143–44, 220n1; and American drummers, 124; and apprentice programs, 19, 140, 150–56, 165, 207n23, 207n25; and bodily discipline, 124, 140, 145, 150, 153–63, *160, 161*, 168–69, 221n11; and *Bon-daiko*, 209n5; and "Chonlima," 166–67; and cocon, 167–68, *168*; and freedom, 159–60, 162; and Gocoo, 221n10; and "Hana Hachijō," 221n7; history of, 146–50, 169, 221n3; and Honō Daiko, 157–59, 161–64, 168–69; increase in number of, 144–45, 220n2; and kabuki, 146–47; and Kodo, 14–15, 108, 140, 150–57, 159, 161–62, 164–68, 207n23; and Korean drum troupe, 58; and "Miyake," 154–55, 221n6; and Miyamoto Daiko, 18; and "new" Ondekoza, 157; and "Ōdaiko," 152, 155, 157, 160, 163, 165, 221n12; and Ondekoza, 144, 157, 159–62, 210n15; and Osuwa Daiko, 144; and race, 124, 145; and Road of Human Rights and Taiko, 45–46; stage costumes of, 145–50, 155–56, 159–60, *160*, 162, 165,

168–69, *168*, 213nn20–22; in Sukeroku Daiko, 19, 207n25; and taiko as new folk performance, 115; unbound, 145, 161, 164; and Wappa Daiko, 221n10; and "Women Play Taiko" (concert), 142–44, *143*, 145, 164, 169; and "Yatai-bayashi," 154, 165, 221n6; and "Zoku," 156. *See also* gender ideologies

woodworking, 70, 128–30, 133

world music, 7–8, 95, 98, 101, 199

World War II, 10–11, 34, 49, 107, 110; defeat of Japan, 119–20, 141; and Den Tagayasu, 61; and Festival Law (1992), 11–12, 116, 207n20; and Korean migrants, 45; and nationalism, 170, 172–73, 180–81, 183; and *The Rickshaw Man* (film), 84; and Sukeroku Daiko, 53

Yagi Yasuyuki, 217n8

yagura (raised platform), 53, 80, 86

yakuza crime families, 37

yamabushi kagura, 211n24

Yamada Chisato, 214n26

"Yamato," 182, *183*, 224n16

Yanagita Kunio, 63, 85

yatai (festival carts), 73–74, 216n5

"Yatai-bayashi," 73–77, *76*, 92, 94–95, 97–98, 102, 135, 212nn2–3, 214n24; and bodily discipline, 137, *138*, 139, 154, 221n6; and women taiko drummers, 154, 165, 221n6

yatai-bayashi (festival-cart drumming), 20, 74–77, 209n1, 211n24, 212nn2–3

"Yodan-uchi," 58, 60, 209n7, 212n2

yōgaku (Western music), 31

Yomota Inuhiko, 81, 83–84, 212n9

Yonaguni-jima, 63–64

Yoron Jūgoya Odori, 216n4

Yoshi (pseud.), 34–37

Yoshida Brothers, 218n10

Yoshiko (pseud.), 153–55

Yoshikuni Igarashi, 172

Yoshioka (in *The Rickshaw Man*), 79, 84–85, 212n8

Yoshitaka Terada, 40

YouTube, 194

Yuka (pseud.), 157–59

yukata (summer kimonos), 155, 157–60

Yumi (pseud.), 154, 221n6

Yumigahama Island (Tottori Prefecture), 211n24

Yumigahama taiko, 211n24

Yuriko (pseud.), 151–52

Yushima Tenjin shrine, 54, 56

Zampa Ufujishi Daiko, 39

Za Ondekoza (The Ondekoza; film), 96

Zeami Motokiyo, 27

zelkova wood, 28, 43

Zen Buddhists, 28

"Zoku," 102, 156

ASIA: LOCAL STUDIES/GLOBAL THEMES

Jeffrey N. Wasserstrom, Kären Wigen,
and Hue-Tam Ho Tai, Editors

1. *Bicycle Citizens: The Political World of the Japanese Housewife,* by Robin M. LeBlanc

2. *The Nanjing Massacre in History and Historiography,* edited by Joshua A. Fogel

3. *The Country of Memory: Remaking the Past in Late Socialist Vietnam,* by Hue-Tam Ho Tai

4. *Chinese Femininities/Chinese Masculinities: A Reader,* edited by Susan Brownell and Jeffrey N. Wasserstrom

5. *Chinese Visions of Family and State, 1915–1953,* by Susan L. Glosser

6. *An Artistic Exile: A Life of Feng Zikai (1898–1975),* by Geremie R. Barmé

7. *Mapping Early Modern Japan: Space, Place, and Culture in the Tokugawa Period, 1603–1868,* by Marcia Yonemoto

8. *Republican Beijing: The City and Its Histories,* by Madeleine Yue Dong

9. *Hygienic Modernity: Meanings of Health and Disease in Treaty-Port China,* by Ruth Rogaski

10. *Marrow of the Nation: A History of Sport and Physical Culture in Republican China,* by Andrew D. Morris

11. *Vicarious Language: Gender and Linguistic Modernity in Japan,* by Miyako Inoue

12. *Japan in Print: Information and Nation in the Early Modern Period,* by Mary Elizabeth Berry

13. *Millennial Monsters: Japanese Toys and the Global Imagination,* by Anne Allison

14. *After the Massacre: Commemoration and Consolation in Ha My and My Lai,* by Heonik Kwon

15. *Tears from Iron: Cultural Responses to Famine in Nineteenth-Century China,* by Kathryn Edgerton-Tarpley

16. *Speaking to History: The Story of King Goujian in Twentieth-Century China,* by Paul A. Cohen

17. *A Malleable Map: Geographies of Restoration in Central Japan, 1600–1912,* by Kären Wigen

18. *Coming to Terms with the Nation: Ethnic Classification in Modern China,* by Thomas S. Mullaney

19. *Fabricating Consumers: The Sewing Machine in Modern Japan,* by Andrew Gordon

20. *Recreating Japanese Men,* edited by Sabine Frühstück and Anne Walthall

21. *Selling Women: Prostitution, Markets, and the Household in Early Modern Japan,* by Amy Stanley

22. *Imaging Disaster: Tokyo and the Visual Culture of Japan's Great Earthquake of 1923,* by Gennifer Weisenfeld

23. *Taiko Boom: Japanese Drumming in Place and Motion,* by Shawn Bender

24. *Anyuan: Mining China's Revolutionary Tradition,* by Elizabeth J. Perry

Text:	11/14 Adobe Garamond
Display:	Adobe Garamond
Compositor:	BookMatters, Berkeley

Milton Keynes UK
Ingram Content Group UK Ltd.
UKHW012352010923
427918UK00007B/314